Love As Human Freedom

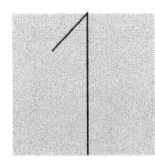

SQUARE ONE
First Order Questions in the Humanities

Series Editor: **PAUL A. KOTTMAN**

LOVE

AS

HUMAN

FREEDOM

Paul A. Kottman

STANFORD UNIVERSITY PRESS
STANFORD, CALIFORNIA

Stanford University Press
Stanford, California

Printed in the United States of America on acid-free, archival-quality paper

Library of Congress Cataloging-in-Publication Data

Names: Kottman, Paul A., 1970- author.
Title: Love as human freedom / Paul A. Kottman.
Other titles: Square one (Series)
Description: Stanford, California : Stanford University Press, 2017. |
   Series: Square one : first-order questions in the humanities | Includes
   bibliographical references and index.
Identifiers: LCCN 2016053302 (print) | LCCN 2016054559 (ebook) |
   ISBN 9780804776769 (cloth : alk. paper) | ISBN 9781503602274 (pbk. : alk. paper) |
   ISBN 9781503602328 (electronic)
Subjects: LCSH: Love in literature. | Love--Philosophy.
Classification: LCC PN56.L6 K68 2017 (print) | LCC PN56.L6 (ebook) | DDC 809/.933543--dc23
LC record available at https://lccn.loc.gov/2016053302

Typeset by Bruce Lundquist in 10/14 Minion Pro.

For Sakura

Contents

Acknowledgments

This project owes a great deal to several institutions: The New School, for a sabbatical and other forms of research assistance; the Internationales Kolleg Morphomata at the Universität zu Köln, for a generous fellowship which made possible a year of reading and writing free from teaching and administrative duties; and the Center for Philosophy and Literature at the University of Tokyo and the Philosophy Department of the Università degli studi di Verona, for visiting professorships that augmented the time I could devote to research. I am also grateful to the audiences who heard sections of this book in lecture form over recent years. I cannot list them all here, but I especially remember discussions at the Committee on Social Thought at the University of Chicago, the Università degli studi di Salerno, the Literaturwissenschaftliches Kolloquium at the Ludwig-Maximilians-Universität München, and the Department of Comparative Literature at the City University of New York, Graduate Center.

I am also indebted to many individuals, a few of whom read and commented on drafts of the entire manuscript. I have benefited enormously from correspondence and conversations with Robert Pippin, and from his comments on a late draft; his encouragement and support are deeply appreciated. Jay Bernstein was the first to hear me talk about this project, and I am grateful for his enthusiastic support and helpful suggestions throughout. Thomas Pavel offered a number of helpful comments on a late draft. Richard Eldridge also read a late draft, and provided some very useful comments and questions. Adriana Cavarero read the manuscript, as well, and made good suggestions. I also remember stimulating conversations and exchanges about the issues raised in this book with Cinzia Arruzza, Christian Benne,

Joshua Billings, Omri Boehm, Chiara Bottici, Judith Butler, Jean Comaroff, Benoit Challand, Andrew Cutrofello, Ewan Fernie, Simona Forti, Bernard Flynn, Oz Frankel, Markus Gabriel, Kristin Gjesdal, Lydia Goehr, Stephen Greenblatt, Espen Hammer, Agnes Heller, Gregg Horowitz, Daniella Jancsó, Anna Katsman, Shoichiro Kawai, Karl Kottman, Jonathan Lear, Leonardo Lisi, Julia Reinhard Lupton, Inessa Medzhibovskaya, Dmitri Nikulin, Adi Ophir, Dominic Pettman, Julia Peters, Terry Pinkard, Ross Poole, James Porter, Meghan Robison (I am grateful to Meghan for invaluable research assistance, as well), Adam Rosen-Carole, Rocco Rubini, David Schalkwyk, Alain Schnapp, Joshua Scodel, Michael Squire, Ann Stoler, Yasunari Takada, Davide Tarizzo, Tommaso Tuppini, Rosanna Warren, David Wellbery, Michael Weinman and Alenka Zupančič. I should also like to thank my students, as well as Emily-Jane Cohen at Stanford University Press.

Special thanks, finally, to my daughters, Sophia Kottman and Helena Kottman, for their cheerful help throughout; and to Sakura Ozaki, for all that her encouragement and understanding has made actual, and now possible.

Love As Human Freedom

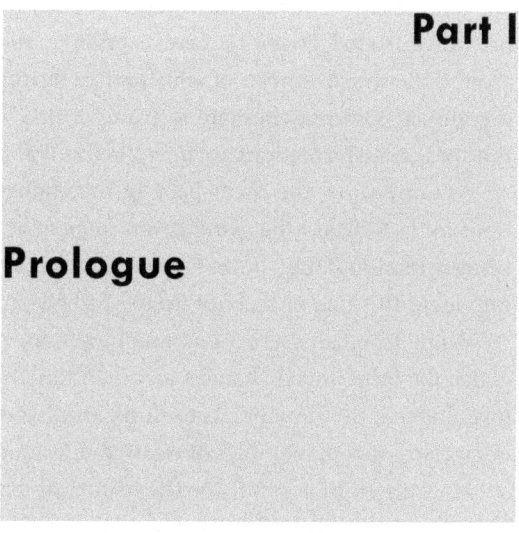

Part I

Prologue

Love must be a lover of wisdom [*philosophos*,
"philosopher"], and, as such, in between being wise
and being without understanding.

Plato, *Symposium* 204b

In recent years, with astonishing rapidity, widespread social opposition to same-sex marriage has evaporated in many parts of the world. Reliable and effective birth control has become increasingly available to individuals around the globe. Millions of women, in the past century, have gained the ability to safely and legally terminate a pregnancy at will. New reproductive technologies, along with new kinship formations, make the propagation of life and the raising of children seem less and less the result of sexual reproduction. At the same time, in many places, we are living through one of the most profound social transformations in human history: the erosion of a gender-based division of labor. The tidal waves of political and philosophical feminism, and the critiques to which entrenched institutions of sexual domination are subjected, are being felt throughout society. Behind this lies the expanded social authority of lovemaking and 'love-based' commitments, in our laws governing everything from marriage and domestic economic life, to the adoption of children, to our schools and medical practices. Virtually no social, civic or political institution is being left untouched by these vast changes. In the face of ongoing violence, naked prejudice, social crisis, regressive politics and institutionalized oppression around the world—much of which arises in response to the developments just mentioned—we may hesitate to trumpet this list of achievements too loudly. But these transformations are nevertheless real and vast.

At same time, the sheer pace of the change often outstrips our explanations for it. Indeed, what would even *count* as an explanation for such immense transformations? This book is an attempt to answer this question, and to get into focus the *kind* of account we need to give to better explain these realities.

While love can seem a perennial topic for poets, philosophers, or theologians, the large social changes just mentioned belie any ahistorical visions of love. Indeed, they compel us to think anew about love as a historical practice, comprised of concrete ways of treating one another that change over time.

How, then, to account for the historical transformations just mentioned? How to reckon with their vast implications? And how might these changes themselves help us to explain anything else? These are some of the questions to which the following pages will try to respond.

Consider a well-known reality, no less astonishing for being common knowledge: for generations upon generations, in many societies around the world, even today, men possessed of the requisite social standing have sexually enslaved women and girls, as well as boys, hermaphrodites, eunuchs and others. And they have done so, not merely in circumstances of sheer brutality, or where might makes right, but as a prerogative bestowed upon them by their civilization. Sexual domination, in fact, has long been endemic in human cultures—a core element of the way many peoples around the world have conceived of themselves for millennia. And although there have been mighty attempts to explain the reasons for this persistence of sexual domination—especially the prevalence of what we sometimes still call patriarchy—we lack a full understanding of *how* such institutions could have come into the world with such staying power. As Simone de Beauvoir's indispensable *The Second Sex* notes: "The world has always belonged to males, and none of the reasons given for this have ever seemed sufficient" (73).[1]

Given the manifestly equal intelligence and capabilities of women, how could there have been so many centuries upon centuries of sexual domination? And what ends were being served by such gender-based divisions—between men and women, men and boys, matriarchs and girls, and other similarly enforced social-gendered roles? The answers to such questions have seemed

obvious to many, as self-evident as the privileges of power in any other form
of social domination. But, I think, the available explanations are still insufficient and impoverished. In their place, then, I will outline a historical dialectic
that claims—and here I must be careful, lest the claim sound exculpatory—that
such institutions of domination were inevitable, however wrong.

At the same time, we lack a convincing account of how anything that might
deserve the name of love—a love-affair, or a loving relationship—between a
man and a woman, say, or between an older man and a younger man, or any
other gender configuration, could have plausibly come into the world out of
such a painful, hierarchically determined history. *How* after all, did human
beings ever come to conceive of themselves as *lovers?* How did we come to
see ourselves as capable not just of sexually dominating another, or of being
dominated by another, but of making love to another, given the enormity of
the painful history just described? And how did our view of ourselves as lovers
come to be so authoritative for who we think we are, to the point of becoming
central to broad forms of social organization? Is our conception of ourselves
as lovers a mirage, or a poetical fantasy, or a delusion induced by dominant
ideologies?

Although my answers to these questions will not come into focus until
much later in the book, in Part III, I want to mark the questions here—so that
the trajectory of what follows is clear from the start. My aim will be to arrive at
a provisional comprehension of our contemporary situation. But to get 'here,'
we have to start 'there'—much further back. The second and third parts of this
book, then, offer an account of love as a historical transforming practice, one
with its own internal dynamic over time. I present love as a fundamental form
of human self-education, a set of practices through which we have cumulatively
taught ourselves that we are rational and free—even if such lessons can never
be learned once and for all.

. . .

The topic of this book, then, is love as freedom.

'Love' and 'freedom' are, of course, notoriously difficult to define. In English,
as in many other languages, 'love' is both a noun and a verb; at once a passionate feeling and a particular activity. Love can refer to someone's relation to
objects in the world, or to a bond between individuals. And different *kinds* of
loving practices have developed over the millennia—familial love, friendly love,
charitable love, and also romantic or sexual love. The terms given to these, in a

variety of historical contexts—*philia, erōs, ahava, caritas, amor*—all continue to inform the use of the word 'love' around the world.

This semantic complexity should not deter us, however, since the difficulties we face in talking about love stem not from words but from questions raised by their usage. If we can bring the right *questions* about love into focus, then we can at least be on our way.

Across the human sciences, since Plato at least, various definitions of love have been formed by posing a very basic question: What *is* it to be a lover? or What is the *nature* of love? Beneath such inquiry there is a fundamental assumption, as old as philosophy and science: namely, that the right way to proceed when faced with something puzzling is to ask, What *is* it? or What is its *nature*? Over the years, we have developed different methods for handling these questions.[2] A historian, for instance, might show how love is historically determined, discussing how people once loved in particular times or places.[3] A literary scholar might consider love to be a poetic theme or invention.[4] A sociologist might define love as the manifestation of the institutional and ideological forces that shape our experiences.[5] A physicist or mathematician might demur that love is not one of the What *is* it? questions that her training has prepared her to answer. And of course there are religious, psychological, anthropological and evolutionary-biological attempts to say what love is.[6]

Many such inquiries have their value, obviously.[7] My approach in the following pages will take a different direction, however.

Rather than try to explain what love is, the question I want to raise is, What does love help us to explain? or What does love make sense *of*?

This may seem an unfamiliar way of proceeding, I realize. But every author, probably, writes with a fantasy of how she or he would like to be read, or judged. And in writing this book, I have set for myself a standard which, I submit, might not be a bad way for readers to evaluate this book, too: kindly assess what I have to say on the basis of whatever sense I manage to make, not just of 'love,' but of anything *else*—what love makes sense *of*.

Indeed, a central claim of this book is that love amounts to a fundamental activity through which we make sense of our world and each other. By 'sense-making,' I mean a satisfying explanation of some phenomenon or another, or a way of justifying actions and practices, or giving an account of something or someone. Our ways of loving one another, I shall argue, do not just presuppose or reflect extant ways in which we understand ourselves and our world. Love *is* itself an enacted attempt at understanding, a practical form of self-education—

one that is communally shared, undertaken with others in ways that change deeply over time.

Some readers may understandably wonder why I want to say that love is a form of sense-making, an expression of our desire to understand—rather than something that arises in the putatively natural affections that exist among family and kin, in humans and in other social animals. Admittedly, it may seem reductive or 'cold' to speak of love as a form of sense-making or 'self-education.' But I think this impression is a symptom of how much we may have over-intellectualized our understanding of what sense-making *is*, or how humans and animals go about it. Too often, we tend to regard sense-making as something that happens 'in the mind,' or in hypotheses and formulas, not in a lover's words or a warm touch. But the heat of passionate life, our coming to feel at home with others, and our messy, concrete ways of loving one another are also ways we make sense of the world and one another over time.

This is perhaps also a good place to mention that I will nowhere insist upon any fundamental difference between humans and animal life. Although I will say no more about nonhuman creatures, I do not claim to delineate any final limits of nonhuman animal life.

My suggestion will be that love should be regarded alongside human practices like philosophy, religion and art as an unavoidable way in which we have made intelligible the deepest threats to the sense we make of our lives. I want to try to show what might be gained by regarding love as a sense-making practice of this special sort. At the same time, if love differs from philosophy or religion or art, then this is because different loving practices show how sense-making is at the heart of how we actually *treat* each other, touch one another, speak with one another, reckon with our bodily life together—and the ways of living we correspondingly achieve and explain. Love is a form of sense-making that develops only in our shared bodily practices and interactions, and the extent to which these can achieve their own kind of 'reflections'; indeed, *that* is how love has been 'taken up' in art, religion and philosophy.

What, then, does love explain, and make sense of?

Love can account for lots of things, as I hope to show, including the enormous social changes just mentioned. I do not mean that love is the *cause* of these changes—rather, I mean to say that love is a self-correcting practice through which these changes were to some extent realized, and through which they might be better explained. Ultimately, I will argue, love is also one way we teach ourselves that we are free and rational—capable of leading lives for which we are at least provisionally answerable and whose possibilities we open for ourselves, while taking on board all the accidents and misfortunes of life in the world.

Admittedly, I can give no prima facie reason why 'leading lives for which we are at least provisionally answerable' should count as freedom. In talking this way, I have in mind a tradition of thinking about freedom that emerged in the German idealism tradition, especially in views presented by J. G. Fichte and later developed by G.W.F. Hegel.[8] In that tradition—and contrary to Christian or voluntarist philosophies, according to which freedom means being able to cause an action by an independent act of will—freedom is understood to be tied to a dependence on certain social relations in which independence is achieved. That is, freedom is understood to entail being in a kind of relation to oneself, as well as in a kind of mutual relation with others, in which one's actions can be experienced as one's own. Hegel saw these sorts of relationships not as natural givens, or as expressions of metaphysical substances, but rather as historical achievements—consequences of certain interactions and collective practices, undertaken over time. So, freedom comes to light as a kind of social achievement. And one question that Hegel's texts raise in this regard is how to understand the *form* of social relations, interactions and dependencies in which freedom is achievable. Hegel intriguingly suggests, in various passages, that love between free individuals—as distinct from the 'love' to which one might be entitled as a member of a tribe or clan—might count as a paragon of such mutual recognition. I will return to these passages at appropriate points over the course of this book—also, at times, to depart and differ from central aspects of Hegel's discussion of love and freedom.

For the moment, however, let me say a bit more about my own approach in the following pages.

■ ■ ■

My first suggestion is that love is a deeply felt historical practice which develops in response to what we (or our ancestors) have taken to be the most profound threats to the sense we make of anything whatsoever—realities and experiences that, if left unintelligible, would threaten our ability to sustain a way of life. Human beings can make it through life fearfully, miserably, meanly, or with heavy hearts; but we cannot hold our societies together without giving some account—however provisional or correctable—for what most threatens sense. We have developed different strategies for doing this, of course. But we have also developed different notions of what *counts* as sense-making—that is, of what we must *do* in order to account for anything. My claim is that love remains one of our most fundamental sense-making efforts, one which attempts to explain not just what 'allows for' explanation, but what *demands* to be accounted for, the most unavoidable burdens on our powers to make intelligible anything at all. In this way, love also expands our notion of what counts as sense-making, in ways I shall discuss.[9]

I hasten to add that, in my discussion, I will not try to offer a new 'theory' of love, or to define love by the lights of established areas of human knowledge. I will, of course, unavoidably appeal to determinations that others have made. But in making these appeals, I wish to bear in mind how different methods of inquiry (philosophy, philology, anthropology, literary criticism, sociology, historical analysis) are as much conceptions of objects of study as they are tools for their assessment. The questions and answers we offer when figuring something out also shape whatever we are trying to know.[10] In discussing texts characterized as literary or philosophical or historical, then, I want to ask what these texts themselves are 'thinking about'—how they make sense of us, not just how we might make sense of them.

Temporal Change: Life and Death

One of most conspicuous 'threats to sense' faced by human beings is the continuity of temporal change. The passage of time erodes the sense we make of anything we perceive, unless we manage to grasp what is 'essential' or constant in such change. Most ordinarily, after all, lovers become 'sense-makers' when faced with changes in people and circumstances over time. We all change over the days and years, just as we adjust to shifting circumstances. Our children grow up before our eyes; our parents grow older. Our beloved becomes more tolerant, or suffers an injury, or changes his political views. Our friend appears lively at some times, and at others she appears mellow. My paramour flirted with me yesterday, but today she ignores me. Unless we can grasp what is essential about one another, over time through all these changes, not only will we fail to 'know' one another, but we will not be able to make sense of anything at all.[11] And, although identifying one another necessarily involves sensuous, bodily apprehension—we cannot look elsewhere, or get 'behind' appearances—this also entails a kind of reflective appraisal, some 'understanding' of one another. As we look into someone's eyes or perceive her body language, we also try figure out her changing moods or interests, and what those changes reveal about *her*.

Because all this entails reflective effort, love must be a concrete, practical attempt to make sense of one another in light of the constancy of temporal change. Different ways of loving one another—different *kinds* of loving practices—are different responses that we have worked out, over time, to different threats to sense. Some responses are necessarily intimate and thus call for certain kinds of touching, stimulation, a heightened sensuality; others are probably more temperate. Lovemaking, for instance, cries out for certain forms of intimate contact. Other loving acts—like care of the dead—call for different kinds of touching, which change over time. And if we feel that certain kinds of love can be violated with the wrong touch, then this is because our need to calibrate the 'right' touch responds to a particular threat to sense that is posed in light of a particular historical reality. To see what love helps us to explain or make intelligible, then, we have to track these threats to sense, and the practical-sensual forms the responses have taken.

And this is not just a private matter—since we may find that what is required in order to make sense of what we are doing with each other, or to carry out certain sensuous interactions, is not (yet) livable in our social-historical world. Immense social-historical transformations may be demanded by—may be explicable only in light of—love's sense-making efforts. Obviously, a book like this cannot 'catalogue' all of these. Nevertheless I hope to make a start, and at least offer the kind of account that should be possible at this point in time.

■ ■ ■

With this in mind, following this Prologue, this book is organized into two main sections. These begin by discussing the *temporal changes* that most profoundly threatened the sense our ancestors could make of their world and one another: Part II begins with the *inevitability of death*, and Part III with the *propagation of life*.

I begin Parts II and III with this pair—individual mortality and the reproduction of life—because the efforts undertaken by our ancestors to make sense of these two profound temporal changes, both in the lives of individuals and with respect to the overall circumstances we all share, have shaped fundamental and lasting forms of human self-understanding. What I mean by this will, I hope, become clearer as we go along. But my overall discussion might be helpfully introduced by stating some issues and topics which will orient my discussion.

In Part II of this book, I discuss the threat posed by the death of individuals to the sense we make of each other *as* individuals. Death challenges our ability to determine who someone *is*, given that person's retreat from life. How are we to reconcile our understanding of someone with what we see happening to him after death? The earliest forms of love—care of the dead, ancestral family love—emerge as a practical-thoughtful response to this challenge. Romantic love, I will suggest, develops in part by offering a compelling alternative to ancestral family love—by furnishing a novel account of the claims of mortality on human individuation, in view of which 'care for the dead' gives way to new positive freedoms for 'loving interactions' among the living. I shall examine ways in which some of our best known love stories—such as those of Orpheus and Eurydice, and Romeo and Juliet—have thought about these issues.

Part III of this book begins with a discussion of how fruitfulness and multiplicity, in our life-form and others, must have puzzled our ancestors. Our forebearers would have had to *learn*—to teach themselves through reflective practice—that our life-form can reproduce through our own activity: a practice we eventually came to understand and regulate as sex. At the same time, this 'lesson' could only have been learned through sexual acts that consolidated and expressed different 'knowledges' and self-understandings. The ramifications of this sexual self-education are immense. I will try to show how sexual activity has historically installed, and (from our vantage today) explains, a number of profound transformations in our self-conception and modes of social organization over time.

For instance: once we understood ourselves to be a life-form that reproduces sexually, we began to treat one another in ways that expressed that understanding. In the third part of this book, I will suggest ways in which such 'treatment' can help us to explain how we came to think of ourselves as (*interact as*) sexually differentiated, and eventually as gendered in social-institutional terms. I will argue that this sexual self-education can explain the duration of deep-seated social institutions of sexual domination, patriarchy and a gender-based division of labor. Along the way, I will also suggest how my account might usefully respond to certain impasses that have arisen in thinking about gender, kinship, the rise of feminism, and new reproductive technologies over the past few generations in the human sciences. And I will offer an account of lovemaking as a distinct world-historical achievement, one that can help us to explain enormous social-historical shifts, from the increasing social authority of love-based commitments to the erosion of a gender-based division of labor.

Such a summary only scratches the surface, of course. Nevertheless, seen in the right way, loving practices can help us to make sense of a host of cultural-historical phenomena that we would not otherwise be able to explain as efficaciously or as fully. Or, at least, this is what I shall set out to demonstrate.

This brings me to another principal claim of this book. Our practical responses to individual mortality and the propagation of life, I shall argue, led our ancestors to 'try out' different self-conceptions of human life as forms of social organization: as family or clan, or as a community of the living and the dead; as sexually differentiated, or socially gendered; as sexual lovers—to name only a few. These are not just different 'interpretations' of given natural processes—death or birth. They are, rather, the matrix through which we have articulated powerful ideas about ourselves and the conditions of our existence.

Indeed, different regimes of love show us that we have not taken sexual reproduction and individual mortality as given facts of the matter that govern social practices—though we can be tempted to think this way—but rather as historically shifting *reasons* for acting that have exerted profound authority in human cultures: organizing our activities, installing our values, directing our actions, and determining our identities and modes of social recognition. And whenever those reasons have started to seem insufficiently explanatory, we have developed new loving practices (new explanations) and hence *new* reasons for what we do to and with each other. By expanding reasons in this way, we expand our freedom and possibilities for acting. In doing this, we have also come to see one another *as* reasons for what we do. This is one development I shall consider at length, in treating sexual love, in particular, as the realization of freedom and self-consciousness.

The organization of this book around these two broad inquiries—individual mortality and sexual reproduction—also suggests a way to think about the historical achievement and development of sexual love, in particular. Sexual love, I argue, develops in response to the explanatory failures of more ancient practical understandings of individual mortality and the propagation of life. And from this, in turn, the social authority of lovemaking and love-based commitments emerges. I will try to show how, looked at in the right way, this development might furnish a more satisfying explanation of consequential shifts in our culture, our values, our ways of treating one another than has yet been made available.

For this kind of developmental account of love as sense-making practice to work, of course, I have to convince you that I am doing more than offering just one of many possible accounts of social transformations. However, this need not mean showing how what actually happened was historically necessary in some absolute sense (e.g. claiming that it *had* to happen this way because of 'the way things are'). Contingency in human affairs can be acknowledged by showing how historical actualities became possible, and even probable.[12] To this end, I shall try to offer a philosophical anthropology—hopefully one that will prove useful for inquiry across the human sciences—in light of manifest realities and social facts.

For all these reasons, I am interested in broad historical changes, and those loving practices that both 'drive' and provide an explanatory matrix for thinking about such changes. I want to think, for instance, about how our ancestors went from organizing their lives primarily around ancestral love and care for the dead to a way of life in which such care is still provided but no longer operates as the uncontested matrix for human self-understanding.[13] And I want to think about the growing authority attributed to sexual love—or what I shall call love-based commitments—over the past few centuries. In trying to account for these immense social transformations, and others as well, I want to understand how the basic values that uphold different ways of life came to *be* authoritative in the first place—why it would be impossible to understand historical societies (internally, as well as at a remove) without grasping the genesis of those values. This requires thinking on a fairly broad canvas (embarrassingly large, at times). But without this *kind* of account, contestable as it no doubt will be, our understanding of 'how we got to be us' is greatly impoverished.

The Erosion of a Gender-based Division of Labor

At this juncture, let me say just a bit more about the methodological ambitions of this book, in order to try to usefully contrast my approach to some current orthodoxies in the human sciences.

Consider an immense social change about which I will have much more to say in the third part of this book. For at least the past generation, in certain parts of the world, we have been living through what is arguably the most profound cultural transformation in human history—the increasing unacceptability of a gender-based division of labor as a principle for organizing our activities.[14] The ramifications of this transformation are vast. To name only a few: in widening areas of the world, unequal social standing for men and women is ever more disputed and even intolerable; the very notion that sexual difference determines (or ought to determine) what we do, or how we treat each other, has come to seem highly questionable in many parts of world; gender identity categories are increasingly experienced and judged to be fluid and malleable; the social intelligibility of kinship and family relations is less and less structured by sexual reproduction; and new reproductive technologies and contraceptive techniques are severing the propagation of life from the regulation of sexual practices.[15] I take these to be undeniable historical developments and social facts which, therefore, must orient what I have to say at relevant points in the following pages.[16] The implications of these facts are being widely discussed and debated across the humanities and natural sciences. Indeed, it seems safe to say that these are subjects of intense discussion across all walks of society—rightly so.

A number of these discussions naturally take the form of polemical defenses of, or attacks on, these broad changes—from the standpoint of public policy, social justice movements, morality, or religious traditions.[17] The force of the contestations themselves signals that we are dealing with 'live' questions that cut across cultural domains in profound ways. So we need ways of reckoning with these issues.

In reflecting on all this, many continue to propose that the contestations themselves reveal the essential nature of the social transformations in question. When it comes to the erosion of a gender-based division of labor, they claim, we are ultimately dealing with power dynamics, or a struggle to control the social agenda. Michel Foucault offered a particularly influential formulation of this, when he spoke of a strict connection between how we 'know' or 'define' human life and social realities, and the distribution of power within societies: a tight link between knowledge and power.[18] Foucault's suggestion—which has been taken up across the humanities—is that the constitution of what is 'real' or 'known' is itself, fundamentally, social power. Knowledge and power are not separable, goes the thinking; rather, through their interlocking, social realities and practical possibilities are determined. For instance, if women are 'known' to give birth, then that knowledge is both expressed in and reflective of the power dynamic it installs (a certain social division of labor). And yet, as this example illustrates, this kind of 'genealogical' approach leaves unexplained the *reason* for any particular knowledge-power nexus.

Genealogical approaches are visible in nearly every area of the contemporary humanities, and can be plausibly traced to certain aspects of the work of Marx, Nietzsche and Freud—the so-called masters of suspicion[19]—and their reactions to the pretensions of enlightenment reason. Genealogists try to unmask the relation between 'power' effects (social-institutional regimes) and holding something to be 'real' or 'true,' often by showing that relation to be contingent, ultimately without reason.[20] In light of genealogical critiques, certain ways of life—such as 'traditional societies,' in which the gendered reality of being a 'man' or 'woman' comes with corresponding practical restrictions—can start to look irrational. At the same time, nontraditional, more 'modern' ways of life—which foresee no need to restrict activities in this gender-based way—can also start to look just as contingent or rationally indefensible as the 'traditional' way of life. A kind of reductive historicism sets in. We tell ourselves that if we had been born in different times and places, we would have thought otherwise about ourselves and the world—as if that is pretty much all one can say.[21]

In the third part of this book, I will try to offer a different way of thinking about the relationship between knowledge (our ways of thinking about the world) and the installation of social power—in light, especially, of gender-based social institutions. For the moment, I want only to introduce a general methodological suggestion, and to sketch an alternative to this 'genealogical' paradigm. My first suggestion is that 'knowledge' (sense-making regimes) could not have the 'power' to shape an entire way of life, or to organize our activities and lend authority to our values and beliefs, unless such knowledge is seen to offer satisfying explanations for our deepest threats to sense. Power dynamics or social authorities are no doubt connected to knowledge (to how we explain 'reality')—Foucault was certainly not wrong about that. But these dynamics—such as 'gender,' or 'sexual reproduction,' or 'individual mortality'—must draw their energy *from*, before they can give energy *to*, our fundamental explanatory exertions. Social authorities are not 'normative'—are not reasons for doing something, or for treating others in certain ways—unless they offer at least provisionally satisfying accounts of our shared conditions. Explanatory satisfaction is not merely an effect of a struggle for control of the social agenda, even if these agendas are invariably set by the way we account for what we take to be reality.

Put another way, profound historical shifts in social-power dynamics—like the erosion of a gender-based division of labor—are no doubt connected to tectonic shifts in our self-understanding, our knowledge or our ways of explaining reality. But the question is whether those *shifts* are, themselves, knowable. Are social-historical transformations intelligible, ex post facto, in light of larger sense-making efforts that are not, themselves, *just* the installation of a new normative regime or social practice?

My suggestion will be that epochal normative collapses can only be explained if such collapses can be seen to result, not just from the perception of 'new realities' that do not fit an earlier knowledge-paradigm, but when those new realities *must* be grasped for the sake of making anything at all coherently intelligible. Profound power shifts—the collapse of our most deep-seated commitments—reflect profound threats to our sense-making efforts *tout court*, and the realization that those threats must be practically addressed, not just for the inner coherence of a particular a way of life, but so that anything whatsoever can be knowable.

This matters for our own self-conception, too. One of the most striking developments in the human sciences over the last generations—and, indeed, in our social world as a whole—has been the attention paid to the importance of gender as a social norm. Following Foucault, and by developing insights first offered by Simone de Beauvoir and others, Judith Butler has forcefully maintained that "knowledge and power are not finally separable but work together to establish a subtle and explicit criteria for thinking the world"; and she has, arguably, done more than anyone else to articulate the implications of this for our view of gender.[22] Seen from one angle, the rising interest in gender (and gender studies) is itself a manifestation *of*, not just a reflection on, the historical development in question. The insight that gender is fundamentally normative—that it expresses our ways of knowing the world, and the 'values' and 'norms' we uphold in light of that knowledge—is not just a philosophical insight, after all, but also a historical realization or new form of self-awareness (it is a reflection of what we now 'know'). The insight that gender is normative, hence unstable and revisable, cannot just be an ahistorical account of 'the way things are'—because part of the insight itself is that, for long swaths of human history, gender was 'thought' to be non-normative (biologically or theologically determined, say). A different 'knowledge regime' was in place. So, we still need to ask: *Why* did gender get installed as a knowledge regime in the first place? And why did gender more recently become a crucial domain for reflection on this kind of normative 'trouble'—and with what implications? By the same token, we should ask why gender has not been just any old norm, but a tremendously powerful norm, according to which entire societies, across the world, have felt compelled to organize their activities. Clearly gender *does* matter, but we ought to be able to account more precisely for its historical reality and power to control social agendas.

In Butler's view, genders are embodiments or practical possibilities within networks of entrenched cultural norms; new possibilities emerge through appropriations or revisions of these norms, in light of their "instability" or "contingency" (or, even, arbitrariness).[23] This contingency is thought to reflect the way in which norms are sustained through the practical delineation of their own limits—the "disciplining" production of a "constitutive outside," "exclusionary matrix," or "hegemony."[24] Although Butler does not speak much about freedom—the way that, for instance, Simone de Beauvoir did—it is clear that she is offering an account of normative autonomy, an explanation of how cultural norms achieve hegemony, become self-disciplining and self-delineating.[25] At the same time, Butler's account presents normative autonomy as if it were an open-ended round of musical chairs, in virtue of which legitimate 'players' are produced (socially as well as psychically) through the exclusion of others—but without any account of why any particular round of the game is being played in the first place.[26] But does Butler's notion of "contingency" really give explanatory satisfaction? Can we not, instead, aspire to explain why we acknowledge certain phenomena as contingent?

More broadly: can we make sense of the duration and failure of certain norms or power formations—such as gender, or the erosion of a gender-based division of labor, or sexual reproduction? Which sites of normative trouble are significant, and why? Significant, I mean, for our overall self-understanding, but also for ethico-political questions like, Which norms do we require in order to make life bearable for ourselves and others?

In order to give a fuller account of how we got here, then, I shall try to explain why a gender-based division of labor is eroding, why gender itself has become a site of increasing trouble, why access to birth control or abortion has become a pressing rights issue over the past few generations, and why the human sciences today cannot proceed without taking gender studies and feminist thought into account.[27] Other issues will be considered, too. Again, I am not suggesting that there is, or need be, any single explanation for these historical circumstances. But the possibility of making sense of deep historical transformations requires an account of how certain social domains—like gender—are inextricably linked, not just to power structures or 'disciplining regimes,' but to fundamental ways in which we have tried to make our lives intelligible, to deep-rooted self-conceptions on whose foundations entire ways of life are based. I am proposing that we see love as just such a fundamental sense-making practice.

Sense-Making

Finally, then, I should say a bit more about what I mean by fundamental sense-making practices, before finishing these prefatory remarks. After all, everything human beings undertake could be said to do some 'sense-making work.'

The historical duration of any practice reflects some 'account' of reality that is implicit in the doing of that activity. Athletic endeavors, for instance, imply some understanding of the laws of physics as well as a basic grasp of widely accepted social 'rules,' or at least a sense of occasion within a particular cultural horizon. Likewise, to take another broad example, the practical success of modern science and technology brandishes the explanatory efficacy of its theoretical insights—and in so doing, brings new historical realities into being.

And yet this last example can also help us to see a limit to the *kind* of sense-making achieved by the natural sciences. We may find ourselves empowered by modern science to bring into being nuclear weapons, medical cures, mechanical demands on our time and attention—but none of these phenomena can be fully explained or evaluated *by* the natural-scientific discoveries that gave rise to them. For instance: I can grasp the 'cause' of the Internet, from an engineering point of view, without knowing what sense to make of the Internet's existence. We can bring a new phenomenon into the world, and even understand the causes for its emergence, without necessarily being able to say what that new phenomenon really *is*. By the same token, the social authority of the scientific method, as a social practice or institution, cannot itself be evaluated by means of the scientific method.

As already mentioned, 'genealogical' work in the human sciences has tried to respond to this impasse. Throughout his career, Foucault undertook to illuminate what he called "a common history of power relations and object relations."[28] He recognized new nexuses of knowledge and power in various practices that might be said to 'define' the modern age—the use of prisons, psychiatry, or the 'science of sexuality.' Foucault saw in these practices (or "disciplines," as he sometimes called them) not merely new rules or codes of behavior, but novel techniques and concrete activities that expressed and achieved unprecedented value-regimes, new human self-conceptions. Such practices are historically significant, Foucault thought, not only because they manifest the endurance of a particular society—in the way that raising a red lantern might be taken to signal the vitality of a traditional Chinese society—but also because they display what a social world *thinks it is* in virtue of its endurance. The building of a temple, or the founding of a school, or the establishment of a constitutional democracy, or the practice of clinical psychiatry, for instance, could all be said to install and make explicit organizing beliefs, values and principles of a society. One measure of this is that these beliefs and values might find new forms of allegiance—new followers and adherents—beyond the confines of the local community whose vitality they indicate, such that these new followers start to treat one another differently over time. Foucault sought to investigate social practices whose historical rise and later fall reflect transformations in the self-understanding of entire social worlds, and whose cessation amounts to upheavals of values and not just changes in our habitual 'ways of doing things.'

Inspired by Foucault, many others have taken to examining the significance of the demise of certain broadly 'significant' historical practices. The philosopher Kwame Anthony Appiah, for instance, has offered a theory of what he calls "moral revolutions." As perspicuous examples, Appiah discusses the abolition of the Atlantic slave trade, of dueling in public, and of the binding of women's feet in China.[29] In a similar vein, others have looked to the abolition of torture, or to the demise of feudalism, or to the practical articulation of human rights or the rule of law, as historically revelatory in this way—namely, as practices that not only express the endurance of a particular way of life but also express the fundamental 'moral' self-understanding of that way of life.[30] Some even see in the developments of modern social history evidence of "moral progress"—expanded domains of individual and mutual recognition.[31]

Of course, one problem is that of deciding *which* practices count as historically revelatory in this way. What *counts* as a significant dimension of 'power,' after all? That is, which customs and activities might be understood not only to require and institute their own distinctive domains—probably all social practices do *that*—but also to do so in ways that perhaps foreground and hence educate us as to the implications of such 'requiring and instituting' more generally? Foucault himself seems to have been uncertain of which (if any) social domains—medicine, psychiatry, prisons, sexuality—aptly display how power operates; though I note that he turned, toward the end of his career, to the history of sexuality for the kind of traction that more distinctly modern institutions (prisons, psychiatry) seemed unable to provide. I will return to this in Part III.

At the same time—to get to the issue I want to raise here—in identifying certain social practices as historically revelatory in this way, it would also be important to consider what these practices can and cannot tell us about *themselves*, what sense these social activities can make of their own successes or failures. Let me suggest one question for further consideration: Can the historical realities brought into being by particular social practices—such as those Foucaultian domains just mentioned—be evaluated, 'corrected' or grasped *in* or *through* the historical reality and continuation of such practices themselves?

Or can that historical reality be grasped, evaluated and 'adjusted' only by the objective-documentable rise or fall of such practices over time.

Consider the suppression of the Atlantic slave trade. Could (*can*) the historical reality brought into being by the slave trade be grasped, evaluated and corrected *by the continuation of the slave trade*? That is, could the slave-trade itself 'adjust' over time, such that it would 'get better' at explaining the historical reality for which it is responsible? I understand the answer to this question to be, "No." Moreover, I understand *that* answer to have justified and required, minimally, the legal abolition of the sale of slaves in Britain, America and other nations (many other steps are in order, too). Put another way, although the Atlantic slave trade was a practice that manifestly displayed the values and beliefs of a particular historical society, the practice of the slave trade itself could not explain or make intelligible the 'historical reality' brought into the world by adherence to those values. The slave trade's eventual failure to make sense of *itself*—to justify its 'reality,' its way of 'knowing' the world—is what rendered it no longer viable, and made abolition historically possible and probable. Put differently, the actual meaning of the legal abolition of the slave trade (abolition's social authority, as distinct from its status as a moral 'ideal') just *is* the cessation of the slave trade, and the efforts we then exert in treating each other differently.[32] Obviously—but significantly—the slave trade turned out not to be a practice through whose practical *continuance* abolition could be actualized.

We are often tempted to understand the suppression of the slave trade, or of public torture, as the discovery of a moral fact—as our awakening to some moral truth, such as the intrinsic equality or dignity of all human lives. Others might regard the slave-trade and torture as ways we *taught* ourselves—through awful lessons—those same moral truths, which had lain dormant all these years just waiting to be discovered and learned. However, these seem highly implausible explanations for these historical realities. For one thing, we fail to explain these practices *as historical realities* if we rely on ahistorical moral truths to explain them—as if our historical failings were part of an ongoing morality play in which we slowly learn, or teach ourselves hard lessons about, how we 'ought' to treat one another given the kinds of creatures we are. All of this is, I think, part of an understandable desire to see things from the point of view of moral facts. This desire is understandable, I mean, as a measure of the perceived threats to sense in the present—a measure of how an unflinching acknowledgment of historical reality can still fail to make that reality explicable. Nevertheless, by trying to open a space for 'critical' deliberation about what we 'ought' to do next, this escape from history is more of a symptom of perceived threats to sense-making than a good response to that threat. Put simply: there are no moral facts, outside history, waiting to be discovered—moral values cannot help us *explain* anything. If we want to explain how we come to have the moralities we have—as Friedrich Nietzsche tried to do, in the *Genealogy of Morals*—then the first thing we have to do is admit that the morals themselves cannot tell us that story.

So, part of the problem lies in what would even *count* as an adequate explanation of a historical reality—and, hence, as a good basis for its correction or adjustment or discontinuance. If the historical meaning of the legal abolition just *is* the cessation of the Atlantic slave trade, first and foremost, and not the discovery of a 'moral fact,' then legal abolition *makes manifest* the slave trade's historical failure and collapse, without being the 'reason for' or 'explanation of' the collapse.

It remains unclear, in other words, what is truly *explained* by the abolition of the slave trade. What has abolition *accounted for*? What sense have we made of ourselves and one another, by showing the slave trade to have been, ultimately, senseless? Can the abolitionist give a good justification for the slave trade's historical duration? He may offer rationalizations or causal accounts— weak excuses about agrarian economics, colonialization, or about man's cruelty to man, or whatever—but it is hard to see how he can *justify* or try to *explain* the historical reality itself just by being an abolitionist. From the point of view of the abolition alone, it would seem, there can be no sense made of the slave trade, no true accounting for it—only deliberations about our immediate next steps, in light of our acknowledged connection to a historical crime.[33]

Many today see this kind of deliberation as the only kind of sense-making left to us. Perhaps they are right. This kind of 'tragic deliberation' in the contemporary human sciences bears certain resemblances to the reflections undertaken by Oedipus, once he 'awoke' to the historical crime he had committed. Whether he intended to commit the crime is, of course, irrelevant from the point of view of his subsequent tragic deliberations. The only question left is, what ought he do now, given what he acknowledges having once done?

Nevertheless, I want to at least suggest that what I am calling 'tragic deliberation' is not the only kind of sense-making available to us. I want to propose that we also practice more fundamental forms of sense-making—which might yield understanding about our connection to our past actions, not only through their abolition or acknowledged criminality, but through their self-corrections and acknowledged successes and failures. If graspable, these sense-making practices might also give us the chance to better account for *how* we make sense—of one another, and of whatever in our world threatens the sense we make of it, including historical crimes, immense social transformations, and accidents and misfortunes.

■ ■ ■

To begin trying to clarify what I mean, I will emphasize one important evaluative question about human affairs which tragic deliberation cannot sensibly ask: *Was it worth it?*

After all, the one question that the abolitionist cannot sensibly ask about the slave trade is whether it was *worth the cost*, the suffering and the damage wrought. In being an abolitionist, he has already given his emphatic answer: "No." Not even his becoming an abolitionist—not even the 'goodness' of that historical development—could justify the past suffering, from the tragic deliberator's point of view. Hence, the abolitionist cannot even *entertain* the question of the slave trade's having been worth it. Analogously, nothing in our present reality allows us to sensibly ask whether the extermination of six million Jews was 'worth it.' Or whether the devastation of Native cultures in the Americas was somehow 'worth it.' And historical traumas of this sort no doubt occur in individual lives as well. (As is often pointed out, one problem with talk of moral progress in human affairs is that it risks 'rationalizing' past crimes in view of an eventual moral betterment.)

Tragic deliberation thus begins by seeing the past as wrong, as a kind of crime—just as it looks to the present and future for the ongoing purgation of that past in deciding our next steps. In short, tragic deliberation may be unavoidable, under certain historical conditions. However, figuring out *which* historical conditions *are* tragic in this way is another task altogether—one that cannot be tackled by tragic deliberation. So, there are limits to tragic deliberation as a sense-making practice; namely, it offers us no way to explain *why* we did what we did, and hence who we might become, in view of a history we can own as ours—no matter its actual outcome.

By contrast, in assessing love's achievements and explanatory power, we cannot avoid asking, *Was it worth it?* This is just as true at the level of 'objective' history as it is for individual 'subjective' love-affairs. In assessing the rightness or wrongness of a particular love-affair—or in assessing a socially sanctioned way of treating one another in a given social world (pederasty in ancient

Greece, the institutionalized sexual trafficking of women and children, family love, courtship, prostitution)—we weigh the historical realities brought into view *by* those practices, taking in all accidents and contingent misfortunes. In this effort—as I will try to show—we not only deliberate about our next steps on the basis of moral judgments about past acts. We also try to ask whether the outcome (the present reality) is *worth* the suffering, the risks incurred along the way, the contingencies and accidents and misfortunes.

I do not mean that we need arrive at a final, shared answer to this question—*Was it worth it?* Our answers might change over time. I mean that we can sensibly pose this question only in the wake of certain undertakings—not just in order to take measure of moral progress, but to weigh an ongoing evaluation of our past. Indeed, there appear to be historical realities in the wake of which we cannot avoid posing the question. And if there are such realities, then we need ways of explaining them—how they came to be, and with what implications. Love stories, and love's own story, can help us in this, I wager.

At issue, then—in ways I hope to clarify in the following pages—is nothing less than freedom, self-justification and self-awareness in human affairs. One way of getting this issue into focus is to consider those undertakings and historical practices that can determine their own worth, or become the basis for their own evaluation—as ongoing, self-correcting, self-educating activities— while taking into consideration all the misfortune and calamity that might befall human beings when they set out on a life-project. In asking *Was it worth it?* we are also asking after the basis for collective self-evaluation, under circumstances where that evaluation cannot be separated from the actual outcome.

Perhaps some undertakings can be assessed or weighed in light of the sacrifices endured—that is, in light of 'values' that are detachable from the worth-it- ness of the undertaking itself, such that the latter can be measured by the former. But others, like love-affairs or large-scale social transformations, perhaps cannot be planned or evaluated in terms of any such cost-benefit analysis. This is another way of saying that the worth-it-ness of certain undertakings—like love— can perhaps only be decided adverbially by their eventual successes or failures, by being 'lived out' as the opening of possibilities for greater freedom in the face of whatever misfortune and hardship may come along. By becoming open to that *kind* of evaluation—that sort of *Was it worth it?* question—past events and interactions appear retrospectively self-educating, free, and self-justifying.

We need set no limits to the possible list of such activities or projects— though it is important to think about which activities are fundamental sense-making efforts and why. Nevertheless there is, I propose, at least one criterion for these kinds of fundamental sense-making practices—namely, the extent to which we continue to hold one another answerable, adverbially and over time, for their eventual successes and failures. By proposing that love qualifies as a way we come to hold each other answerable—and by trying to demonstrate why and how—this book aims to enliven the possibilities for freedom and sense-making which love enacts and tests.

Part II

Love of the Living and the Dead

Who is it that can tell me who I am?

Shakespeare, *King Lear* (1.4.217)

Getting to Know One Another

Those we love manifest certain qualities to whose charms we are not immune. His lovely hair, for instance, might strike our fancy. Or perhaps her awkward laugh and quick wit stand out to us. These properties matter a great deal because, unless we can identify them, we cannot distinguish their possessor from everything else that exists. Inasmuch as we take our bearings largely from the way things ordinarily look to us, we cannot discern other people—let alone love one another—without relying on describable characteristics, even if these amount to little more than the kinds of identifying markers used by scientists to determine that something is a 'such and such.'[1] There is a bit of scientific observation in every love-affair.

Determinable features are not *all* we love about each other, of course. With enough experience, we come to understand that figuring out who another person 'really is' means more than simply being able to observe his Gallic nose or describe his funny walk. However, we come to understand this not because there exists some ineffable, singular 'lovability' about people that transcends appearances and mere description. We learn this, rather, through the routine perception that who people really are simply cannot be adequately accounted for through observation and description alone. Others are not necessarily as they seem to be at any given moment.[2] Who someone really is must be sought out, imagined, conceived, made subject to conjecture and reflective thought—not just available to sensuous apprehension or empirical proof. At the same time, we obviously cannot abandon observation and description—or look 'under' or 'behind' a person's appearance for his true essence—without losing sight of the other person, *his* manifest qualities. More generally, then, we discover that we need a way to distinguish who someone is 'really' from what is not essential to him—even as we learn that we cannot rely on a gap between 'appearance' and 'being,' or 'seeming' and 'truth,' to do that work for us. As a matter of practice, love cannot proceed without the reflective work of separating the essential from the inessential—*nor* without our reflecting, as we go along, on just how we go about determining and recognizing what is essential. How quickly lovers must become philosophers.

Truth be told, of course, human beings engage in this kind of reflection all the time—in everything from scientific accounts of natural phenomena to the military-political work of 'knowing' one's enemy. Our ability to discriminate what things are from how they seem at a given moment is what makes us more than mere 'sensors' of random appearances. We are self-aware inasmuch as we manage to distinguish how things are from how things appear. And different kinds of love, different loving *practices* and bonds, help us distinguish the essential from the inessential. While it might seem an undue generalization to start by speaking of love in this highly abstract way, there is something to be gained, for the time being, by considering love in the most generous sense of the term—that is, as the name for any number of ways that human beings have treated and recognized each other over history, as family, friends, ally or foe, fellow citizens or sexual lover. So, for the moment, I will use the term 'love' undefinedly and proleptically but, I hope, comprehensibly.

Not only do different forms of love manifest our various attempts to make sense of one another—so, too, the very fact that we elaborate, over time, different loving practices (familial, charitable, friendly, sexual) means that what is involved in making sense of each other is also something we want to figure out. It would be absurd, after all, to suggest that lovers become 'sense-makers' or philosophers just by stroking their chins thoughtfully, or by parsing the essential from the inessential into neat mental categories through intellectual labor alone. The messy business of loving other human beings—the ways we treat one another, touch one another, what we do to and with one another, and how all this changes over time and history—all this is a way of 'doing' philosophical work. Love as a practice, in other words, must be a fundamental kind of sense-making. And the human bonds to which we give names—'friend' or 'brother' or 'partner' or 'lover'—express our understanding of one another, a shareable self-conception.

Of course, whatever sense we make of one another can be disappointed or frustrated, or fail utterly. We can *mis*understand ourselves and one another, despite our best efforts. But if this is so, then considering love as a historical practice—one that changes and develops over time and in history—should teach us about how we have succeeded and failed to make sense of each other, and what the implications of this self-education amount to, at this point in our shared history. This book is devoted to this broad consideration.

Most ordinarily, lovers become 'sense-makers' when faced with the inevitability of temporal change—for example, when confronted with the transformation of people and circumstances over time. Undoubtedly, each of us changes with the passing of days and years, just as we adapt to fluctuations in the circumstances of our lives. Our child grows up. Our lover's hair falls out. His moods shift. Nevertheless, unless we apprehend him over time in spite of these changes, we could not continue to 'know' him, for example, as someone we care about. Identifying who he 'really' is must involve not only sensuous apprehension, but also a reflective grasp of him—in his ever-changing appearance—as well as some sense of how we arrived at that understanding. The more we care to get to know him, the more we do this. After all, if someone who claimed to understand me had grasped *only* certain external features of my life—such as the facts of my life-story, my basic likes and dislikes, my stated hopes and dreams, facts turned up by an Internet search—then it seems fair to say that she could not yet claim to really understand *me*. She would only have understood these features—not what these features themselves make manifest or 'show': namely, who *I* am. To understand *me* she would have to do more than just perceive or apprehend my external manifestations—she would have to think about these things, reflect on them. Not just in silent contemplation, but also in more thoughtful interactions. To more deeply know me, in other words, she would have to concretely treat me, or speak about me, in ways that somehow made her thoughtfulness manifest.

The practical business of loving each other, then, means searching for a way to make sense of one another as ever-changing—while looking for ways that these changes 'reveal' our beloved. If this ongoing pursuit involves thought-ful work on our part—if it amounts to something more than waiting for a di-vine revelation, or 'moment of truth'—then love is a concrete, practical effort at making sense of one another, as temporal creatures, possessed of qualities, with whom we interact in historically transforming circumstances. After all, our ev-eryday *interactions*—including moments of thoughtful repose, or our efforts at finding the right words, the right gesture—are the only way for this practical effort at understanding to proceed. By the same token, whatever sense we make of one another is expressed in how we treat or 'love' one another, and how that treatment changes over time. Transformations in our concrete practices of loving one another, over the days and years, thus amount to profound and im-portant revisions in our sense-making efforts—our attempts at understanding ourselves and others, our collective self-education.

To be in any kind of love-relation—a friendship, a family, a tribe, a sexual romance—is be answerable, in deed if not in words, for the very fact of being in the relation. And being answerable cannot just mean saying, 'she has nice teeth' or 'we are family'—where being answerable must, at a minimum, imply that 'she is family and *I* see that as a reason for doing this or that.' To be bound to another, or to treat another in a particularly 'loving' way, is to be answerable for the sense one makes of that other person, of one's relation to them. Our ac-tions express 'senses made,' just as our sense-making takes shape in our actions.

For example, if I am asked what it is to belong to others as 'family,' then the answer I give must be practicable—what I 'think about' my family members *is* what I do for and with them, our shared answerability for what we do. To take another instance: when, in the third act of Shakespeare's play, Hamlet confronts his mother with the image of "two brothers," and challenges her to tell him the difference between the two men—"Ha! have you eyes?"—he is not just examin-ing whether Gertrude can apprehend qualitative differences between his father and his uncle; he is interrogating Gertrude's reflective judgment, *her* under-standing of what she is doing with Claudius following the death of Old Hamlet. "What judgment / Would step from this to this?"[3] And while Gertrude may be unable to produce a verbal answer that will satisfy Hamlet, the implication is that unless Gertrude can demonstrate *some* thoughtful answer, she has no self-consciousness, hence no agency in the affair at all.

We cannot really get to know someone, in short, just by compiling a list of what we 'know' about him: by cataloguing his attributes and deeds, from the banal (how he takes his coffee) to the less banal (the defining deed of his life), or merely by describing his important attributes—his unusual intelligence, his deep-seated insecurities, his penchant for music.[4] For one thing, it might be helpful to hear what *he* thinks about what he has done, or about who he is—say, by catching his conscience in a moment of introspection or self-analysis. This might be helpful, not because it would offer a glimpse into the 'real' person that 'transcends' all of his appearances, but because it would give us another way to think about an overarching connection *between* his various deeds and appearances. Such accounts can take many forms, of course. Biographers, storytellers and poets, for example, might thoughtfully present the unified story of a protagonist's life as something more than a fragmentary chronicle of 'what was said and done' or a list of 'descriptive qualities.' So, too, one friend might listen to another tell her story over coffee, not just as a detached audience, but with a delicate mixture of empathy, sympathy and distance adopted for the sake of heightened understanding. These are also acts of love—where by 'love' I still mean, very generally, practical attempts to make sense of others, such as take place in acts of mourning, eulogizing, or friendly conversation.

The first suggestion I want to make is that we take a giant step in the direction of achieving such self-understanding just by seeing that this is what we are doing as lovers—when we realize, in other words, that our efforts at understanding one another do not lead to some truth 'beyond' or 'behind' appearances, but to a richer understanding of the reflective, practical effort required in order to 'get to know' ourselves and others at all. We take another giant step, I think, if we can see these efforts as provisionally successful efforts at sense-making, hence as somehow rational—even if what we think we know about one another can never claim to be definitive. And we take a further step—to anticipate the theme of this book—when we see our efforts at understanding one another as also a way of coming to grips with the concrete challenges of mutuality and recognition in human affairs.

All of this is, admittedly, very general. Nevertheless these remarks will, I hope, prove useful in light of what I have to say next.

Loving the Dead

Now, there is one temporal change from which no living creature is exempt: death. And this makes individual mortality unavoidable for thinking about love who we really are in light of changes over time, and hence a necessary place to begin thinking about love as a practice. So, this is where I propose to start.

The threat that death poses to any sense we make of one another lies, first, in the way that an individual's death confounds our apprehension and identification of that other person.[5] The problem, again, is not just one of determinate identification. We can still 'identify' a dead body as 'so-and-so' or 'such-and-such,' at least for as long as distinguishing qualities and features remain perceptible. The problem, rather, is the larger one just discussed: How to thoughtfully demonstrate who we think this other person *really* is, or *actually* was, in light of his or her retreat from the company of the living? This required our ancestors (as it still requires us) to try to understand this 'change' called death—not just to observe it. After all, just witnessing an individual's passage from life to death threatens our efforts to make sense of that passage.

For one thing, we are left asking: what happens to someone when he dies? Does he withdraw into nature? Does his death show that—no matter who I thought he was, particularly—he belongs to an indifferent life-process of birth and decay? Is human life just an interlude in a biological cycle of generation and rot? How can we reconcile our understanding of someone's individuality or particularity with what we see happening to him after death? How can we understand someone as self-consciously active in the world—answerable for what he does—if his activity appears to end, not in any perceptible completion of a deed, but in the cold cessation of his movement?

To compound matters, we obviously cannot learn from a dead person, a corpse, how he *himself* assesses the change he just underwent, from being alive to being dead. Whereas we might gain some understanding of another person by asking him how he felt about losing his hair or becoming a parent, or by watching his facial reaction at the moment he is accused of a crime, we cannot expect a dead person to show or tell us what he thinks about his transition from life to death.[6] No one can report to us, in the first person, about death as an experience to be undergone or a deed to be performed. So, too, no one can be held responsible for being mortal. Death, rather, seems to de-individuate the dead one—by rendering him "quiet," as Hegel has it, or "without breath," as in Aristotle's summarization of a well-known ancient Greek characterization of death.[7] Whether one dies violently or of illness or old age, the passage from life to death itself appears to be a 'universal' natural process, since no one avoids it forever. Death looks like "nature's theme"—as Claudius calls it, in *Hamlet*—rather than something done or experienced by a particular person. If the 'universal' passage from life to death is something fundamentally unknowable, unreportable—if it is only an impersonal 'natural' process—then death threatens any sense that we might make of each other as individual existences. Our ability to demonstrate who we think someone essentially *is*—as distinct from anyone else—is thrown into question.[8]

In sum: because we cannot ask the dead to undertake that sense-making, the task of explaining—of demonstrably thinking about—an individual's 'life-to-death change' must fall to us, the living. What we 'do' for the dead one— bury him, mourn him, avenge him, leave him for the dogs, sing his praises—*is* how we make sense of him as belonging to us, to self-conscious life and not just to the unthinking movements of the natural world. For instance, by caring for the dead body, we stave off the natural processes that de-individuate the corpse. We preserve that body's distinctive features through embalming or special garments, so that the human community might then accomplish that destruction by burial or cremation—and thereby turn a natural process into a human deed.[9] Ritual acts of caring for the dead, such as those codified in the early Egyptian Book of the Dead, are assertions of conscious life against what seems to us like nature's mere flow and time's passage. Such rites install the intergenerational life of a community to which individuals might intelligibly belong, and in view of which they can be understood *as* individuals, as a member of a shared form of life rather than just as specimens of a natural species. Conscious life, in its finite 'subjective' form (individual lives), is rescued from oblivion by being 'objectified' or codified in ritual-institutional practices through which we engage one another and show how we understand each other.

Contrary to what some philosophers maintain, then, death itself does not individuate us any more than birth does. Individuation is a social-historical achievement, occasioned by the threat to our sense-making posed by mortality, and made real by our ancestors through communal practices.[10] In *Phenomenology of Spirit*, Hegel offers a philosophical-anthropological account of this when he suggests that the constitution of the ancient family as "ethical [*sittliche*] relation" responds to this task. The family, or "blood-relationship," as Hegel calls it, was—in ancient times, especially—particularly suited to this job, since the challenge for any blood-uterine relationship (such as that between Jocasta, Antigone and Polynices) is to show how they are bound as individuals not only because of an inscrutable fact of nature (maternal birth, or death and decay) but by their practical duty to one another: above all, the duty to care for one's *own* dead.[11] In our care for the dead, we show that who we think the deceased 'really is' is not fully defined *for* him (or for us) by some given set of natural facts or attributes, but by the way we thoughtfully *treat* him. When Isis collected Osiris' body parts to mummify them, when Achilles mourns Patroclos or drags Hector's body through the dust, when Antigone buries Polynices, when Hamlet "lug[s]" Polonius' "guts into the neighbour room" or when he seeks revenge for his father's murder, or (to anticipate a work to which I will return) when Ennis tries to retrieve Jack's ashes at the end of Annie Proulx's *Brokeback Mountain*, they are all demonstrating what they think of the dead individual, in his very being. As this short list shows, *how* we make sense of one another changes radically over time.

As Alexandre Kojève put it, this kind of love, "is first realized in and by the ancient Family." And since this love "does not depend on the *acts*, on the *activity* of the loved one, it cannot be ended by his very *death*. By loving man in his *inaction*, one considers him *as if* he were dead. Hence death can change nothing in the Love, in the value attributed by the Family. And that is why Love and the worship of the dead have their place in the pagan Family."[12] Obviously, the "Family" to which Kojève is referring is not the modern, bourgeois nuclear family, nor the ancient Roman family or any other localized kinship practice. At issue is the emergence of a historical practice of 'love'—care for the dead—as the requisite for any self-aware form of life, any rule-following set of practices through which individuals engage each other.

Loving the Living

As it happens, all this results in a profound threat to the sense we make of one another. For the ancient family's care for the dead can only 'love' individuals in their very being—the physical 'thereness' of someone—and not in view of any self-expressive, self-conscious activity we might undertake other than ritual care for the dead. And if we have only one overarching 'reason' to love one another—namely, the threat that death poses to the sense we make of self-conscious life, as just discussed—then, as a practical matter, we love one another the same, dead or alive. We treat and love the living *as if* they were dead.[13] Similarly, the formation of militaries and warring states around the 'sacrifice' of individual lives to the *polis*, shows the worth of the living individual to be most fully revealed in his death. If the aim of caring for the dead, in militaries as in ancient family life, is to demonstrate that the natural process of death changes nothing in our love—nothing in our thoughtful assessment of the dead individual—then there is nothing that one can do to individuate oneself *apart from die*, especially if that death is particularly memorable or brave or honorable. But if that is true, then in what sense do we apprehend each other as, 'think of each other' as, really living or as having lived at all?

Our ancestors were, of course, troubled by these questions, and went on to learn that ritual love of the dead is inadequate to the task of making full sense of one another—though no culture can do without it. For one thing, what if there is disagreement about the dead one's standing in the community, about who we think the dead one *is*? What if, as happens in Sophocles' *Antigone*, there are some who think that Polynices should be treated to burial; while others, like Creon, think that he is really an enemy to the *polis*, and as such is someone whose corpse should be left untreated? At issue, as Hegel's famous interpretation of Sophocles' tragedy made clear, is not only the latent conflict between family and *polis* that is brought to light, but the way in which this is revealed through the incompatibility of the practical requirements that inhere in the life of the family and the life of the *polis*. The conflict, in other words, is laid bare by the practical failure of burial rites alone to adequately determine who Polynices really was, in view of what he did while he was alive. The questions did not go away: How are we to understand *him*? How are we to think about the connection between the various features of Polynices' existence (his family, his upbringing, his life-circumstances) and his actions (his military allegiances)? And who do we think *we* are (Antigone, Creon, Ismene; *polis*, family) in light of our enacted response to these questions? Confronting all of these problems means taking an evaluative stance on burial, since keeping one's commitment to bury the dead now requires Antigone to be held individually answerable for it.

The need to make sense of individuals in their living activity also accounts, at least in part, for narrative or poetic or artistic efforts to testify to some connection between human actions and human agents. If storytelling is, along with care for the dead, a primordial human practice, then this is probably because poetic testimony (like Sophocles') demonstrates thoughtful reflection on who someone really is (or was) in view of various features of their existence and their deeds.[14] At the same time, to the extent that poetic efforts are necessarily commemorative or memorable, they also drive home the importance of mortality for our conception of human agency. Inasmuch as no one 'lives to tell' about his passage from life to death, again, any artistic-narrative presentation of an individual as he 'really was' is, finally, offered from the point of view of a human community that survives the death of that individual.[15] "Death is the sanction for everything that the storyteller can tell," as Walter Benjamin put it, "he has borrowed his authority from death."[16]

At the same time, if what we owe the dead is not something on which we can universally agree—if individual mortality is not an "authority" around which a coherent way of life can be indefinitely carried out, or through which it forever can understand itself—then this does not mean that our responses to death cease to carry explanatory weight. It just means that our understanding of individuals in light of their death is open to revision, to new active responses. Our responses to the deaths of others, after all, tend to be thoughtfully improvised and historically self-reflective, not just unthinkingly dutiful.[17]

Such innovations can be seen anywhere one cares to inquire into the history of human practices rooted in the authority of individual mortality—from the shifting elaboration of tomb markers in Egypt and epitaphs and funerary portraits in ancient Rome to the range of cultural narratives, eulogies, chronicles, séances, obituaries and ceremonies that register not only a ritual connection between the living and the dead, but also an ongoing 'rethinking' of our shifting connection to those very rituals. We can leave it to specialists to tease out the historical details of these shifts.[18] Likewise, under certain social conditions, our response to individual deaths becomes a subjective work of memory or mourning that is increasingly untethered from the practical, communal issue of what one does with the dead body, even as that concrete issue never fully disappears— a dilemma that Freud understood to be expressed in Hamlet's predicament.[19]

The point I wish to make here, at any rate, is more general: the claims of individual mortality on the sense we make of ourselves are subject to immense upheavals, in light of new challenges to our self-conception—challenges which require ever more self-aware sense-making practices, more imaginative and thoughtful responsiveness among the living. Rule-based funerary rites—those fundamental social obligations that obtain by virtue of being essential to our self-conception as conscious beings—tumble into the issue of how living individuals take up that self-conception. "We with wisest sorrow," says Claudius, eulogizing his dead brother with this thought in mind, "think on him / Together with remembrance of ourselves" (1.2.6–7).[20]

This means that our innovative responses to individual mortality amount to our 'trying out' different self-conceptions of human life. The history of funerary practices is not just different 'interpretations' of the natural process of dying—it is a matrix through which we have articulated new conceptions of ourselves and the conditions of our existence, including the passage from life to death. So, to avoid misunderstanding, it is not the cold 'fact' of death, but rather self-induced transformations in our practical responses to individual mortality—our *thinking* about the deaths of individuals—which account, at least in some part, for transformations in our culture, our values, our ways of treating one another.

With this much in mind, we are in a position to at least provisionally propose an initial axiom: human activities are not just bounded or governed by the fact of individual mortality, but also by our practical efforts at self-understanding—which must have included our practical attempts to explain who we are in light of temporal changes, like birth or pregnancy or death. If human activity is determined by our own practical-reflective efforts at self-understanding—by our attempts to explain ourselves and our circumstances, for which we are answerable in the first person—then how we 'think about' ourselves is expressed in the historical horizons of our practical possibilities.

To demonstrate this, rather than just assert it, I want to track sexual love as a practice through which we can be seen to have 'taught' ourselves that our activities are not governed or determined by any external power, or fact of nature, but by our own self-conscious sense-making efforts and practices. I will give a fuller account of this in Part III, but for the moment I propose to think about how sexual love develops in the terms just discussed: that is, in response to the practical crisis in the 'objective', duty-based domain of family love.

Vincit Amor

I wanted to endure my grief, and I will not deny that I have tried to bear it. But Love has conquered me.

posse pati volui nec me temptasse negabo: vicit amor

Ovid, *Metamorphoses* (8 CE)

Everyone remembers the tale of Orpheus and Eurydice, mostly from its primary ancient Roman sources, Virgil's *Georgics* (c. 29 BCE) and Ovid's *Metamorphoses* (8 CE).[21] Eurydice ("doomed girl," *moritura puella*) dies on the day of her wedding to Orpheus. In the fourth book of Virgil's *Georgics*, the tale is told by Proteus to the beekeeper Aristaeus, who learns that his own troubles (he has lost his bees) are the result of Orpheus' anger at his role in Eurydice's death.[22] Eurydice is the victim of what looks like blind fate: Aristaeus' covetous pursuit, Eurydice's flight from him, and the fatal snakebite to which this leads.[23] Orpheus descends to the Underworld to retrieve the dead Eurydice, initially wins her back, and then loses her again during their 'ascent' to the world of the living when he turns back to look at her.[24] This much of the story is familiar enough.

However, not everyone remembers that Orpheus was not always known as Eurydice's lover. In fact, Orpheus had first been famous as an archetypal figure for musicianship and singing—a fame that seems to predate the first mentions of his involvement with Eurydice by some centuries.[25] Think of the numerous representations of Orpheus charming the gods and animals with his lyre.[26] Only later did Orpheus come to be known as the hero of one of the best-known love stories ever.[27]

Consider, first, the way in which Virgil describes Orpheus' response to Eurydice's death. Orpheus grieves Eurydice without publically mourning her. He performs no funerary rite in her honor.[28] In explicit avoidance of the community's rites, Orpheus soothes his "lovesick heart" with a song performed for no one but himself:

> [Eurydice's] friends, the Wood-Nymphs, filled the high peaks with ululation, and these wailed, too—the heights of Rose Mountain and the lofty Whole-Earth range in Thrace, and King Rhesus' war-loving land, and tribes on the Danube, rivers in Thrace, the North-Wind's wife. Orpheus, strumming his hollow-shell lyre to soothe his torn heart, sang you, sweet wife, sang you to himself on the lonely shore, day in, day out, sang you at sunrise, sang you at sunset.[29]

Orpheus does not deny the fact of Eurydice's death or individual mortality, of course. Nor does he contest the finality of Eurydice's eventual return to the Underworld. As Ovid tells the story, he asks only for "possession of [Eurydice's] few days as a boon":

> We mortals and all that is ours are fated to fall to you, and after a little time, sooner or later, we hasten to this one abode. We are all on our way here, this is our final home, and yours the most lasting sway over the human race. (*Metamorphoses* 10.32–35)[30]

In this way, Orpheus rejects—he 'determinately negates,' as philosophers would say—the sense that traditional practices make of her death.[31] His "lovesick song" laments not just the loss of Eurydice, but also the failure of communal rites to make her death culturally meaningful to *him*.[32] "I wanted to endure my grief," says Orpheus, "but love has conquered [*vicit amor*]." The point, I think, is not that love is somehow a more powerful emotion than grief—as if these were competing passions in tug-of-war within Orpheus' heart.[33] Love is not just a passionate impulse or all-powerful *amour fou*, by which Orpheus is swept away or to which he simply 'cedes,' but a novel practical possibility—one that emerges improvisationally in Orpheus' search for a response to Eurydice's disappear-ance, a response *other* than caring for her corpse or singing a mourning song.[34]

This is why, instead of singing *of* the dead—as one might expect of Orpheus-the-singer in more ancient figurations—Orpheus' song here becomes a direct demand, carried *to* the dead, to "the portals of the Underworld." As in earlier figurations, Orpheus' song continues to enchant and gather an audi-ence.[35] However, in Virgil's and Ovid's accounts, the Underworld denizens are so dumbstruck by Orpheus' new love-song that they bring to a halt their own ritual practices, opening a space for Orpheus' song to set a provisional course for what happens next.[36] Virgil does not tell us what Orpheus sings, exactly, though we perceive the affective force of the song. In Ovid, however, Orpheus' song is made explicit: "I wanted to endure my grief," he says, "and I will not deny that I have tried to bear it. But love has conquered me. . . . if the fates deny this privilege for my wife, I am resolved not to return. Rejoice in the death of two" (*Metamorphoses* 10, 25–27, 38–39).[37]

Orpheus' Turn

With this, we come to the decisive point in the story: Orpheus' fateful turn-around.

So far as we know, Virgil's poem is the earliest source to represent Orpheus as suffering the loss of Eurydice twice, due to his having turned to look back.[38] Yet we do not learn from Virgil the terms of the 'pact' between Orpheus and the Underworld; we learn only that Persephone imposed a condition, a *lex*, ac-cording to which Eurydice would have to follow Orpheus during their ascent.[39]

Interpretations of Orpheus' backward glance abound. Indeed, Ovid's own retelling of Virgil's tale is itself an interpretation of Orpheus' turn. Yet, so far as I am aware, the following account has not yet been considered.

Because Orpheus' appeal to the gods was 'successful'—Eurydice is released—he now finds himself in a kind of trap. His predicament is not, as we might be tempted to think, hidden in the famous condition: "that he should not turn his gaze backward" (*ne flectat retro sua lumina*; *Metamorphoses* 10.51). Rather, the quandary lies in this: if the lovers were to *complete* their return to the world of the living, then the fate of their relationship would once again be subjected to the social authority of individual mortality, a way of life organized around the 'care for the dead' from which Orpheus had now distanced himself. Orpheus' "success," that is, would only return them to the same historical self-conception from which his song had sought to free them.[40] The trap, in short, is inherent in the very granting of Orpheus' plea—namely, to "renew the life-thread of Eurydice." "We all fall back who are born mortal" (*Metamorphoses* 10.18).

This did not escape Virgil and Ovid. Both depict the silent ascent as taking place on a liminal path that—in contrast to the river Styx (Death)—does not neatly divide and connect the living and the dead so much as represent a domain that, effectively, belongs to neither. This is emphasized, among other things, by the way in which the tenebrous play of earthly light and Underworld darkness ("on the edge of light") renders indistinct the precise boundary between the living and the dead—all in marked contrast to depictions of the Underworld found in Homer's *Odyssey*, Book 11, or in Plato's Allegory of the Cave, where the emphasis falls on the sensuous perception of light and shadow, on the 'passivity of seeing,' rather than on the subject's active turning or 'taking in.'[41]

Orpheus, for his part, also seem to understands that the ascent through this liminal space demands a conclusion that is now up to him. The gods' injunction—"if he turned his eyes, the gift would be lost"—is not the expression of a divine power *over* Orpheus. Just the reverse, the injunction effectively evacuates the gods' power to determine the outcome, leaving matters to Orpheus—in an admission of atheism, or secular-rational authority, so to speak. Until, or unless, the lovers complete their return to the world of the living, no 'higher power' than Orpheus himself can finally separate him from Eurydice, or decide his response to her death.

Both Ovid and Virgil emphasize that Orpheus knows, in advance, the consequences of turning around. Because Orpheus can connect his actions to a foreseeable outcome, we should consider his turn as self-conscious, self-expressive—not as sheer impulse, or as the involuntary expression of some skeptical urge.[42] Orpheus, I wager, knew what he was doing—or at least, he sought to connect his action to what he knew about the condition (*lex*) under which he alone was acting. At the same time, the consequences of Orpheus' action—of his 'turn-around'—are not made known by the communal values that his deed upholds, or fails to uphold, but rather by what these consequences reveal about *him*, his experience and understanding of Eurydice's disappearance from life. Ovid's description should be read, I think, as bearing this out:

> Afraid of failing, fearful and eager to see, he turned his loving eyes [*hic, ne deficeret, metuens avidusque videndi flexit amans oculos*]. (*Metamorphoses* 10.56–57; my translation)

As I read these lines, Orpheus' anxiety was not directed toward whatever was happening behind him, but rather toward his own action. Orpheus was aware, not just of what Eurydice may have been doing, but of what *he* was doing. He expresses his *own* fear of failure—and, therefore, his temerity and self-awareness. Why should the traditional translations and interpretations not, at least, reflect this possibility?[43]

Instead of responding to Eurydice's death with the ritual act of burial or mourning—whereby, as we saw, Eurydice's death would change nothing in the love she is accorded—Orpheus sees her death as having changed everything for him, for them. *His* estimation of Eurydice has not been left unchanged by her death. How could it be? She was alive one moment, his new bride, and dead the next. Whereas the community understands Eurydice to belong to them, as an individual, alive or dead, Orpheus cannot be satisfied with this judgment. He cannot be satisfied with funerary rites or mourning songs. Some other way of 'loving' her must be sought, however improvisatory.

But he must finally fail in this effort. Not because her body cannot be treated lovingly, but because, when it comes down to it, *he* cannot allow *himself* to love Eurydice's body the same as when she was alive, knowing what he knows: she has died.

He turns his eyes to see her dead, then. So that it is his understanding—his perceptual grasping of her disappearance from life—through which her loss is realized. In this way, his distinct, non-sanctioned relation to her—his love— remains valued above any ordinary worldly life.

> Dying a second time, she made no complaint against her husband; for of what could she complain save that she was beloved? (*Metamorphoses* 10.59–61)

It goes without saying that we still care for the dead by encoding rule-based procedures for such care. The depth of our self-conception as a community of the living and the dead explains the endurance of the practice, in its manifold transformations over the years. Love of the dead remains an unavoidable activity against whose horizon the significance of rule-based, duty-bound institutional forms of life in human self-understanding generally can be considered.

By the same token, whenever our routine interactions—whatever we are supposed to do for one another—fail to adequately explain or capture our self-understanding, new ways of interacting improvisationally emerge. And, I am suggesting, when such failures touch upon our most fundamental institutional commitments, the burden of answerability falls with greater weight onto in-dividual subjects, who are called to make fuller practical sense of one another as temporally changing, mortal creatures as best they can. This was Orpheus' predicament.

Most of the time, the stakes are low enough for this to go more or less unno-ticed. For instance, if simply saying a ritual "thank you" to my friend fails to cap-ture my indebtedness, or the depth of our friendship as I see it, then I can try to come up with some other display of gratitude. I can send flowers, or arrive with a bottle of wine. And if that improvised display is then accepted by my friend *as* gratitude, or as a sign of our lasting friendship, then my 'reason' (my gratitude, our friendship) justifies the act. I need not explain myself further. No new reason is articulated in such cases, of course—it is still just gratitude; only new ways of adhering to that reason emerge.

However, like Orpheus, one might act improvisationally, in a way that ap-pears unjustified by any socially recognized 'reason'—in a way that seems to express no shared understanding or self-conception. Ovid and Virgil called this new way *amor*. What then?

Well, one possibility is that one might be understood to be acting irrationally—at which point one cannot be held accountable for any action (the defense could only offer an 'insanity' plea). Virgil's Eurydice, for one, under-stands Orpheus' turn to be just that: a moment of madness, *furor*.

Alternatively—and this is the scenario that interests me—one might suc-ceed in getting others to take *oneself* as the provisional reason for the act. In this case, one might be taken to have acted self-expressively—as if Orpheus were the promissory note for a fuller explanation that is forthcoming, so long as Orpheus can become more fully known or understood. In this scenario, it is not a socially shareable 'value' or 'reason' that explains the action—instead, *Orpheus* becomes especially answerable for what he does, since his impro-vised attempts at sense-making are the only possible justification for what he has done. Orpheus becomes the reason for which his own turn is accepted as an action—and not as an irrational twitch, or bodily reflex. And if Orpheus is not taken to be mad, then he is individually answerable for his turn, for Eurydice's separation from him—a state of affairs that has not been lost on modern poets who rightly have gone on to imagine Eurydice's posthumous interrogation of Orpheus and his act.[44] Orpheus became a romantic lover, I am suggesting, precisely by becoming individually responsible for his own 'take' on Eurydice's death.

To become an amorous lover is one way we can become self-explaining or self-justifying. This happens, I am proposing, when we make ourselves answerable for acts that are not fully intelligible, or justifiable, in terms of extant, shared reasons for acting—familial, economic, military, or communal duties and values—which are justifiable only in light of the failure of such norms. More broadly, the issue is how we respond to one another—not just as people whose actions are taken to express known reasons for acting (established duties, commitments and values)—but also in view of one another *as practical reasoners*, who find we can offer no further justification other than our improvised attempts to make sense of things. This opens the possibility, at least, of a way of life that accords to the practical demands of becoming answerable to one another the same importance and centrality that our ancestors attributed to care for the dead.

It goes without saying, I hope, that we are still looking for ways to do this 'working out'—so, my point is not just to argue *that* we do this. This much should be clear—in everything from the articulation of new political systems, new domestic arrangements, and new economic regulations to expanded legal protections. If we manage to hold one another responsive to the question Why did you do this? and if we expand the potential occasions for such responsiveness, by enacting critical viewpoints on our fundamental commitments and duties, then we are entitled to say: the *more* we make ourselves responsive (the more we see *ourselves* in the reasoning behind our acts), the freer our activities.

My aim here is to try to better understand *how* we do this, how we learn that *we* do this, and with what implications.[45] It is in this light that we might profit from seeing love as a fundamental activity through which we have taken up the demands of mutual answerability, and taught ourselves that this is what we are doing. Not because love is the *only* practice through we do this, but because love has been an activity through which we have taken up the demands of mutual answerability by putting into question our most widely accepted reasons for acting—starting with care for the dead, arguably the most fundamental and historically persistent human duty. One of the lessons of love is that no shared self-conception, no matter how rationally compelling—not even what we owe the dead—can declare itself definitive or entirely capable of satisfying or justifying the challenges of answerability and mutuality.

The tensions in this predicament are raised to a fever pitch in arguably the most influential love stories in the world: Shakespeare's *Romeo and Juliet* and, its precursor, Ovid's "Pyramus and Thisbe."[46]

Pyramus and Thisbe

Pyramus and Thisbe lived in contiguous houses, in the city which Semiramis is said to have surrounded with walls of brick.[47] Being young and beautiful, living as next-door neighbors, they could not fail to notice one another.[48] At first, familial and neighborly ties sufficed to sustain an "acquaintance," but over time love grew (*tempore crevit amor*), such that the lovers not only fantasized about one another, but also sought to actualize these fantasies in the world, and to gain social-familial sanction for their relationship.[49]

We do not learn from Ovid why their parents forbid them to marry. (In contrast to Shakespeare's *Romeo and Juliet*, for example, there is no apparent history of conflict, no "ancient grudge.") Of course, societies *can*—and routinely do, through the incest taboo for instance—legitimately oppose certain sexual relations on economic or other grounds.[50] However, while this prohibition might lead to an opposition between the bonds of *erōs* and *philia*—a tragic conflict that was not unknown in ancient times, as the myth of Phaedra's ill-fated desire for Hippolytus makes clear—this is not the predicament of Pyramus and Thisbe.[51]

Indeed, the lovers do not even need to leave their family homes in order to carry on their affair. As Ovid makes clear, their ardor flourishes in the discovery that their passions *cannot* be prohibited by their families— "What no parents could forbid . . . they burned with mutual love" (*Metamorphoses* 4.61–62). From the parents' point of view, the lovers' desires are a matter of indifference, since they are 'merely' subjective.[52] Pyramus and Thisbe thus carry on their affair as part of their daily domestic routine—whispering, communicating by "nods and signs," and talking to one another through "a slender chink in the wall" shared by both houses. Even in restrictive and traditional settings, family life accommodates the existence and expression of subjective passions—however awkwardly. Ovid's memorable description of the "chink" in the wall is a perfectly apt depiction of this. We learn, for instance, that the fissure belongs to the houses' original structure—it is not a hole punched open by the lovers, nor the product of natural wear and tear.[53] At the same time, we learn that—prior to Pyramus and Thisbe—no one had noticed this particular opening:

> This chink, which no one had noticed through all these years—but what does love not see [*quid non sentit amor*]?—you lovers first discovered and made it the channel of speech. (4.66–70)

Openings for passionate expression can be discovered within duty-based social structures, without necessarily posing any existential threat to the structure's integrity.

Thus, the chink in the wall—love's discovery—allows for improvised, passionate interactions *within* domestic life (indeed, *thanks* to domestic life) without, however, being reducible to familial-domestic duties. By pressing their lips and ears to the partition, the lovers are not obviously performing any recognizable family obligation, after all, but neither are they rejecting any. Like teenagers with smartphones, they are exploring ways in which the strictures of family life furnish a context that supports, even invites, self-expressive acts. At the same time, the lovers' whispering and heavy breathing at the wall opens a perspective *on* the domestic context that would have otherwise remained invisible. For one thing, they learn that family life does not know its own fault lines, so to speak; openings for new practical possibilities may yet be discovered. So, the lovers prize the wall and its chink as a kind of 'chat room.' "So, separated all to no purpose, they would talk" (4.78).

Now, one thing chat rooms teach us—one reason we keep chatting—is that experiences of sexual desire are not reducible to the sensuous experience of seeing or touching, or being touched by, another person. The concrete technical medium of the chat room itself, after all, promises not direct carnal knowledge, but the eroticism of increased *understanding*—the desirability of making oneself known to another, and of knowing another. It speaks to the pleasure we take in *knowing* another—in our *sapience*, as well as our sentience. "Love looks not with the eyes, but with the mind; And therefore is winged Cupid painted blind." [54] The deeper and more satisfying the knowing, the longer the conversation, the more gratifying the pleasure. At the same time, by trying to understand what the other 'wants,' the lovers develop an erotic attachment not just to the other's body, but to the promise of that greater understanding. As in Plato's depiction of our erotic attachment to knowledge in *Symposium*, about which I shall have more to say, the chat room today remains a practical context or medium through which we can also teach ourselves about the implications of our desire to know one another, and our erotic attachment to such knowledge. [55]

One way we do this—still today (with new smartphone apps)—is by reflecting on the possibilities and limitations of a given 'chat' medium itself, when it comes to expressing or enacting what we know, or want to know, about one another. Pyramus and Thisbe, for instance, reflect on the chink in the wall by addressing that medium not only as a constraint ("O envious wall") but also as enabling their erotic discourse ("We owe it to you, we admit, that a passage is allowed by which our words may go through to loving ears"; 4.76–77). In other words, Pyramus and Thisbe explore the expressive possibilities and limitations of the medium—they figure out what it allows them to do and say. And in this way, they look for what *kind* of sense they can make of one another through this medium.[56]

It sometimes happens, as we know, that a desire to probe the expressive capacities of a medium—a hole in the wall, a letter, a smartphone—ends up taking precedence over a desire to understand how the medium helps one to make sense of anything else. Think of the obsessive attachments people can develop to their communication devices. In music, too, it sometimes happens that a composer or performer will try to express, so to speak, the 'expressive limits' of their instrumental medium—as Franz Liszt tried to do with the piano.[57] Rock guitarists often do this, usually to tedious effect. When this exploration of the instrument happens in a 'chat room,' a sort of fetishistic attachment to the medium can take root—the caress of the iPad, or the telephone—in ways that obscure, or even undermine, the erotic understanding afforded by the conversation: "I kiss the wall's hole, not your lips at all" (*A Midsummer Night's Dream* 5.1.200).

Yet, such explorations of the medium can also lead to a frustration, or bored exhaustion, with its expressive capacity; or simply to an adequate grasp of a medium's practical limitations. When this happens, we redouble our search for practical, concrete conditions that afford a more adequate pursuit of our desire to understand, to better get to know someone or something.

. . . *poteris nec morte revelli*

Whom death alone had power to part from me, not even death shall have power to part from me.

quique a me morte revelli heu sola poteras, poteris nec morte revelli

Ovid, *Metamorphoses* (8 CE)

Given their material and social constraints, and their boredom with the "wall," this search requires Pyramus and Thisbe to "elude their guardians' watchful eyes and steal out of doors," so as to make a date "in the open country" at Ninus' tomb (*Metamorphoses* 4.85–88).

Ovid's tale distills the practical-philosophical predicament to its barest outlines: If family or civic life responds to our need to make sense of one another as individuals, in view of profound temporal changes like death (metamorphoses, as it were), then any effort to make further sense of one another in view of *other* things we come to know (our desires and passions, our personal histories, our subjective stances on the world) must likewise increase practical possibilities for that sense-making and give greater positive freedom.

Surreptitious courtship—making a date—is a familiar form for such positive freedom, and was already so in Ovid's time. Indeed, Ovid's own *Ars amatoria*—a textbook devoted to the objective, pragmatic considerations that arise in extra-marital courtship—gives an elaborate account of what is required, concretely, of those who might wish to get to know one another better under widely known social constraints.[58] (This was a theme that occupied Roman poets from Catullus to Horace, and Ovid, in particular, throughout his career.[59]) In this context, however, Ovid cuts straight to the heart of the question under consideration: how are lovers to account for what they have learned about one another, as individual agents, in death as in life? How are the 'free' improvisations of courtship to establish themselves, objectively, as a way of life?

Even at this general level, it is not hard to see that this is a question with which we are still grappling today—as we work out new marriage regulations and kinship formations, and bestow greater social authority on 'love-based' relations. So, of course, the answer Ovid provides is hardly conclusive—historically or philosophically. I will return to these issues in more detail. However, Ovid's vision is instructive in that it shows what is minimally required for any realization of freedom: namely, a way to make fuller sense of the deepest threats to the sense we make of one another as individuals, starting with the passage from life to death.

To get the problem into sharper view, Ovid sketches a kind of limit case. As is his procedure throughout the *Metamorphoses*, Ovid invites us to reflect on more ordinary circumstances, in the terms these extreme cases help to provide.

What happens, he asks, if one of the lovers dies—or is thought to have died—in the very act of improvised courtship, in the attempt at leading a self-expressive and self-directing life? What sense is Pyramus to make of Thisbe's disappearance from life? Will he see her death as the end of an individual life? Or will he also see her death as the end of a shared project, the closing off of practical possibilities?

Recall: the lovers tear themselves away from the walls of family and city in order to carry out their project of heightened mutual understanding, in view of the satisfactions that project promises. Thisbe arrives early at the appointed location, where she sees a lion whose "jaws are dripping with the blood of fresh-slain cattle." Fearful, she steals away, accidentally leaving her cloak on the ground behind her. With its bloody jaws, the lion tears into the cloak, which Pyramus then finds and takes as evidence that Thisbe has been killed. In contrast to Orpheus, who accomplished his self-expressive deed only after Eurydice's death—not *with* her in life—Pyramus and Thisbe had pursued their course together. Which means Pyramus sees in Thisbe's bloody veil a sign not only of her physical demise, but also of the failure of their shared undertaking. Rather than curse the lion, or the gods or fate or rotten luck, therefore, Pyramus curses *himself* as the one who killed her by courting her: "Oh, I killed you, poor girl, in that I bade you come forth by night to this dangerous place, and did not myself come hither first" (4.111).[60]

We can get an even clearer picture of the stakes by taking one further step back.

The age-old view of human life, which I have been attributing to the ancient family, is the notion that death threatens the sense we make of individual lives because it lays bare our irrevocable vulnerability to temporal change—paradigmatically, the passage from life to death. According to this view, death—like temporal change generally (aging, illness, hunger)—expresses natural demands over which we have no control, or that lie outside the bounds of human agency and understanding. There is no way to render one's life, even as one tries to 'direct' it, immune to these threats, to the external demands of death, of nature, of time's passage. At best, according to this ancient doctrine, we can only respond to this threat to agency and understanding—the deepest threats to conscious life—by doing ritual deeds that transform these natural processes into human facts, through institutional rites of various kinds.

At the same time, starting with Orpheus' turn, I have been trying to excavate an emergent, alternative view of this predicament—or an alternative way of living it out—in which we can see what is, while not immune to death and temporal change, at least resistant to the deep threats to our agency and self-understanding that death and change pose. I have been offering various terms for this immunity—practical understanding, improvisational acts, self-expressive deeds, self-consciousness, freedom, love—all culminating, at this point in my discussion, in the courtship efforts (the self-determining 'life-plan') of these two young lovers.

In Pyramus' and Thisbe's actions—flirting, chatting, making a date—I see immense stakes: an attempt to determine for themselves their practical possibilities and self-knowledge, in the face of institutional life and natural peril. At the same time, they are attempting to understand themselves as capable of such an effort.

Here is where the conclusion to Ovid's tale can help us explain matters further. For, if Pyramus and Thisbe's 'project' is to have any reality, any value or authority, then they must be able to withstand the gravest threats to the sense they make of their lives and activities—the starkest of these being death, decay, bodily ruin, disappearance from life. After all, Pyramus and Thisbe cannot avoid such peril or misfortune, or be magically immune to destruction. Sooner or later, death awaits—and disaster can always strike any of us. A lion suddenly tearing Thisbe to shreds is a suitable image for this, from a Roman point of view at least.

The question, however—which Pyramus' response helps to formulate—is whether one can justify to oneself and to others what one *does*, or has done, with the living, given the ever-present threat of such destruction. At stake is how we make *ourselves* answerable for whatever comes to pass. Answerable not just to nature, or gods, or the dead, or our ancestors, I mean, but answerable to one another; and not just for obligations and duties (gratitude, fidelity to ancestors, obedience to laws), but for having acted self-expressively and for accepting what else might happen along the way. Can we hold ourselves answerable for the fact of holding *one another* answerable—in a world where lions lurk, where no one gets out alive, and where our plans can go terribly wrong because of arbitrary events?

In an elemental sense, as Ovid knew, all of this is at stake whenever we 'make a date' for the sake of getting to know one another better, without the support of any deeper social sanction (economic, professional, familial, civic). Whence, we might say, the sheer existential thrill of pursuing a love-affair. To make one's way to a far-flung locale at midnight, just because one has made a 'date,' is something one does, not just to 'keep promises made,' but to make such promising and oneself as promiser the final justification for one's activities. It is a gambit to open practical possibilities and positive freedom for ourselves as self-aware agents in a hostile and perilous world. After all, the lovers cannot honestly say that they find themselves in the shadow of Ninus' tomb by accident—not even the sheer chance of having become acquainted, or of having been neighbors in the first place. They have chatted for hours upon end, and they have thought matters through, however intemperately. They cannot take themselves out of the equation, whatever happens, and *that* is what sets the stakes.

All this means that Pyramus must now assess—in light of Thisbe's bloody death—whether their love-affair was worth it. And to evaluate its worth, he must try to decide whether the outcome is something that merely happened *to* them—blind accident, cruel fate, a hungry lion—or whether the failure is expressive of 'their' action (or, at least, 'his' action). To evaluate what has happened, in other words, Pyramus must struggle to distinguish between those events that are extrinsic to their undertaking, and those that are intrinsic to its success or failure.

Of course such evaluative work is, in everyone's life, extraordinarily difficult to do. Contingent events—the weather, delayed trains, illness—play a role in the success or failure of any life-project. And yet a failure is still a failure, just as a success is a success. Those who fail or succeed are implicated, either way, even if they 'give in' to fatalism and start to see themselves merely as playthings of higher powers. Nothing excludes giving in to fatalism from being a human possibility, of course. And yet fatalism cannot be caused. It must be given in to, even cultivated, on the basis of our understanding of any connection between what we do and what happens. (Roman stoicism was one prominent form of fatalism in Ovid's day.[61])

Not giving in to fatalism, then, means somehow claiming whatever happens as one's own personal success or failure, even in the face of seemingly arbitrary circumstances. It means establishing and demonstrating some interconnectedness between what one does and what happens in the world. And under conditions of utter failure, this means having to see one's project as having come undone through one's participation in it, one's self-expressive role in the events in question. Furthermore, this 'owning' cannot be accomplished through mere lip service, but must also be objectively demonstrable—or else one's actual role in the events in question remains unclear and undetermined.

Pyramus, I take it, does not give in to fatalism. Indeed, Ovid presents something like a limit case for what *not* giving in to fatalism can demand. Pyramus must see Thisbe's death not merely as an external event in the world—an obstacle or extrinsic misfortune—but as a direct expression of his active role in what happened. ("Oh, I killed you.") Thisbe's death is not just the end of her physical life; it is the end of their plan, their shared project.

From an outsider's perspective, of course, Pyramus' (ultimately suicidal) conclusion can seem quite a stretch. At least, we can imagine a stoic spectator trying to talk Pyramus out of his despair by saying, "*No, it was not your fault. Look . . . there was a lion . . . You could not have known. There was nothing you could have done . . .*" Such a spectator would not be wrong, in any absolute sense. But—and this is key to what happens next—the spectator would nevertheless have to *convince* Pyramus that he bears no responsibility for what happened to Thisbe. He would have to *move* Pyramus out of his 'participant-agent' stance and into the 'spectator' stance—which means that the spectator must suppose (to begin to comfort Pyramus at all) that Pyramus already inhabits the participant-agent position. Even if Pyramus were to 'accept' the spectator's words of comfort, he could only do so by moving himself from his initial stance—"I killed"—to a new self-expressive stance or action; for instance, by declaring that, yes, lions are neither predictable nor stoppable and that he is not responsible for that. So we are already on the terrain of free, self-conscious subjects. At the same time, to the extent that a person shifts his stance *to* the stoic position, his positive freedom is restricted, and he is left with diminished worldly projects, beyond a cultivation of his 'acceptance' of things.

Of course, Pyramus' history as a participant in this story—like anyone's history as an agent in a complex world—is enmeshed in a tangle of events and circumstances in which the results of human actions are formed and occasioned by things that are not.[62] And the question is: Is Pyramus' own role in that tangle so limited as to be perceptible only in those moments where he 'gives in to fatalism,' or stoically absolves himself of having contributed fundamentally to whatever happens? Or, alternatively, is his role more decisive, such that it is necessarily shot through with, or implicated by, 'whatever happens'—lions and all?

Consider these stakes as Ovid sets them. If, on the one hand, Pyramus moves to the spectator-stance and absolves himself of having played any decisive role in Thisbe's death, then his self-conception as an agent in the world is correspondingly limited to a kind of sad regret at not having been *freer* to determine the outcome. This kind of regret might involve Pyramus' wish that things had been otherwise, but it does not mean he will wish that he had *acted* otherwise. By moving himself to the spectator-stance, he would free himself from that latter wish—and hence, free himself from the worry that his actions or his project could have made much difference (or that they might yet make a difference). This is, again, how one gives in to fatalism or cultivates a certain kind of stoicism.

If, on the other hand, Pyramus simply says that he *feels* guilty, but does nothing that demonstrates his own sense of responsibility, then we have reason to doubt his answerability and his positive freedom. His answerability for what happened must be demonstrable or else it remains idle conjecture. So Pyramus does something extraordinary. "'Tis a coward's part merely to pray for death," he cries, "Drink now my blood, too" (4.115–18). With this, he plunges his sword into his groin, where death comes most painfully to mortals, as Homer says (not into his side or breast, as many translations squeamishly indicate).[63]

Pyramus' suicide can, of course, be seen as excessive, irrational, or overly self-berating. But if we regard Pyramus' behavior as entirely irrational, then what notion of rationality are we committing ourselves to? Can Pyramus be-have rationally only by neatly detaching his deeds from the tangle of real-life circumstances in which he must act, if he is to act at all? Assuming—as I think we must—that such detachment is never achievable, then does not rational be-havior require somehow seeing one's actions *in* that tangle, at least to the extent that one continues to act in view of a life-plan at all?

Ovid not only sees Pyramus as free, self-aware and rational; he goes a step further, by refusing to treat 'natural' occurrences and human activities as inher-ently separate.[64] Pyramus' blood spouted high into the air, like a broken pipe spewing water, Ovid tells us—so that the hanging berries turned dark forever with a "purple hue" (4.125–27). If our acts are enmeshed in the tangle of worldly circumstances, then the tangle of the world—natural occurrences included—is indelibly marked by the role we play in grasping everything that happens under the sun.

Was It Worth It?

If Pyramus takes himself to have played a decisive, 'not-just-fated,' role in Thisbe's death, that does not mean that he thereby knows what his role is, ex-actly. (It will become known, too late, that Thisbe was not killed by a lion at all.) By implication, one need not—in order to know that one has a role in world events, or just in order to have a role at all—know what one's role in events and circumstances finally amounts to. Even assuming one *could*—by getting a kind of God's-eye viewpoint—gain knowledge of the precise extent and meaning of one's role in world events, this would just amount to giving up one's role as a participant in favor of becoming a privileged spectator (as happens to Scrooge in Dickens' *Christmas Carol*, for instance). Knowing oneself to be a partici-pant, then, means *not* being able to fully know what that participation finally amounts to, or has resulted in—a predicament which, of course, complicates the kind of responsibility one can reasonably 'assume' along the lines of the discussion above.

As everybody knows, this is something about which Greek tragedy offers one powerful way to think. And the 'tragic' viewpoint is not without relevance to Ovid's tale. Since Pyramus cannot know—from a God's-eye point of view—the precise scope of his role in what happens, it falls to him to determine or express how he sees himself implicated in what has come to pass, with whatever foresight or hindsight he can muster. Figuring out the extent of one's involvement in world affairs, by rational deliberation and from a constitutively limited (all too human) viewpoint, is of course part of what it is to be a human agent generally. Such figuring out can take various forms, as tragedy teaches—for instance, in the work done by Oedipus in *Oedipus the King*, or the continuation of that work in *Oedipus at Colonus*.

Yet, although Pyramus probably 'knows' that he cannot reasonably hold himself directly responsible for the lion's hungry assault on Thisbe, he also fails to convince himself that he played no role in the overall circumstances of Thisbe's death. She had come to meet *him*, after all. In this sense, I think, Pyramus and Thisbe's adventures present us with a novel problem—beyond those presented in Greek tragedy, at least.

Consider one instructive contrast between Ovid's tale and Sophocles' tragedy: When Oedipus tried to figure out the extent of his involvement in his father's death and his family's ruin, he did so by deliberatively looking back on what happened. In this way, Oedipus discovered that he was implicated in a crime in ways he had not known; and—once he learned of his involvement—he changed his life-plan and self-conception accordingly. However, while it contributed to his next steps, Oedipus' deliberation was not a matter of deciding whether he was 'right' or 'wrong' to have killed his father. The murder was wrong. It was agreed by all to be a crime. Oedipus, thus, did not have to evaluate his prior action—he had only to grasp his connection to the deed.

By contrast, Pyramus' suicidal deliberation was not just a determination of his connection to what happened. He also had to assess the rightness or wrongness (the success or failure) of his original life-plan, the love-affair itself—the courtship, the whispering, the promising, the attempt at a self-determined future. In judging himself responsible for Thisbe's death, Pyramus was not, like Oedipus, simply claiming responsibility for a death that he never intended to bring about. Looking back, he had to acknowledge and weigh the connection between his and Thisbe's love-affair and its outcome: Thisbe's bloody death. Pyramus had to judge the love-affair itself—its initial possibilities, its risk and final cost, and to ask himself a question Oedipus could never ask: *Was it was worth it?*

So, what would make a love-affair 'worth it'? What could justify or redeem the risks that must be incurred in trying to carry out a self-determined form of life?

At a glance, such questions might seem to lead toward age-old notions about how human beings weigh values, or determine what is of value. According to one well-worn line of thought, we discover what we value by being willing to fight for it, to kill for it, to sacrifice for it, or to work for it. Or—it is sometimes said—we value whatever we would risk our life for. This way of thinking leads, first, to the reasonable conclusion that our values (including the value of living itself) are not decided by 'life itself,' or by any fact of Nature, but by us—by what we hold ourselves to *doing* for the sake of what we hold dear. By the same token, according to this view, we know that we *hold ourselves* to our commitments and values only in the wake of this deep existential crisis, where ultimately life and death are at stake.[65] Living creatures may desire to persist in their own being, but that has not prevented at least some of us from risking our lives—from leaping in front of a bus to save a child, giving a kidney to a sibling, or challenging someone to a duel. Conversely, such experiences may teach us that we find life itself to be valuable in light of what we *do* in order to stay alive, such as sacrifice our dignity, or work as a slave. At any rate, all these familiar notions lead to the conclusion that values are ultimately determined by what we would willingly 'give up' for their sake—to the point of staking life itself. We sacrifice our time and energy—or our scruples—for what we value, says this theory. Or we give our body, our life. Or we sacrifice our children on some altar or other. And that is how values get institutional traction, or normative authority. Let me call this the 'sacrificial' theory of value.

The notion underlying this theory is that 'value' or meaning can only be determined, ultimately, through the staking of individual lives, either one's own or another's. Values are thought to be undeterminable, unknowable—incapable of orienting our commitments or actions—without an evaluation of life itself, in the face of death. According to this sacrificial view, the 'worth-itness' of any undertaking is thus decidable, ultimately, only in view of individual mortality—death, the absolute lord.[66] Here we meet again the normative authority of individual mortality.

■ ■ ■

With this in mind, we are now in a position to approach the 'value' question differently, and see how Pyramus and Thisbe's predicament, as I have tried to present it, not only puts the sacrificial theory of value into question, but also offers a way to realize, and reflect on, greater positive freedom in human affairs.

The first issue for positive freedom, I want to argue, is whether an undertaking can determine its *own* value, or be the *basis* for its own evaluation—even when that undertaking has not yet been granted broad recognition as a worthy task or activity.[67] After all, in asking the question *Was it worth it?* we are also inquiring into the basis for any such evaluation, under circumstances where that basis is not always clear. In the case of Pyramus and Thisbe, I want to say, it is significant that the worth of their relationship cannot be determined in the age-old, sacrificial ways just outlined—even though the kind of courtship in which they are engaged is not yet as authoritative for their social world as it is for our own.[68]

Sacrificial thinking is of no help, for one thing, because it is too late for Pyramus to ask whether he would die for Thisbe, for the chance to carry out his affair with her. True, he may have staked something—even his life—just by making his way to Ninus' tomb. But the question he is asking *now* is not simply whether he should have taken the risk, in the 'abstract' (trying to forget what he now knows). The only question now is whether the affair was worth it given the failure of the whole enterprise, given all the misfortune, and in light of what he now knows. Pyramus can no longer ask what he would give up for a chance to pursue the affair with Thisbe, since the affair itself is no longer possible—and it is in light of *that fact* that his assessment must now unfold.

In light of this failure, then, whatever Pyramus gave up (his time or energy, even his life or safety) cannot decide for him the value or the meaning of the love-affair's pursuit. Indeed, the 'value' of the love-relation was never determined by whatever life-staking moments it might have called for (although those cannot be avoided). I am tempted to say, further, that the 'thrill' or the existential mood of a love-affair arises not in the risk or stakes the love-relation demands—its potential or actual costs—but, rather, in the overshadowing of *that* thrill by another: the joy taken in the affair's pursuit itself, the experience of possibilities for further activities opening up.

In contrast to Denis de Rougemont's well-known claim that sexual love is fundamentally "adulterous" (or death-bound),[69] I would say that Ovid's tale offers, among other things, a way to think about the difference, at the experiential level, between the actualization of a love-affair and what turns out to be merely a diversion or discreet tryst. As Ovid well knew, a sexual tryst can always be assessed and weighed merely in light of the costs paid, the sacrifices made—

just as adulterous meetings can be 'planned' solely with an eye toward risk-management and sacrificial thinking. However, a sexual love-relation cannot be thus planned or evaluated. Its worth can only be decided by the love-affair's eventual success, by its being lived out as the opening of possibilities for greater positive freedom in the face of whatever misfortunes and hardships the world delivers. A love-relation can only be valued in light of the practical possibilities it eventually realizes—its positive freedom—not in view of whatever costs may be exacted or calculated along the way. So, too, it is only by *becoming open* to that kind of evaluation (*that* kind of *Was it worth it?* questioning) that a series of events and interactions can look, retrospectively, like a love-affair at all, like positive freedom. All of which is to say, the *undertaking itself*—love—becomes the measure of its own worth, although we still have to understand how this happens.

For a start, it matters a lot what the lovers have taken themselves to be *doing*—what the shared and individual understanding of the pursuit *is*. Perhaps they set out to conceive and raise a child—only to find that this proves impossible for one reason or another. In this case, the failure to conceive and raise a child may mean the collapse of their shared project altogether. Or perhaps they find something else to do together. Either way, that failure to raise a child must prompt the question *Was it worth it?* and my suggestion is that an answer to that question cannot come from any cost-benefit analysis, or sacrificial form of thinking under the shadow of life and death as absolute lord. Only the failure (or success) of the project can decide the project's worth—and this is true, from the lovers' point of view, regardless of whether the project was a child, or the renovation of the kitchen, or a political revolution, or a walk in the park.

At the same time, I want to suggest, there is at least one criterion for the kind of activity or project that can sustain a love-affair, and that is the extent to which it provides the lovers an undertaking for whose success or failure they can hold each other answerable. To be capable of sustaining a love-affair, the activity or project must, I want to say, be something for whose success or failure the lovers manage to hold *each other responsible* above all—beyond the various ways in which they might also simultaneously be responsible to other social powers (to the bank for a mortgage, to political parties for solidarity, to an employer for work), *and* while taking on the various misfortunes that might occur along the way, such as illness or any other kind of bad luck.[70] We need set no limits to the possible list of such activities or projects, though it would be important to think about which activities cannot qualify and why.

This means that—in the ambit of what I am calling the pursuit of a love-affair, or positive freedom beyond sacrificial thinking—our worldly activities themselves call for new forms of reflective evaluation. In my view, the scope of such an evaluation—for economic theory, political analysis, and social thought generally—has never been adequately appreciated or explored. It would, I suspect, require the elaboration of a fuller practical philosophy than we have available. (I hope to find occasion to pursue this further; but this is not the place.)

Here, I want to note that Pyramus and Thisbe's project was, so to speak, manifestly open-ended, and therefore it helps us to see the stakes just outlined with greater clarity. Their life-plan, after all, was not to have a child or to buy a house or start a revolution, but simply to *pursue a shared undertaking* by holding one another accountable, by *being* accountable to one another: starting with making a date. They measured their investment in what they were doing not in terms of the life-costs or sacrifices, but by making themselves answerable to one another. This undertaking would have been worth it, I want to conclude, only if making dates and holding one another answerable had continued to open practical possibilities for action that, in the absence of such mutual answerability, would not have become actual. Only its ongoing success could have validated the undertaking, just as only its failure could devalue it—wherein failure can be sudden and irrevocable, while validation can be adverbial, moment-to-moment.

Their efforts, as we know, did not work out. A distinctive feature of a love-affair, or a provisional attempt at leading a free life, is that the effort can fail. And the possibility of such failure cannot be excluded from the prospects for success. As already emphasized, this failure can result from sheer misfortune—such that even such contingencies, all the bad luck in the world, can be owned at the heart of the failure. And of course, eventually, the death of one of the partners will put an end to the whole activity.[71] Thisbe's death, after all, is the end of their shared project—just as any individual death means the cessation of a love-affair. But this means that it is the truncation of the affair—*its* end—which gives the death its significance and meaning, not the other way around.

In contrast, consider the norms or values for which people sacrifice themselves or stake their lives—ideals like equality and justice, God and country, morality, money, the safety of loved ones, the rule of law, or religious tradition. These values cannot, by definition, be laid low by an individual death—for their value and normative endurance is, ultimately, measurable by the sacrifice of individual lives for which they can call. Sacrificial think-ing sees in an individual's death, at bottom, a chance to evaluate normative commitments.

The lover, however, sees in his beloved's death the cessation of a shared proj-ect, whose final outcome calls for evaluation. Death is no longer the absolute lord, in light of whose authority our deepest commitments are weighed. Our mutual answerability can also determine what an individual's death means. How far we have come from our initial collective attempts to reckon with indi-vidual mortality! Thus, Thisbe follows through:

> I will follow you in death, and men shall say that I was the most wretched cause and comrade of your fate. Whom death alone had power to part from me, not even death shall have power to part from me. (4.152–53)

Romeo and Juliet

All the issues discussed thus far are gathered up in Shakespeare's *Romeo and Juliet* (1592). In ways that, I hope, can help us better think about a number of further implications.[72]

As he will go on to do in *Richard II*, *Hamlet*, *Macbeth*, *Othello*, *Coriolanus* and *Cymbeline*, Shakespeare frames the central action of *Romeo and Juliet* by depict-ing an aborted duel. Although the play opens with the Capulet and Montague men preparing to fight to the death, Shakespeare wastes little time in making sure that we understand "Verona" to be a social world in which such sacrificial scenes are impractical, and where more peaceful undertakings are being culti-vated. Shakespeare seems to have thought life-and-death struggles—the horizon for the sacrificial theory of value just discussed—to be unworthy of our primary dramatic interest, and best presented as moments to be eventually overshad-owed in the course of the play.[73] In *Romeo and Juliet*, life-and-death battles yield to love-relations—"Thou shalt not stir one foot to seek a foe" (1.1.78).[74]

From the start, both Montague and Capulet readily acknowledge that they must find ways, other than fighting, to pass the time—"'tis not hard I think / For men so old as we to keep the peace" (1.2.2–3). To this end, they hold feasts and arrange marriages to mark the coming of spring. As in Ovid's tale, the context for the action is primarily domestic: ancient families set against a civic horizon and state authority that enforces the peace. For his part, having gladly missed the "fray," Romeo finds it difficult to pass the time—"Ay me, sad hours seem long" (1.1.159). The cause of the sadness that "lengthens Romeo's hours" is "not having that which, having, makes them short" (1.1.162).

> Benvolio. In love?
> Romeo. Out.
> Benvolio. Of love?
> Romeo. Out of her favour where I am in love. (1.1.163–66)

That "love" here means sexual desire is obvious enough. Romeo desires to 'have' Rosalind (1.1.206–14). Which is why Rosalind need not appear on stage; she is a mere lack—as Romeo says, a "not having."[75] Romeo is, at this stage, just this desiring 'emptiness'—"Tut, I have lost myself. I am not here. / This is not Romeo; he's some other where" (1.1.195–96). And because Rosalind appears to Romeo as *forever* lacking, he regards himself as condemned to an existence of unsatisfied longing.[76] So long as he remains gripped by this desire Romeo lives fatalistically: "She hath forsworn to love, and in that vow / Do I live dead, that live to tell it now" (1.1.221–22).[77]

As Benvolio understands, Romeo just needs to "forget" Rosalind and take an interest in someone else. So long as he is alive libidinously to the world and to others, one lack can always be replaced with another:[78] "Tut, man, one fire burns out another's burning / One pain is lessen'd by another's anguish; / . . . Take thou some new infection to thy eye / And the rank poison of the old will die" (1.2.45–50). Such are the pleasures of the 'life' to which Benvolio and Mercutio seek to return young Romeo. It is, after all, no accident that they arrive at Capulet's house as masquers. A masque is a sufficiently pleasing way for a veritable parade of substitutable objects of desire to appear—"On, lusty gentlemen" (1.4.113). At the same time, the masque is more than a merely formal charade. In the absence of "quarreling" or duels, the masque has now become the *content*, so to speak, of Verona's social world: the waxing and waning of appetites, dancing, eating, looking, liking. If 'life' amounts to finding satisfying ways of substituting one desire for another, then ritualized revelry is the most self-aware form of life to which one might aspire—"A visor for a visor" (1.4.30).

Although she does not yet desire anyone in particular, Juliet is, like Romeo and his companions, aware of herself as sexually desiring. And with news of her betrothal to Paris, Juliet approaches the masquerade, like the others, ready to be moved by *erōs*: "I'll look to like, if looking liking move" (1.3.97).[79] Thus moved, Romeo and Juliet swiftly progress from looking to speaking to caressing to kissing (1.5.92–109). I think we can safely take this moment to be one of sexual consummation—or as close as Shakespeare can get to showing us the lovers having full sexual relations on stage—"You kiss by th' book" (1.5.108).[80] As befitting a masque, however, this is still an anonymous desire—oriented toward a substitutable object. Both are probably disguised when they meet. Nothing at this point distinguishes Romeo and Juliet's encounter from the seduction between any other Capulet and Benvolio or Mercutio.

What ends up distinguishing Romeo and Juliet is that—unlike Benvolio, say—they are not satisfied with the "satisfaction" offered by the masque and its anonymity. Romeo and Juliet do not want to remain unknown to one another.[81] Like Pyramus and Thisbe—and to recall the issue we have been tracking throughout—Romeo and Juliet want to better get to know one another, and that desire for understanding is manifestly erotic. They have not had enough of one other, sexually—"O trespass sweetly urged, / Give me my sin again!" (1.5.108–9)—and part of what spurs them on is a desire to better know *whom* they desire. All this generates the elemental challenge with which I began my discussion: how are the lovers to understand one another?

First things first, of course. Each must descriptively apprehend the other, by identifying distinctive features and characteristics—by learning as many relevant facts about the other as possible. So, Juliet interrogates the Nurse, "What is yond gentleman?" (1.5.126); and Romeo asks a servant, "What lady is that, which doth enrich the hand / Of yonder knight?" (1.5.41–42) And—to return to the discussion in the first pages of this section—this quickly leads to the realization that 'who' the other person is cannot be known just by learning that she is beautiful and a Capulet, or that he is a Montague who kisses by the book. So, our initial questions find their place: Who is Juliet? And who is Romeo? How are they to be individuated and 'known' by one another?

As I tried to show in my earlier discussion, these questions tumble into the form of life I was calling the ancient family, the community of the living and the dead. Within their respective households, after all, Romeo's and Juliet's individual 'beings' are acknowledged as such. Indeed, they are socially identifiable only inasmuch as they belong to a house, tribe or family: "Is she a Capulet?" (1.5.115), and again, "His name is Romeo, and a Montague" (1.5.135). And the families attach an absolute value to Romeo's and Juliet's individuality, no matter how they behave. The first indication of this absolute value is marked simply by their proper names.[82] But the deepest is the one we have already discussed: the 'love' shown to them by their families after their deaths. When we see Juliet's parents mourn her death after her ingestion of the potion, or at the play's end, we perceive that they acknowledge Juliet's particular value to them, no matter what she does or has done. Because this kind of "love"—as Kojève and Hegel reminded us—"does not depend on the *acts*, on the *activity* of the loved one, it cannot be ended by his very *death*."[83] Not only does Juliet's death fail to transform her family's recognition of her particular value, her death affirms that all along she was treasured as an individual inasmuch as she was, to them, 'as good as dead.' As Capulet says: "life, living, all is Death's" (4.5.40). Just as parents often look upon their children with the greatest tenderness and appreciation when they are asleep, so too Juliet's (first) death counterfeits "a pleasant sleep" in order to trigger the family's most solemn act of loving care. "In thy best robes, uncover'd on the bier / Thou shalt be borne to that same ancient vault / Where all the kindred of the Capulets lie" (4.2.110–12).

Juliet's predicament is particularly stark in this regard—since Romeo is afforded, by his gender and status, a relative freedom of movement in Verona. Within the more austere restrictions of the Capulet household, Juliet is a mere extension of her father's actions, as witnessed by her betrothal to Paris. For instance, when Juliet seeks to negate the demand that she marry Paris—"Hear me with patience but to speak a word"—her father will have none of it:

> get thee to church a Thursday
> Or never after look me in the face.
> Speak not, reply not, do not answer me. (3.5.151–63)

Because she cannot even "speak" the word "no" to her family, Juliet comes to see that her life is valued by her family only because she is, to them, already as good as dead—as we hear in Lady Capulet's words: "I would the fool were married to her grave" (3.5.140), and the later characterization of the family tomb as a "womb of death" (5.3.45). "Talk not to me," Lady Capulet tells her daughter, "for I'll not speak a word. / Do as thou wilt, for I have done with thee" (1.5.202–3).

Since Juliet has no individual life outside of the family, how is she to act self-expressively *within* the life of the family? Actually, very little is required, nothing more than a hospitable gesture. It is enough for the family to admit within its fold, for a time, some guests from the larger community.

> Tybalt. Uncle, this is a Montague, our foe:
>   A villain that is hither come in spite
>   To scorn at our solemnity this night.
>
>   . . .

Capulet. Content thee, gentle coz, let him alone.

> . . .

He shall be endured. (1.5.60–75)

Because Romeo does not appear at the feast as an enemy, but as a "virtuous and well-governed youth" about whom "Verona brags" (1.5.64–65), his presence bears witness to an openness *within* the ancient family that, like the chink in the wall between the houses of Pyramus and Thisbe, had been there all along and had simply remained unnoticed. This turns out to provide Juliet and Romeo with all they require—a chance to encounter one another within family life without, finally, needing to relate to one another *as* family.[84] So, contrary to a common misinterpretation, Romeo and Juliet are not divided by Capulet-Montague enmity.[85] When Romeo and Juliet each learn of the 'house' to which the other belongs, they do not despair. As I hear her words, Juliet gives this strange news welcome:

> My only love sprung from my only hate
> Too early seen unknown and known too late
> Prodigious birth of love it is to me
> That I must love a loathed enemy. (1.5.137–40)

"What satisfaction canst thou have tonight?"

It is my lady, O it is my love!
O that she knew she were!

Shakespeare, Romeo and Juliet, 1595

"What satisfaction canst thou have tonight?" (2.2.126) asks Juliet, and the question is a sincere and urgent one. The satisfaction they seek, I have been suggesting, is to better understand who the other is, to more fully know themselves and one another ("too early seen unknown and known too late").

Most immediately, they have had to learn to identify one another. Romeo does not stumble upon Juliet in the darkness, after all. He has purposefully sought her out. Speaking first—in "the numbers that Petrarch flowed in"— Romeo rhapsodizes the sight of Juliet's body: "The brightness of her cheek would shame those stars / As daylight doth a lamp" (2.2.19–20). He tries to apprehend and describe her beauty as best he knows how—poetically. However, the limits of epideictic speech are immediately apparent. Romeo's sonnet can grasp Juliet only as sensuous object, not as an active *subject*. ("She speaks yet she says nothing: what of that?"). So, when the beautiful apparition speaks—

"Ay me"—Romeo must halt his rhapsody and try to make sense of Juliet in her activity: "She speaks. / O speak again bright angel" (2.2.25–26).

Romeo catches Juliet in a moment of introspection, as she thinks aloud.[86] More specifically, he catches her trying to understand who *he* is—"O Romeo, Romeo, wherefore art thou Romeo" (2.1.33). To better understand Juliet, then, Romeo must also grasp how she understands him. And in listening to her, the first thing he learns is that what Juliet knows about him (his name, his family) is not sufficient *for her*—not a good enough way of 'knowing him': "So Romeo would, were he not Romeo call'd, / Retain that dear perfection which he owes / Without that title" (2.2.45–47). In Juliet's view, they cannot adequately know one another by name, or in the terms that family life makes available[87]—"Deny thy father and refuse thy name."

As mentioned, one issue is the inseparability of sense-perception and reflective understanding. Juliet and Romeo both need ways to apprehend the other person—and these 'ways' are not limited to linguistic or discursive-mental categories (proper names or the stuff of Juliet's thoughtful musings). Their knowledge of one another is sensuous knowledge, after all—kissing and touching are perfectly discriminating, judging, 'knowing' ways of their experiencing one another as individuals. This is not just passive or receptive sensation; it is also an active knowing—and in this case, it is also the expansion of a desire to know one another more fully.

> What's Montague? it is nor hand, nor foot,
> Nor arm, nor face, nor any other part
> Belonging to a man. O, be some other name!
> What's in a name? that which we call a rose
> By any other name would smell as sweet;
> So Romeo would, were he not Romeo call'd,
> Retain that dear perfection which he owes
> Without that title. Romeo, doff thy name,
> And for that name which is no part of thee
> Take all myself. (2.2.40–49)

When Juliet smells a rose, she knowingly apprehends a *rose*, and not a daisy, irrespective of what she calls it; even if she must also name it, so that it—the "rose"—can thus be determined by its smell. By using its name, she is able to say what it *is*, instead of just sniffing around. But because the sweet smell is one way Juliet knows a rose to be a rose, it would be wrong to conclude that she first 'senses' and then 'judges' ('ah, *that* is a rose'). Her sensory awareness, rather, orients her (discerningly) in the midst of temporal change and the continuous onslaught of the world on her senses. And this orientation affords her *self*-awareness, inasmuch as 'she' can pick out a rose among the scents her nose detects, or determine what things are in light of how things appear—or tell the difference between Romeo and another man.[88]

At the same time, Juliet's thinking unfolds in a concrete, practical context. 'Her' thinking about the world—about roses and Romeo, Capulet and Montague, hand and foot, being and appearing—is not just the upshot of some spontaneous, inner faculty possessed by Juliet or any self-aware creature. Juliet thinks about Romeo in the wake of, and in response to, the whole evening's activity: the masque, the kissing, the *erōs*, the naming. Those activities were also ways of thinking about the world, in that they enacted certain self-conceptions (for instance, who the masqueraders took themselves to *be*). And now, as the evening stretches toward morning, she finds that "Romeo" threatens the sense that those earlier activities could make of him, and of her. She desires to know him further, then. And in thinking all these things through, Juliet is trying to get matters straight, not just because 'knowing' Romeo better would solve a puzzle, but because she *wants* to know Romeo, actively and erotically.

Unlike a rose, of course, Romeo can listen to Juliet's account of him, or he can catch her in a reflective mood. He can also introduce himself or make himself known—by communicating to Juliet who he 'takes himself to be.' Or he can try to remain hidden. Shakespeare thus presents Romeo, at this very moment, with the task of figuring out whether—or how—to make his presence known to Juliet under the "mask of night." And Shakespeare leaves Romeo with another challenge, too, which is whether or not to present himself to Juliet, while *bearing in mind* what he has heard her say. So, when Romeo eventually speaks up, it matters that he also shows he was listening:

> By a name
> I know not how to tell thee who I am:
> My name, dear saint, is hateful to myself
> Because it is an enemy to thee.
> Had I it written, I would tear the word. (2.2.53–57)

Unless one knows the voice, it would be disconcerting to hear, "By a name / I know not how to tell thee who I am," spoken by an unseen intruder. But just as she can determine a rose by its smell, Juliet immediately identifies Romeo by his sound—"My ears have yet not drunk a hundred words / Of thy tongue's uttering, yet I know the sound" (2.2.58–59). Juliet cannot see Romeo, though he can see her. So, the dialogue in the darkness—with its different sensible attunements (to voice, to vision)—shows how mutual identification works in the deliverances of the senses, irrespective of the words used.[89]

"So separated all to no purpose, they would talk," wrote Ovid of Pyramus and Thisbe at the chink in the wall. Romeo and Juliet find, however, that "stony limits cannot hold love out, / and what love can do, that dares love attempt" (2.2.67–68). While the risks and dangers remain—"The orchard walls are high and hard to climb, / And the place death, considering who thou art, / If any of my kinsmen find thee here" (2.2.64–65)—Romeo and Juliet have a chance to explore the implications of their undertaking, a luxury foreclosed to Pyramus and Thisbe by the lion. And whereas Ovid does not tell us what Pyramus and Thisbe said to one another, exactly, Shakespeare allows us to listen while Romeo and Juliet arrive at the central issues: mutual answerability, and the practical possibilities or positive freedom it opens.

The first thing for which Romeo must answer, of course, is "How camest thou hither, tell me, and wherefore?" Romeo's response—"By love, that first did prompt me to inquire; / He lent me counsel and I lent him eyes" (2.2.62, 80–81) —makes explicit that his purpose is the one we have been tracking: the desire to understand, as an erotic pursuit. Both lovers are made answerable for this desire, because they tell one another that they know they are acting on it (not merely being driven impulsively by it). Given how often the play is misunderstood as the mere intemperance of youthful impulses, it is important to recall that Juliet holds *herself* to what Romeo overheard her say—"Fain would I dwell on form; fain, fain deny / What I have spoke" (2.2.88–89)—even as she asks Romeo to what, exactly, he thinks he is committing himself by talking with her.

Of course, it was Shakespeare who elsewhere wrote, "When my love swears she's made of truth / I do believe her, though I know she lies" (Sonnet 138); and perhaps no other writer has found as many ways to explore the equivocations of love-oaths.

> Dost thou love me? I know thou wilt say "Ay,"
> And I will take thy word: yet if thou swear'st,
> Thou mayst prove false; at lovers' perjuries
> They say, Jove laughs. O gentle Romeo,
> If thou dost love, pronounce it faithfully. (2.2.90–94)

However, oaths and contracts are unsatisfying, to Juliet, only to the extent that they make the lovers answerable to an external authority, rather than to one another. And only time can tell just how answerable they will be to one another.

> Well, do not swear. Although I joy in thee,
> I have no joy of this contract tonight:
> It is too rash, too unadvis'd, too sudden;
> Too like the lightning, which doth cease to be
> Ere one can say "It lightens." Sweet, good night.
> This bud of love, by summer's ripening breath,
> May prove a beauteous flower when next we meet. (2.2.116–22)

At the same time, if contracts bring no joy, there is at least the immediate satisfaction of discovering that they are thinking the same thing; that their desire to understand one another is mutual. Hence, Romeo's response to Juliet's question, "What satisfaction canst thou have tonight?"

> Romeo. Th' exchange of thy love's faithful vow for mine.
> Juliet. I gave thee mine before thou did'st request it,
>   . . . I would it were to give again.
>
>   . . .
>
> And yet I wish but for the thing I have.
> My bounty is as boundless as the sea,
> My love as deep: the more I give to thee
> The more I have, for both are infinite (2.2.126–35)

The young Hegel referred to this moment as a paradigmatic expression of mutuality in human affairs.[90] But the older Hegel would also want to know what practical entanglements and concrete possibilities are called for by the lovers' vows.[91] Consider that, in asking Romeo to swear he loves her, Juliet is not asking Romeo to declare what he will do in order to prove that he loves her. She is asking what, exactly, loving one another (holding one another individually answerable) allows them both to do, and which would otherwise have been impossible. What practical possibilities does their love-relation open, or actualize? Indeed, although Romeo and Juliet do not consider this question explicitly here, they will soon face how their love-relation will require (or enable) others to do things which they would not otherwise have done. This becomes a pressing question, for instance, when Juliet must ask the Nurse to take certain steps, or when they are compelled to involve Friar Lawrence, or when Romeo feels entitled to tell Tybalt to "be satisfied" (and put away his sword) on the basis of "the reason of . . . love" (3.1.69, 71).

All of which is to say, Romeo and Juliet seek to make themselves answerable to one another—to take on a life-plan or project, along the lines of my discussion earlier, anti-fatalistically, come what may.[92] And at the same time, they also seek to make their mutual answerability *authoritative* for others. They want to realize what I have been calling a 'love-based' commitment, which means they eventually would need their commitment to be authoritative for those around them—to be a reason for others to act differently, to be a basis for new practical possibilities in Verona. Rather than seek authorization *for* their marriage (from the family or the state or the church), therefore, they seek to make their love-based marriage itself a form of social authorization. Friar Lawrence—who acts on the lovers' behalf, and not the church's behalf, when he marries them in secret—also sees this as a plausible hope: "In one respect I'll thy assistant be; / For this alliance may so happy prove, / To turn your households' rancour to pure love" (2.4.86–88).

All of this requires concrete undertakings, of course. And this is why Romeo and Juliet are not content to say good night with declarations of love alone, without making specific plans to carry forward the very next day.

> If that thy bent of love be honourable,
> Thy purpose marriage, send me word to-morrow. (2.2.143–44)

"Parting is such sweet sorrow"

As everyone familiar with the play knows, things do not go according to plan. But when do things ever go fully according to plan?

As already discussed, there is no way to neatly separate our actions and life-projects from the various misfortunes that can cause them to go terribly wrong. Tybalt's murderousness, the Friar's lost letter, Romeo's banishment—these are all events that clearly contribute to the outcome with which everyone around the lovers must reckon. However the central question, as before, is whether Romeo and Juliet's role in what happens is somehow decisive—even taking in all contingencies—and, if so, *how* it is decisive? Or put another way, does their project succeed or fail? Was the love-affair worth it to them? And on what basis might we hope to answer these questions?

To try to begin, let me make an assertion—which I trust can be accepted as true about the historical world depicted in the play: Shakespeare's Verona is not a world in which 'love-based' marriage commands the kind of social authority that it has come to command in the years between 1592 and the present.[93] Shakespeare's "Verona," in other words, is a social world in which Romeo and Juliet's project, as described above, is bound to be enormously difficult and, in all probability, unsuccessful. Perhaps, as the Friar hopes and prays, Romeo and Juliet's secret marriage—undertaken without their parents' knowledge or blessing—might change the way things are done in Verona, at least in part.[94] But the odds of success are long, given the obstacles—starting with Juliet's betrothal to Paris. Even in the moments of their wildest optimism, Romeo and Juliet themselves seem keenly aware of the dangers and pitfalls, and the lack of social-institutional support for their undertaking.

By the same token, though I am not sure it even needs saying, the predicament of Romeo and Juliet is not a 'timeless' predicament, but a historically conditioned one. Matters would look quite different today (misapprehensions, such as *West Side Story*, notwithstanding). Indeed, one of the aims of the third part of this book will be to explain the increasing social-institutional authority of sexual love and love-based commitments, and the implications of this for our self-understanding. *Romeo and Juliet* helps us explain some important stages of that broader account I am trying to offer.

So, in asking the question *Was it worth it?* I am not only asking after the circumstantial feasibility and value of their undertaking: marriage, perhaps with a view toward the kinds of goals the Friar has in mind. I am also asking about Romeo and Juliet's affair as they experience it, or try to live it out, under difficult social conditions—and I am asking what value *that* experience and those efforts can have. What are we to make, in other words, of the role Romeo and Juliet themselves play in what comes to pass?

Consider two moments in which we see and hear the lovers alone. The first comes at the end of the balcony scene, where we left off a moment ago. Shakespeare seems to have been tempted to conclude the scene with the exchange of vows; hence, the next lines: "I hear some noise within. Dear love, adieu" (2.2.136). But ending the scene here would have meant showing the lovers to be merely subject to the return of worldly demands and intrusions. And because, I want to suggest, such intrusions do not fatalistically determine Romeo and Juliet's interactions, Shakespeare does not let us off the hook. "Stay but a little," Juliet tells Romeo, "I will come again" (2.2.140).

So, Romeo stays. And stays.

As it happens, no external demand really compels them to part. Instead, the "parting" *itself* becomes their project, and the conclusion of the balcony scene depicts exactly this. It is a familiar scenario: namely, the task of saying good night—"Three words, dear Romeo, and good night indeed"; "A thousand times good night" (2.2.142, 154). And then, a moment later:

> Hist! Romeo, hist! O for a falconer's voice
> to lure this tassel-gentle back again. (2.2.158–59)

For what purpose does Juliet lure him back? Merely to ask at what time she should send the Nurse to him.

> Romeo.　　　　　　By the hour of nine.
> Juliet. I will not fail.
> [*Awkward pause*]
> Juliet. I have forgot why I did call thee back.
> Romeo. Let me stand here till thou remember it,
> 　　Remembering how I love thy company.
> Juliet. *I* shall forget, to have *thee* stand there still,
> 　　Remembering how *I* love *thy* company.
> Romeo: And *I'll* stay still to have *thee* still forget.
> 　　　　　　　　　(2.2.165–75; my stage direction and emphasis)

We know how these conversations go. They mark the rhythm of an exchange caught up in the endless demands of mutuality: *You* say good night; no, *you* say good night. *You* hang up; no, *you* hang up.

> Good night. Good night. Parting is such sweet sorrow
> That I shall say good night till it be morrow. (2.2.184–85)

Similarly, we later catch the lovers aloft at Juliet's window, perhaps in bed. This time, there is no resigned, tearful acceptance of the necessity of saying good-bye. On the contrary, the lovers begin with a bald-faced denial of the external demands that they supposedly face. "Wilt thou be gone?" begins Juliet.

> 　　　　　　It is not yet near day.
> It was the nightingale and not the lark
> That pierc'd the fearful hollow of thine ear.
> 　　　· · ·
> Believe me, love, it was the nightingale. (3.5.1–5)

"Therefore," continues Juliet defiantly, "stay yet; thou need'st not to be gone" (3.5.16).

None of this should astonish us. We routinely defy the world's demands, the passage of time—by pushing the snooze button on our alarm clock, or by pushing it twice. Or by making love in the morning before heading off to work. To be free agents in the world is to be perfectly capable of making day night, or night day.[95] This is not a disavowal of the 'real' limitations of Romeo and Juliet's worldly position. Rather, the lovers come (together) to the realization that these limitations are not fully 'limiting' so far as they are concerned. External obstacles do not disappear, but they do not determine the lovers' experiences and interactions absolutely. At this point, then, Romeo takes Juliet's wager, and raises the ante:

> Let me be ta'en, let me be put to death,
> I am content, so thou wilt have it so.
> I'll say yon grey is not the morning's eye,
> 'Tis but the pale reflex of Cynthia's brow.
> Nor that is not the lark whose notes do beat
> The vaulty heaven so high above our heads.
> I have more care to stay than will to go.
> Come death, and welcome. Juliet wills it so. (3.5.17–24)

Here Juliet pauses. The 'reality' with which she must contend is not only the Prince's decree or the earth's rotation or individual mortality, but also the 'reality' that night and day are what she and Romeo take them to be. In truth, Romeo need not leave at that moment; she need not stay. Juliet, we recall, has promised to "follow" Romeo "throughout the world," and there is not much to prevent her from slipping off to Mantua with him at this point (2.2.148). All that is required is all that was ever required—that they stake their lives; that they not flinch in the face of death. And yet, Juliet hesitates.[96]

Consider, it is not the fear of death that will separate Romeo and Juliet. Romeo's next words—not death—are what truly terrify her: "How is't my soul? Let's talk. It is not day" (3.5.25).

"Let's talk." With these words it becomes clear that what actually divides them is the very freedom that has afforded them such exhilaration. For Juliet must now look over and see, simply, Romeo himself. No night to hide her blush; no father to deny; no name to doff; no walls to climb; no—let us face it—no excuses. How are the demands of mutuality to be met?

If nothing external divides them, then their separateness must be actively negotiated, not passively suffered. Figuring out when to stay together, or when to move apart, is one of the demands of mutuality. In this instance, Juliet does not hesitate. She banishes Romeo herself. "It is [day], it is. Hie hence, begone, away. . . . O now be gone" (3.5.26, 35).

After watching Romeo descend from her window following just "one kiss," she tells him, "Methinks I see thee, now thou art so low / As one dead in the bottom of a tomb. / Either my eyesight fails, or thou look'st pale." To which Romeo replies, "trust me, love, in my eye so do you. / Dry sorrow drinks our blood" (3.5.55–59). To many readers, this has seemed a 'foreshadowing' of the play's final scene. I take the moment to be far more prosaic. Romeo and Juliet are, in effect, 'breaking up.' They are coming to grips with the demands and practical possibilities inherent in being answerable to one another.

Juliet is anything but suicidal at *this* moment. For the first and last time Juliet faces a sunrise, a future, that appears to her open and undecided—full of practical possibilities. Perhaps they "shall . . . meet again" (4.1.51). She faces the new day with aplomb: "Be fickle, Fortune. . . . But send him back" (3.5.62–64).

■ ■ ■

In light of everything just suggested, we can now offer a provisional answer to the question *Was it worth it?* A love-affair is worth the trouble, it seems, if it opens practical possibilities and positive freedom, occasions for doing things and ways of interacting, which would not otherwise have been possible. And this is true, even when those practical possibilities amount to little more, ultimately, than the chance to break up mutually, to send one another off with a farewell on good terms—as opposed to being forcibly separated or coerced into a union. Even in Juliet's break with Romeo, we see not the invisible hand of fate, but the minimal freedom and possibilities for action that love-affairs might open. And this seems to be enough.

But even more than this has been made possible by their love-relation. For a start, Juliet is now in a position to more fully and self-consciously, explore what 'family life' makes possible for her—in ways she would not have seen or thought possible without her affair with Romeo. Romeo, too—given that he has been banished, but not executed—is left with at least the prospect of returning to Verona where, minimally, there will be one less Capulet out to kill him. Although Mercutio has been lost, and although Romeo must head out for Mantua for a time, there is every reason to think that the Friar is not entirely wrong to imagine, for Romeo, a future "time"

> To blaze your marriage, reconcile your friends,
> Beg pardon of the prince, and call thee back

> With twenty hundred thousand times more joy
>
> Than thou went'st forth in lamentation. (3.4.150–53)

Individually and collectively, Romeo and Juliet have realized a set of practical possibilities that would have been unavailable were they not to have
held each other answerable as lovers in the ways described above. And they
have done this, while taking on the various obstacles and misfortunes that
have come their way—Tybalt's aggression and death, family discord, Romeo's
banishment.

Yet, as Juliet acknowledges, Fortune is fickle and will have its say. Her new-
found positive freedom will be put to the test, by the news that her mother
cannot wait until after breakfast to share: she must marry Paris on Thursday,
and be thus folded back into the bonds of the ancient family. *This*—we might
think—is what drives her to suicide. And it is true that she would rather die
than marry Paris: "Shall I be married then tomorrow morning? / No! No! This
shall forbid it. Lie thou there. [*She lays down a knife*]" (4.3.22–23). However, it
is not exactly right to conclude only that. Rather, because these alternatives—
suicide or marriage to Paris—would merely decide the fate of her individuality such as it is already acknowledged and valued by her family, this choice
itself appears to Juliet as unfree, unsatisfying. Either way, she would belong
to the Capulet clan as an inactive body. In seeking a "remedy," therefore, what
Juliet wants is a 'third' option—something other than this marriage or suicide. Because the Nurse offers no help, she turns to the Friar in desperation.

In light of this, we can demystify the Friar's medicinal remedy. "If," says the
Friar,

> Thou hast the strength of will to slay thyself,
>
> Then it is likely thou wilt undertake
>
> A thing like death to chide away this shame,
>
> That cop'st with death himself to 'scape from it. (4.1.72–75)

Note that the Friar's plan does not require Juliet to oppose her family. Instead,
it exploits the fulfillment of the family's highest duty in order to make possible
for Juliet a life beyond her value to them. The point is not to make her immortal, of course, but to separate her life and eventual (real) death from her
family's power to assign her life its final value—not by denying the family the
chance to care for her corpse, but by letting the family accomplish precisely
that. The Friar's plan would free Juliet by reconciling her to the family, letting

her be as 'dead to them' as she has always been. Inasmuch as Juliet's family 'loves' her in her very being, she does belong to them as a valued body. She has to acknowledge this debt. So, she must 'die' to them, be buried and mourned. Of course, because this death will be counterfeit—"a thing like death"—it also turns the family's most sacred act of love into a ceremonial sham. In this sense, the ruse exposes the gap between their blindness to *her* (her self-realization, her freedom) and their perception of her individual bodily vitality. By allowing Juliet to seem to her family precisely as she has always seemed to them—a sleeping beauty, as good as dead—the strategy depends upon nothing more than the family's inability to distinguish between their dozing child and their dead child.

At the same time, the stratagem also shows how much Juliet's practical possibilities have shrunken, and how quickly. Escaping to Mantua with Romeo is no longer one possibility among many; it looks like the only way out.[97] And, although Juliet initially jumps at the chance, the severity of what she is undertaking dawns on her. By making a mockery of her family's care for her dead body—by turning family love and its valuation of her into a charade—she also loses a communal context for her action—"My dismal scene I needs must act alone" (4.3.19). Her project becomes the negation of the social authority of individual mortality, for the sake of seeing what else meeting the challenges of mutuality with Romeo might make possible.

As everyone knows, the plan fails. Romeo is given word of Juliet's death, rather than word of the Friar's (new) plan. Given what Romeo understood his practical possibilities to be—and since those were tied to eventual reconciliations in Verona, contingent upon the acceptance of his marriage to Juliet—Juliet's death leaves him with severely diminished prospects, at least as far as he can see. His efforts have failed and—like Pyramus—he is left with the question of whether to give in to a kind of fatalism, or else to reflect on how, at the heart of the failure, contingencies and all the bad luck in the world might be owned. I have already noted Romeo's anti-fatalism, but it was never more forcefully expressed than in his response to the news of Juliet's death: "Is it even so? then I defy you, stars!" (5.1.).

The end of his prospects with Juliet gives her death its weight and significance, not the other way around. Like Juliet, Romeo refuses to see death as the "absolute lord," in light of whose authority our deepest commitments are weighed.[98] Our commitments—our mutual answerability—can also determine what an individual's death means. This is exactly what Romeo sets out to demonstrate by undertaking to kill himself—not in Mantua, but in the Capulet tomb, where he can lay his youthful, bloodless corpse alongside Juliet's.

> Thou detestable maw, thou womb of death,
> Gorged with the dearest morsel of the earth,
> Thus I enforce thy rotten jaws to open,
> And, in despite, I'll cram thee with more food!
> [*Opens the tomb*] (5.3.45–48)

Like Juliet, Romeo denies the traditional authority of individual mortality and family love, for the sake of seeing what else meeting the challenges of mutuality might make possible, all while accepting the collateral costs along the way.[99] "Well, Juliet, I will lie with thee tonight. / Let's see for means" (5.1.34–35).

As it happens, each manages to see in the other's dead body not the calm, cold repose of death—*rigor mortis* or the foul stench of decay—but an individual warmth and vitality. Romeo's lips are still warm and supple to the kiss; his body shows no wounds or blemishes. And Juliet?

> O my love, my wife,
> Death that has suck'd the honey of thy breath
> Hath had no power yet upon thy beauty
> Thou art not conquer'd. Beauty's ensign yet
> Is crimson in thy lips and in thy cheeks
> And Death's pale flag is not advanced there. (5.3.91–96)

In this outcome, Romeo and Juliet are not just the passive beneficiaries of good timing or strange fortune. They have each acted purposefully, with a project in mind—ingesting potions and poisons, laying plots and taking risks, with unwavering resolve and fearlessness, and without any lawful authorization or communal justification. What in ancient "Verona" could have justified what they have undertaken to do?

Without avoiding misfortune, they did not give in to fatalism. And where they failed, they also made it their business to claim that failure at the heart of a shared project. Human freedom is realized not only in the ritual negation of external, alien necessities—love for the dead—but in life's denial of necessity's impersonal externality. "Thus with a kiss I die" (5.3.120).

Part III

From the Propagation of Life to Lovemaking

Fruitfulness and Multiplicity

From these first men, stupid, insensate, and horrible beasts, all philosophers and philologians should have begun their investigations . . . and they should have begun with metaphysics, which seeks its proofs not in the external world but within the modifications of the mind of him who meditates it. For since this world of nations has certainly been made by men, it is within those modifications that its principles should have been sought. And human nature, so far as it is like that of the animals, carries with it this property, that the senses are its sole way of knowing things.

Giambattista Vico, The New Science (1744)

Man gives significance to the sexes and their relations through sexual activity, just as he gives sense and value to all the functions that he exercises; but sexual activity is not necessarily implied in the nature of the human being.

Simone de Beauvoir, The Second Sex (1949)

In the course of the biblical narrative, fruitfulness comes before sex.

"Be fruitful and multiply and fill the water in the seas and let the fowl multiply in the earth," commands God in the first chapter of Genesis, before making the same demand of Adam and Eve: "Be fruitful and multiply and fill the earth and conquer it" (1:23–24).[1]

This follows the revelation that

> God created the human in his image
> in the image of God He created him,
> male and female He created them. (Genesis 1:27–29)

Not only does fruitfulness precede sex, but Genesis 1 also introduces sexual difference in connection to the propagation of life, rather than in relation to sexual activity.[2] This is true of the ancient Greek view, too, as expressed by Aristotle in the first lines of the *Politics*:

> First, there must be a necessary conjunction of persons who cannot exist without each other; on the one hand, male and female, for the sake of reproduction, which occurs not from deliberate purpose, but—as is the case with the other animals and plants—from a natural striving to leave behind them another that is like oneself.[3]

"Striving" between men and women, for Aristotle, originates in the "natural" (*physikón*) demand for species-level reproduction, not in "deliberate purpose" (*proaíresis*) or as sexual acts.[4]

Of course, these passages from Genesis and Aristotle reveal more about the worldviews of our ancestors than they do about any natural facts or timeless truths. And thanks to modern naturalistic-scientific accounts of how certain life-forms regenerate, we now have a different picture of how reproduction and sexual differentiation (eggs and sperm) are causally linked. However, modern scientific explanations are just one way humans have made sense of fruitfulness and multiplicity, pregnancy, male-female relations, the having of children and so on, over time. Explanatory adequacy changes—and at issue here will be the very *kind* of account we need to give, or that our ancestors needed to provide, in light of pressing threats to sense. It is worth remembering, after all, that no naturalistic-causal explanation of the link between sexual differentiation and reproduction could have helped our ancestors fully respond to the deep threats to sense posed by the propagation of life: temporal change, fruitfulness and multiplicity, identity and difference. Not only because they lacked 'modern scientific knowledge'; but because the questions at hand—What *is* the reproduction of a life-form? What *is* a life, given the constancy of temporal change?—still cannot be fully settled just by learning about the birds and the bees.[5]

By the same token, although it is patently absurd to imagine that the only possible answer to the question *Why did you and your sexual partner have a child?* remains *We were following our species-level instinct (or God's command) to be fruitful and multiply,* Genesis and Aristotle were not wrong in any ahistorical or scientific sense. Rather, the link expressed in these texts between a supposedly 'originary' sexual difference and species-level reproduction took root as a *historical* self-conception; in a view of human life once held by our ancestors. And it is worth considering its depth and significance.

This is not to wave away naturalistic accounts of sperms and eggs, when it comes to explaining biological reproduction in mammals like us. But we should resist ontologizing the distinctiveness of a naturalistic or biological explanation in terms of a hard dualism between nature and culture, mind and body. Indeed, as we proceed, we can start to see a kind of continuum between the reproduction of biological life—*both* how humans have reproduced *and* how humans have perceptually grasped reproduction over time (these will turn out to be dialectically intertwined)—and social-historical-cultural transformations over time.[6]

Thus, the first question I want to ask is: *How* did sexual difference take root in the minds of our ancestors as connected to reproduction and procreation? What on earth were our ancestors thinking about in Genesis 1? What did they need explained?

Obviously, when dealing with ancient texts, there are vast hermeneutical obstacles to answering such questions. Still, with some imagination and a "fusing of horizons"—as the philosopher Hans Georg Gadamer used to say—we should be able to make a start.[7]

■ ■ ■

Consider, first, a well-known ambiguity in the passage from Genesis 1 cited above. The ambiguity concerns whether God first created *him* in the singular (*adam*), or whether God immediately created *them* in the plural ("male and female").[8] Was Eve created along with Adam (such that the sexual difference between Adam and Eve is the condition of possibility for further human multiplication), or was Eve made *for* Adam *as* the first instance of multiplication (such that further fruitfulness is seen to require that first instance)?[9]

One possibility is that regularly observed anatomical-bodily differences—between 'Adam' and 'Eve,' say—threatened sense, and therefore demanded explanation.[10] It could not have gone unnoticed by our ancestors, after all, that creatures like us exhibit distinct bodily characteristics. Some of these traits recur with very high degrees of regularity in individuals: hands, teeth, and navels. Other traits might seem typical of particular groupings of individuals or 'peoples': eye color, skin hue, or hair texture. Still other features can be observed to characterize roughly one half or the other of us: penises or vaginas.[11] What kind of effort at sense-making *must* the apprehensions of such traits call for?[12] What kind of explanation do perceptions of bodily differences *require*, that is, if we are to make sense out of anything else about our lives and their conditions?

Well, one answer is that sometimes such apprehensions and descriptions are themselves enough—enough, that is, to give explanatory satisfaction. Indeed, many ancient texts (Aristotle's works and Genesis are no exception) simply offer taxonomical descriptions—quantitative and qualitative markers—which can and do tell us an awful lot about living bodies.[13] Problems only arise when we start to suspect that what living bodies *really are* cannot be captured by such observations and descriptions.

At the most abstract level, this is why so many philosophers have felt compelled to articulate sense-making not just as empirical description but in terms of some distinction between what appears and what 'really is' [*ontos on*], between seeming and being. Think of the distinction between the "ideas" and sensible appearances in Plato; body and soul in Augustine; thought and extension in Descartes; substance and attributes in Spinoza. Such distinctions, in other words, are called for whenever static description and apprehension alone will not explain whatever it is that we want explained.

As noted, one conspicuous aspect of our apprehension of living bodies is that we also perceive changes in bodies over time. Not only do all living creatures manifest certain features, these characteristics also transform day by day, year by year. We all shift shape and size. Some of us do this by becoming pregnant and giving birth—a bodily change to which Socrates, incidentally, attributed our striving for "immortality" (which he also thought explained the desire for offspring).[14] Perhaps most dramatically, all living bodies eventually cease to *be* living, in spite of how they *appear* today—equally, living bodies can be observed to have started living.

This apprehension of temporal change threatens any 'sense' made of the world by the descriptions and apprehensions of traits—such as those I just mentioned—because it leads us to infer that we cannot explain changes in bodily appearance on the basis of how we apprehend individuals at any particular point in time. For instance, I cannot even say—that is, I cannot even *describe*—how my young friend Eve's appearance will change in the future on the basis of my present apprehension and description of her features, let alone *explain* who Eve 'really is,' in light of how her shape-shifting alters my apprehension of her. And furthermore, my apprehension of Eve's difference from Adam at any particular moment is not even the whole *apprehension*. I must also consider any distinction between Adam and Eve in light of these temporal changes. All of which is to say, if we want to explain who Adam or Eve is—or even if we just want to give a fuller description of them as 'changeable'—then we must do more than merely apprehend and describe anatomical difference.

Perhaps this is why Genesis 1 and Aristotle spend little time describing such static differences in much detail. Indeed, although the naked fact of 'characterizable differences' between living bodies is certainly noted by the biblical 'narrator' and by Adam and Eve themselves, that apprehension is not what the story itself aims to make intelligible. Instead, both texts pass immediately to the phenomenon they really wanted to explain: *species-level reproduction, fruitfulness and multiplicity*.

To say it all at once, what Aristotle and Genesis 1 were trying so hard to grasp, in the passages under consideration, is not the fact of sexual or anatomical difference but the reality of reproduction and propagation.

If nothing else, this should be evident from the emphasis in both texts on fruitfulness, multiplicity and procreation—in living creatures generally, and human beings specifically.[15] In reproduction, the constancy of temporal change in living bodies—from pregnancy and birth to maturation and death—becomes a pressing problem.[16] After all, something more than direct apprehension of physical transformation is required in order to *understand* reproduction. Even if our ancestors could observe *that* bodies change, grow and die, or become pregnant and bear children—and even if some inference could be drawn between certain sex acts and species-level reproduction—it was not possible for our forebearers, who lacked microscopes, to 'observe' *how* species-level reproduction really worked in the scientific sense that we accept today. More to the point: the dialectical relationship between ideas about human procreation and the life-forms and practices which such ideas give rise to, and result in, is of course complicated and dynamic. Indeed, this dialectic lies at the core of modern anthropological inquiry.[17] So, to avoid confusion, let me emphasize that my aim here is neither to arrive at chronological, geographical or cultural determinations about when and how human beings educated themselves about sexual reproduction, nor to make universal declarations. In speaking of "our ancestors," for instance, I am speaking heuristically. Instead, I will propose some interpretive hypotheses about human sexual self-education in order to get into view the overall *kind* of phenomenological-retrospective account that, I think, we should be trying to offer, while also grounding these hypotheses in readings of specific texts.

One thing, in particular, must have eluded the direct apprehension of our ancestors: namely, how offspring come to resemble their parents. It was no doubt noticed *that* offspring are "likenesses" of parents, and hence members of a species.[18] Our ancestors must have apprehended these likenesses over time, over generations.[19] Think of how Athena 'sees' Odysseus' face in Telemachus, his son. But *how* exactly was this relative 'permanence' of the species to be grasped—especially, in light of how individual members of a species change over time? This was not a problem that could have been solved through physical apprehension alone. Some further reflection—some hunt for identity among differentiated semblances, such that something essential might be reflected *in* these seemings—was needed. Our ancestors needed to make intelligible the link they saw between temporal changes in individual bodies and the reproduction of species-level life-forms.

Now, it should be understood, this was not just the theoretical challenge of grasping the 'essence' of things behind 'appearances.' The real issue is the sense-making work done by such essences—and the way such sense-making can orient a whole way of life, as a matter of practice. I would go so far as to say that who our ancestors understood themselves to be at a certain stage of consciousness—what they took the whole world to 'really' be—hinged, in large part, upon their reflective understanding of reproduction and bodily change. And this is registered in the power of the 'answers' by which they expressed their understanding—namely, kinship formations, gender and gender-based divisions of labor. Only in recent years has the power of these ancient answers begun to show signs of waning.

What, then, was the answer they gave? How did our ancestors make reproduction in certain life-forms intelligible? By now, you will have guessed perhaps an initial—though not the final—answer: the articulation of sexual difference, especially 'male' and 'female.'

At root, I want to suggest, the perceptual grasping of sexual difference—male and female—is one *outcome* and articulation of our ancestors' efforts to understand the reality of reproduction, temporal change in individuals, and species-level life-forms. Sexual difference is neither symbolic order, nor contin-

gent norm, as others have argued; it is a fundamental way in which human beings have perceptually grasped reproduction.[20] To avoid confusion, by this I do
not mean to suggest that our ancestors first 'perceived' reproduction with their
senses and then 'conceptualized' sexual difference, through mental activity, as a
way to explain it. Reproduction is not a blind "intuition," to use Kant's language,
that got conceptualized or intellectualized by sexual difference. Rather, to borrow from John McDowell's interpretation of Kant, "conceptual capacities are already operative in the deliverances of sensibilities themselves."[21] In other words,
the threat to sense-making that inhered in reproduction, as lived-perceptual
experience, was made intelligible at the level of perceptual experience through
the conception of sexual difference. Sexual difference *was* (and remains) one
historical-conceptual 'taking in' of the world, at work in the lived experience
of reproduction, at a certain moment of consciousness. Sexual difference is a
lived, felt, historically determined way we make sense of the 'reality' of fruitfulness and multiplicity; it is not just itself the 'reality' that is being explained.

This might seem an unnatural way of putting things. But recall that both
Aristotle and Genesis 1 invoke 'male and female'—that differentiation, that
pairing—as a kind of 'perceived understanding' of fruitfulness and propagation
in certain life-forms. The articulation of sexual difference and its social-institutional authority, therefore, should be seen as taking root not in any originary
misogyny, or in the 'othering' of women—though that came to be one effect of
this authority—but as a practical effort to explain to ourselves the propagation
of life-forms, including our own. The endurance of our notion of sexual difference, in other words, is not just the result of its "disciplining power" (to use
Foucault's term) but of our need for it as an explanatory concept. Indeed, the
disciplining power of sexual difference should be seen as, among other things,
one symptom of the depth of *that* explanatory need. In the ancient link between reproduction and sexual difference, a complex interpretive framework is
at work, not as a purely 'mental' or 'intellectualized' process, but as the embed-
dedness of conceptual work *in* our bodies' sensibilities.[22]

All such 'lived' sense-makings are historical, inasmuch as they take root
in material circumstances, or respond to determinate threats to sense that
need not be timeless. It is therefore important to underscore that sexual difference as registered in Genesis 1 or Aristotle can *cease* to be explanatory;
it can become a record of past sense-making efforts. Our efforts to understand our worldly condition are subject to radical revisions, corrections and
transformations—for instance, in light of new problems that threaten sense, or

when our responses to such 'new problems' turn out to be incompatible with, unpracticable in light of, our original account.[23] This happens when we perceive that the reproduction of life *appears* to work differently from the way we originally apprehended it—as happened following the invention of the microscope and the development of new views on the insemination of an ovum[24]— or when we show ourselves capable of safely terminating pregnancies before the offspring are born, or in view of the emerging possibility of cloning human life in laboratories. In light of such 'new' lived experiences, the 'concepts' on display in in Genesis 1 or Aristotle can start to look insufficient. The surest sign of this is the extent to which those who insist on the timeless explanatory power of the Bible in the face of historical change can come to look irrational, ideologically willful or violent.

I will return in the following pages to considerations of more recent ways that we have tried to make sense of reproduction. For the moment, however, let me pull together two conclusions on the basis of my discussion thus far.

First, if the notion of sexual difference was articulated—as I am suggesting—in order to make sense of species-level reproduction, then transformations in our lived experience of reproduction can result in changes to (and hence reveal the mutability *of*) the articulation of any allegedly 'original' sexual difference. Second, self-induced transformations in the way we articulate and *explain* reproduction—the earliest, probably, being a connection between certain sex acts and reproduction—likewise have implications for the normative authority of sexual differentiation. Their fates are connected.

Eve's Knowledge

Now, if sexual difference has been a perceptual-conceptual understanding of reproduction and species-propagation, and available for reflection as such, then this is not necessarily because a connection between certain sex *acts* and reproduction has always been grasped, too. The propagation of life could have been provisionally explained or grasped by our ancestors, at least initially, just through a dimly perceived connection between reproduction and the enigmatic existence of the sexes.[25] At a certain level of experience and awareness, in other words, species-level reproduction could be attributed to sexual difference as divine or natural 'fact,' rather than to specific sexual practices or sensuous experiences.[26] Traces of this attribution are still legible, not only in the Christian myth of the Virgin Mother or the myth of Gaea, but in the evidence attesting to various fertility cults according to which the father played no part in the child's conception; or in Hesiod, where Aphrodite is said to have been born of Uranus' severed genitals; or in the tale of Athena springing from Zeus' head. And then there are the kinds of stories children tell themselves about 'where they came from.' Likewise, in this kind of mythical thinking, the propagation of human life is often described in terms of agricultural fertility or the life-cycle of nature, as in the myth of Demeter, for example.

Because sexual difference was not yet seen as connected to anything that human beings actively *do*, this early form of consciousness presents the sexes as mysterious and inscrutable. The sexes were thought to just be there, as 'created' or 'actually living.' This is why sexual differentiation, and its perceived-conceptualized connection to reproduction and fruitfulness, was often articulated *in and as* our early stories about our gods.[27] The sexes accrued to themselves this kind of ontological status (caught somewhere between bodily immanence and divine transcendence) so long as sexual differences or the sexes were held to be inscribed in the divine-natural order of things, independent of activities we might regulate. If the pregnant body and the arrival of children, for instance, was not yet experienced as connectable to any act for which humans might be responsible, then this was because humans were regarded (and regarded themselves) as unfree, as victims of abduction, as vessels bearing some external power of Nature or divine force. Think of Zeus and Europa, for instance.

Again, this whole worldview provides explanatory satisfaction and practical intelligibility only so long as the link between certain human acts and the arrival of offspring is only imperfectly grasped. For just as soon as a connection between certain acts and pregnancy is felt, perceived—or even suspected—this earlier way of thinking starts to lose its grip. So, whence the suspicion that reproduction in humans results not from sexual difference, or special-level 'behaviors,' but from certain *deeds* for which human beings can hold one another responsible?[28]

It is, I think, safe to assume that a suspicion could only have arisen, over time, through the first-personal experience of having sex, or being penetrated, becoming pregnant and giving birth—although such first-personal experience cannot be fully detached from possible social contexts (such as the coercive enforcement of female chastity).[29] Only by undergoing that particular bodily change in the wake of certain experiences—and hence, over time, coming to perceive-grasp that bodily change as the *result* of certain acts for which we can hold each other accountable—could this connection between individual bodily change, reproduction, and special kinds of experiences have been conceptualized. The first to grasp this must have had such experiences.

Let us, then, call this Eve's knowledge.

We need not, I think, attribute Eve's knowledge to the exercise of any special cognitive faculty that was somehow missing from other life-forms which can also be observed to reproduce sexually.[30] It is enough to begin with the assumption that Eve was curious, although not idly so. She was inquisitive because *failing* to make her world intelligible made it impossible to distinguish *herself* as a distinct being in the world, as a matter of practical coping with her surroundings. This demand for intelligibility is not just the caprice of Eve's disembodied intellect, in other words, it is rooted in the bodily conditions of her experience. Like her ancestors and many fellow creatures, Eve needed to make sense of bodily change and reproduction—above all, her own bodily change, her own offspring. And what now threatened sense—Eve came to see—was precisely that earlier concept according to which offspring just arrive in virtue of sexual difference or divine-natural facts of the matter. This viewpoint simply started to make no sense, for Eve, as soon as she began to perceive a connection between certain experiences she had or underwent—with Adam— and certain *other* experiences: menstruation, pregnancy and the births of her children. This meant that Eve had to begin to single out certain experiences as procreative, or potentially so. And this in turn required a heightened, reflective awareness *of those* experiences, a special perceptual grasping of their distinctive characteristics.

Leaving aside for the moment the experiences of pregnancy and childbirth, we might ask: Was the experience of Adam's nearness one of violation, or pain? Of tenderness, or pleasure? Was it an experience to be feared, dreaded? Or to be anticipated, even desired? And what else would Eve have to know or learn— about herself, about Adam, about her world—in order to even begin to sort through these questions?

Some might be tempted to see Eve's experiences as sufficient for the emergence of what Foucault sometimes called *ars erotica*: "truth drawn from pleasure itself, collected as experience, analyzed according to its quality, pursued according to its reverberations in the body and the soul."[31] But, I think, we should resist this temptation. For one thing, presuming that Eve experienced "pleasure itself" seems rather problematic. For another, sensuous experience alone cannot be the basis of a cultivated practice, it cannot make that practice intelligible, nor become a "quintessential knowledge . . . transmitted by magisterial initiation."[32] Even if we want to speak of "pleasure itself" as a physical experience that, like pain, can be intensified or modified or expressed (vocally, for instance, as in Aristotle's account)—it is far from clear how such intensifications, modifications or expressions can, on their own, structure the intelligibility of cultivated practices, social rituals or 'erotic art.'[33] Moreover, to speak of "pleasure itself" is not yet to grasp pleasure as specifically erotic or sexual, since that distinction requires the prior apprehension of distinctly *sexual* experiences and practices, which could then be cultivated as pleasurable (creating the further difficulty of parsing the cultivation of pleasure from pleasure itself). And that apprehension has not yet been made.

Indeed, for the moment, only one thing seems certain. Eve had to grasp, practically, that distinct experiences she had with Adam were connected to, necessary for, the intelligible reproduction of the life-form to which she belonged. Unless she had undergone certain experiences with Adam—unless they had "known" each other, as it is put in English translations of Genesis 4:1[34]—there would be no fruitfulness and multiplicity. This much, at least, she now grasped.

Note that such experiences need not (yet) have been undergone, by Eve, as distinctly *erotic* or sexual in order for her to apprehend their connection to bodily change, pregnancy, menstruation, birth. Consider the way in which the language of ancient poetry often presents sex as intelligible only through fertility: "Plow my vulva . . ." says Inanna the goddess of love and fertility.[35] If anything, I will suggest, Eve's knowledge—her practiced, sensuous sense-making—allowed sexual practices to emerge *as* distinct practices and experiences, as further efforts to make human life intelligible. More on this in a moment.

Eve's knowledge, next, demanded seeing Adam in a new light. At the very least, Eve now had to see that Adam's involvement was somehow necessary too. Necessary, I mean, not only for species-level reproduction, but for the sake of making reproduction—as well as *Eve's* own life and experience—intelligible. Unless she could understand Adam's actions and experiences, in other words, Eve could not perceptually grasp what she was going through, who she was— nor what life-form to which she belonged. Conversely, the way Eve could touch or be touched—hence the kind of body Eve was—is dialectically connected to the kind of practical self-education she might undergo.[36]

Who, then, was Adam to Eve? What was Adam doing or experiencing, from Eve's point of view? Was the experience in question merely a kind of bodily process, an ejaculatory event to be endured by both sides in the 'natural' course of things, the way that we feel compelled to seek nourishment and eat when famished, or the way the turning of the seasons can compel behavioral changes? Was Adam gripped, from time to time, by a muscular reflex or instinctual appetite for which Eve was somehow the satisfaction? If so, was it by *being* the satisfaction for Adam's appetite that Eve came to be fruitful herself? Such are the kinds of questions Eve must have posed, *in* the felt experience—for instance, by shrinking from Adam's touch, or by seeking him out. Which means, in turn, that Eve could not begin to understand Adam unless she could figure out who or what she was to him. Who was Eve to Adam, then?

For if Eve were nothing more to Adam than the satisfaction for his appetite—if she were *only* fruit, or merely 'fruitful'—then she would be indistinguishable from the plants of the garden. But she must already have perceptually grasped that she was distinct from the fruit of the garden, from mere fruitfulness—not just because of the way she moved about, but because she herself could productively distinguish among the trees and fruits of the garden, and forage therein. She could select and discern, and take her bearing *from* the plants rather just occupy space *as* a plant. She could even determine the goodness or badness of particular fruits, their relative appeal or value; and indeed, on that basis, she could offer fruit to Adam, or decline to do so.

But what exactly was Eve offering to Adam? Mere fruit? Her judgment about the goodness or badness of particular fruits? Did Adam see Eve only as a kind of fruit-judger? Or were they just driven by their appetites alone?

What if Eve offered Adam not just something to eat, nor just her judgment of a fruit's quality and worth, but something else entirely?

Imagine: Eve happens upon a fruit whose goodness was unimpeachable in her eyes, but which she knew she *ought* not pick and eat—because someone had told her not to, on pain of death. "You shall not eat from it and you shall not touch it, lest you die."[37] Leaving aside any theological worries about the source of the prohibition, Eve sees that she has been presented with a *reason* not to pluck the fruit. In light of this, she must make a judgment, not just about the worth of the fruit, but also about the worth of the prohibition—whether that 'reason' is, finally, a reason *to her*. And, at the same time, she must weigh the worth of her very life, since the stated penalty is death. In deciding whether to share the forbidden fruit with Adam, then, she puts her self-conception to a practical test *in* her act. She discerns and assesses not just the fruit but herself, her reasons for acting. By picking the fruit and offering it to Adam, Eve offers not just fruit, nor a species-level behavioral response to instinctual hunger, nor rational deliberation, but her own *self-conception*. She offers herself.

And if Adam partook—if he shared not just fruit, but also Eve's having given herself to him—then they both offer themselves to one another. They install a shared self-conception. Indeed, Adam need not have agreed with Eve's reason for picking the fruit in order to acknowledge that she did so for reasons of her own and that he accepted this: that is, he accepted her, as she offered herself.

Not only this, but it seems clear that Eve wanted to *know*. She desired *knowledge* for its own sake, over and beyond whatever ignorance it might alleviate. At the very least, she wanted to know what would happen if she plucked the fruit, if she and Adam ate. *This* desire for knowledge is not just her need to make her world intelligible, as discussed a moment ago; it is also an expression of knowledge's worth, as such, in Adam's and Eve's eyes—an expression of the *kind* of passionate attachment human beings can have to knowledge. (I will return to this desire to know in a moment.)

At any rate, neither can any longer feign total ignorance of what they are doing. If nothing else, they must acknowledge that *they* partook, that they acted on the basis of something other than instinctual appetite or fruit-judgment. They can no longer take themselves out of the equation. And *that* is the penalty for acting. By acting and suffering for reasons they accept—hence on the basis of a self-conception, not just out of hunger or reflective deliberation—each falls into their agency, and shares forbidden fruit. As a consequence, they must now regard themselves as actors in the world, not merely because they transgressed a law and suffered a consequence, but because they acted on the basis of who they take themselves and each other to be—rather than just on the basis of what they took the fruit to be.

How do Adam and Eve learn all this?

Through their experiences as *sexual* agents. What else is the story of the forbidden fruit about? Sex is one way we fall into our humanity.

Sexual activity and experiences articulate a self-conception, in virtue of which we attach ourselves to one another and the world. One cannot have sex without taking *oneself* to be *doing* just that, without undergoing *that* experience as a kind of self-education. Sex is not just the fulfillment of instincts or pleasurable sensations, nor a blindly sensual bodily experience, nor a process of rational calculation. Rather, as Adam and Eve learn, sexual experience teaches them their status as both subjects and objects in the world. Erotic activity has no external cause (blind hunger) nor does it just express our reflective deliberations (fruit-judging). Sex also implicates us as agents and self-evaluators, as acting subjects and bodily objects. And, although Adam and Eve may not fully realize it yet, it already starts to become clear that reproduction, too, can belong to the domain of contestable reasons *for* sexual activity. It is not just the external 'cause' for sexual activity. I will return to this at a later point in this book. For the moment, we can see that Adam and Eve have already taken the fate of the reproduction of the human species out of God's hands, by grasping their role in the fall.

Sex is self-education, then—a way in which we offer one another, and articulate for ourselves, a self-conception over time. And because we cannot take ourselves out of the equation in sex, it is a practical dimension in virtue of which we might start to take responsibility for what we do. Not "guilt and dreaded shame"—as Milton's well-known interpretation sees it—but practical responsibility.[38] Sexual acts and experiences are ways we share and test our individual and collective self-conceptions; they are not just divine or biological processes or impersonally shared pleasures.[39] Indeed, Adam and Eve now grasp what had, previously, escaped their comprehension. They now see that what they needed to understand—the reproduction of human life—is not just a matter of mere fruitfulness and multiplicity, nor a mysterious process that is somehow connected to the different 'sexes.' Rather, human propagation cannot be understood without coming to grips at the same time with our sexual *agency*, with what we can *do* with one another sexually and otherwise, what we undergo sexually, and with reasons we accept as such. Only with this understanding, by the same token, do the social cultivation of erotic activity and distinctly sexual possibilities even become possible—as a practical-historical achievement, that is, and not as just the impersonal sharing of sensations, however indelible.

To be clear, then, this new 'knowledge' of the connection between reproduction and certain *sex* acts, sexual reproduction, is not the scientific discovery of a timeless truth or biological fact—as should be clear from the fact that the reproduction of human life is less and less determined, nowadays, by what we do with one another sexually.[40] Rather, Adam's and Eve's new knowledge brought about a fundamental and profound historical shift in our self-understanding as human beings—one with far-reaching consequences. Minimally, we had to give up our prior 'knowledge,' according to which the reproduction of human life followed upon certain given or divine facts, like sexual difference, as distinct from concrete sexual practices. More importantly, we had to now see ourselves as sexually reproducing inasmuch as we are sexual agents—actors in the world, beings on whose sexual activity individual fates and the fate of our shared way of life will be decided. Sexual practices must, therefore, be seen as cultivatable and regulatable. The expulsion from the garden of ignorance amounts to taking up the burden of this irreducible normativity, and accepting that even the continuance of our species-form of life depends on our activities and experiences, on reasons we can offer, accept or reject as such.

At this junction, then, at least several related points can be gathered up before we continue.

First, the 'discovery' of ourselves as sexual agents and objects is not just the upshot of weighing and rehearsing erotic desires or fantasies, of impersonally sharing pleasures, or of reaching biological maturity, whether psychic or somatic. Rather, it is a matter of self-induced transformations in our self-understanding, which result from our lived efforts to make our worldly condition intelligible. Second, our 'new' knowledge—that we can and do reproduce sexually—is not only the discovery of biological-natural facts, or the observation of species-level behavior, but also the achievement of a heightened awareness of ourselves as 'reason-giving' agents in the sharing or testing of self-conceptions. (This is one reason why ethnographic investigations into the question of what and when certain cultures came to 'know the truth' about sexual reproduction are ultimately unhelpful: they miss the dialectical way in which sexual practices and sexual self-education are dynamically intertwined). Third, in light of this self-conception, we now grasp that the conditions under which our life-form is reproduced are connected to what we do with one another and how we do it, sexually and otherwise, and are not merely signs of nature's caprice or God's will.[41] Hence, fourth—to pick up the argumentative thread of this book—the history of human sexual practices should be regarded not only as a social reckoning with natural or bodily facts, nor only as the civilized-technical overcoming of natural-bodily limits, but also as a way we have achieved and grasped, over time, the depth of our normative autonomy: freedom.

Sex as Civilization

Our ancestors' sexual attempts to make sense of fruitfulness and multiplicity resulted in their 'giving up' the view that reproduction is a divine gift or natural process—a giving up which, I am suggesting, gave rise to a new shared self-conception: namely, that human life is sexually reproducing. The extent to which this view of ourselves as sexually reproducing has determined our possibilities over broad swaths of human history is difficult to overestimate. Indeed, so powerful is this self-conception that we can be tempted to view sexual reproduction as an external, biological fact of human life, rather than as a revisable historical self-conception.

In a sense, it can be difficult to see how we could have come to see ourselves as agents in the world *unless* we came to understand ourselves as sexually reproducing.[42] For, the enduring authority of sexual reproduction *also* led to our apprehension of a distinct, regulatable domain of sexual practices—in virtue of which, I now want to say, gender roles, sexual identities and erotic possibilities have been articulated and developed.

To avoid confusion, this is not at all to say that sex was originally procreative—much less that sex was originally heterosexual (we have not yet addressed questions of gender difference; more on that shortly). It is only to say that the *intelligibility* of certain human acts as distinctly *sexual*, hence as cultivatable and regulatable, took root in efforts to make sense of reproduction and procreation. If reproduction— fruitfulness and multiplicity, temporal change in individual bodies—could not be explained, then no regulatable social sphere, no intergenerational form of life, could come into view as such.

This initial explanation required, minimally, grasping certain practices or sex acts as potentially consequential—profoundly so, since the known consequences touched upon individual propagation, bodily transformation, procreation and the multiplying of our life-form. To repeat, this grasping was accomplished not just through feats of disembodied intellection, but through sexual self-education over time, by getting pregnant, through certain concrete experiences or practices, by being held accountable. In time, those acts and experiences were seen as expressive of agents, not of impersonal causes, reflective deliberations or divine forces, and in this way came to be distinguished as *sexual* acts—inextricably tied to webs of practical responsibility (in the non-Miltonian sense discussed above), social regulation and a reckoning with consequences.[43]

The first step in the regulation of sexual practices must have been practiced attempts to determine those sex acts that might lead to pregnancy and birth, and to distinguish these from those sex acts that—although they *feel* akin to potentially procreative sex acts (penetration, genital contact and stimulation, certain forms of bodily arousal and contact)—cannot lead to pregnancy and birth. In other words, the first step must have been a practical bid to make *further* sense of the connection between certain sexual experiences and reproduction.

Here, only self-conscious exertion—the collective, self-aware practicing of sex as a distinct activity—could have yielded to our ancestors' reliable knowledge of links between certain kinds of sex acts and reproduction. Sexual experience is not just guided by bodily sensation, then, not merely reflective of what we know about the world; it *is* a kind of 'grasping' of the world, as well as an embodied expression of what we think we know. Equally, sexual experiences and acts are what is (coming to be) known. Sexual activity has been both the practice under investigation, as well as a practical mode of investigation; the objective act under collective scrutiny, and the shared subjective act of scrutinizing; the phenomenon to be made sense of, and a way of making sense of it.

Indeed, one *reason* for sexual activity—one reason for having sex—must have been its explanatory power, the expanded self-understanding (individual and collective) that the activity itself yielded. This self-understanding was both 'objective'—it amounted to richer comprehensions of concrete social-material conditions, such as the demographic composition of a society and its potential for increase—and 'subjective,' because it helped individuals to see how to take up their particular place or role within those concrete social-material conditions, self-expressively as well as dutifully. Sexual acts could now be *practiced*, in other words, in ways that led to fuller understandings of how 'human life' and societies might be governed and regulated, *and* to fuller understandings of how individuals—particular sexual agents—belong to a social realm of rule-governed interactions.

Sex, I want to say, belongs to a subset of human practices that do not just descend from the values and rules of a specific society, but that also express and work out *why* those rules get established in the first place, and how individuals might 'live within' those rules. Sexual practices are not *just* normative like all other cultural practices, therefore. In speaking of the "history" of sexual practice, then, I do not just mean to say that sex acts merely express the values or mores of a particular society—those rules which take hold just by being collectively recognized as binding. No doubt, specific sexual practices are culturally shaped in this way. But I mean, further, that sexual activity is one way we historically *achieve* moral regimes as such, and reckon with the implications of that achievement. And I am suggesting that this reckoning with unavoidable collective and individual issues—such as how to regulate the reproduction of life, or how to behave as subjects in a regimented social world—was not just philosophical, religious, juridical or artistic. It must also have taken the form of self-induced transformations within our sexual practices, at the sensuous-experiential level, not just at the level of regulation.[44]

Moreover, if a necessary part of this reckoning amounted to drawing distinctions, through repeated trials and errors, between potentially procreative sexual acts and nonprocreative sex acts, then the drawing of that distinction was also how sexual activity as such—*its* distinctiveness as an activity—was first brought to consciousness. The first basis for the social regulation of sexual activity—hence the first reason for sex acts, in virtue of which other reasons can get traction *as reasons*—was this 'learned distinction' between procreative and nonprocreative sex, between those sexual experiences that were taken to be potentially procreative and those that were not. This distinction, in other words, must have given rise to both objective rules governing sexual interaction *and* subjective ways of adhering to, bending, or transgressing those rules.[45]

That said, not all sex needed to have been seen as socially consequential in the same way. For instance, the Greek perception of a difference between comedy and tragedy in human affairs might have been an attempt to make sense of how sex sometimes leads to tragic outcomes; whereas in comic experiences, sex can appear *as* the happy outcome. However, if certain sexual experiences were known to be potentially consequential—minimally, because potentially procreative, and in this sense socially significant and authoritative—then the whole field of human sexual activity and sexual possibilities must henceforth have been determined and articulated by this shared knowledge, this shared self-conception: namely, that our propagation as a species is connected to sexual acts that we can, and do, regulate. Only in light of this socially authoritative self-conception of human life as sexually reproducing could sex itself have come to be regarded as a distinct practice, as something for which we can be held responsible, not just something we suffer as a species-level instinct or natural 'event.' The whole fraught sphere of erotic life—the civilizing and regulating of sex as a distinctive practice, its "repression" as Freud would say—has its beginning and first stage in the explanatory force of sexual reproduction.

Gender and Reproductive Regulation: Stages of Life

I am proposing that learned distinctions between potentially procreative and nonprocreative sex must have been not only the initial basis for regulating sexual activity—and hence for regulating a range of other, related activities—but also the basis for the *further* development of sexual practices and social organization.

At this point, then, we can start to be a bit more specific about how sexual practices unfolded, subsequently, and what else they have taught us.

Again, once offspring were understood to result from certain kinds of sex acts, then our ancestors must have noticed that not all sex acts result in offspring. *What*—they must have wondered—could explain the discrepancy between those potentially procreative sex acts that result in offspring and those that do not? How to *account* for sexual reproduction, as distinct from just apprehending it? How to explain, that is, what makes sex acts sometimes also procreative acts? And how to explain what we are experiencing or doing sexually when we are not procreating, since on such occasions we seem to be engaged in something intelligibly related to procreating (however faintly intelligibly) and yet no offspring result?[46] How, indeed, to explain erotic practices? What might *we* explain and learn through our erotic practices?

One immediate apprehension must have already been part of Eve's knowledge: namely, that offspring result from bodily changes which can be observed and experienced in certain individuals only at certain stages of life. This question of *which individuals*, therefore, could not be answered without also answering the question, *which stage of growth and life*? For not only did our ancestors have to distinguish between individuals with certain anatomical characteristics, but among those individuals they also had to apprehend stages of temporal growth and maturity and their perceived connection to propagation: menstruation, for instance, or the widening of the hips. The apprehension of measurable growth as a way of drawing anatomical distinctions must have begun to figure in the regulation of sexual reproduction and social organization.

To say it all at once—this apprehension of age and individual growth must have gone hand in hand with the ascriptions of gendered social status to individuals endowed with certain anatomical features: female, male, eunuch or hermaphrodite.[47] Recall, as just one well-known ancient witness among many, Sappho, and how her poetry so often describes women not only in terms of physical beauty or social standing, but also in terms of age and fertility. Think, too, of the numerous rituals across cultures that require the practiced demonstration (often sexually articulated) of a maturation threshold: becoming a 'man,' 'warrior,' 'citizen,' 'marriable woman.'[48]

The articulation and regulation of different sexual practices among all individuals—now distinguishable by age and growth, by anatomical features as well as other qualities (such as beauty or vigor)—must therefore have proceeded on the basis of a further learned distinction: Not only do certain sex acts result in offspring, but such acts must be performed by or with fertile individuals. The regulation of sexual practices *tout court* and the struggle to make erotic acts intelligible must, consequently, have required an especially strict governance of fertile bodies—not just because they were immanent bodily vessels or 'bearers' of offspring, but also because fertile bodies were *embodiments of what could be known* about erotic practices, embodiments of what *must be known* in order for any further sense to be made of what we are doing with one another sexually.

Where offspring were held to result from 'vital essences' connected to ejaculation, for instance, the social regulation of such emissions took effect, and certain kinds of *ars erotica* became possible. Where offspring were seen as birthed in connection with, say, individual bodies that produce milk, then other regulatory regimes resulted.[49] The point to be made is not that these early beliefs were stable or uniform across ancient societies, or even that they were internally coherent—no doubt, competing explanations abounded. Rather, the point is that these different knowledges became normatively binding for certain agents at certain points in time.[50]

To be clear, not just *any* explanation or 'wisdom' could become normatively authoritative over the long haul. True, local wisdoms about the connection between childbirth and the frequency of ejaculation, or about the implications of the weather during menstruation, can hold cultic authority for adherents. Such knowledges can even turn out to be scientifically verifiable. However, in order to hold broad social-institutional authority for human self-understanding over the historical scope I am trying to consider here, such norms must *also* be intelligibly structured by something other than fervent adherence.[51] *Broad norms*— such as a gender-based division of labor, through which human self-understanding has been determined across historical eras and local belief structures—also require for their intelligibility and *durée* something repeatedly observed and experienced by individual bodies over long periods of time, such that *this observed repetition becomes an unavoidable burden upon our powers of explanation.* The intelligibility of long-lasting authoritative norms, in other words, is structured by that which—in virtue of objectively observed 'reality' and collectively lived 'experience'—*demands* explanation, rather than just *permits* explanation. Unless certain realities and experiences are adequately explained, the conditions of our shared existence are threatened. Our explanations of our *most pressing* or widely repeated realities and experiences hold the greatest normative sway, and thereby have shaped our self-understanding most profoundly over the long haul.

One such reality, I am suggesting, must have been the observation and experience that offspring are born of certain bodies, and not others. The apprehension of *certain* bodies as meaningfully distinct from other bodies—not just unmeaningfully 'different'—was necessary for the regulation and intelligibility of sexual reproduction, not just for the reality of reproduction. And it seems plausible that this distinction was drawn by observing those who give birth, and out of the experience of giving birth: in virtue of this active embodying of reproductive capability. I shall assume that these lived apprehensions, or perceptual-graspings, are the source of the normative connection between an identifiable 'female' fertility and the *social gender of* 'woman,' or more precisely, the gendering of maidens, young women, and fertile women.

This, then, is the genesis of social genders. Whether this initial cleaving between fertile female bodies and other bodies was first articulated as yin and yang, man and woman, or as some other nomenclature, the point is we are dealing with a social apprehension and ascription whose power is rooted in its tremendous explanatory force, its necessity for the intelligibility of the practice of sexual reproduction, hence for the intelligibility of fundamental aspects of our worldly conditions generally.

In practice, then, the social regulation of fertile female bodies and their activities must have subsequently determined the articulation and understanding of all other erotic acts, in virtue of which further social-gendered ascriptions could then take hold: older woman, virgin, young man, eunuch and others. This initial subjugation of fertile female bodies to strict laws, observations and sexual regulations is, I believe, the basic foundation for the historical oppression of women, for a gender-based division of labor as well as for the earliest social articulations of gender. These stem, I contend, not from any deep-seated "will to dominate woman" (Beauvoir), nor from the "arbitrary," non-necessary attribution of the gender "woman" to "the female body" (Butler), but from our ancestors' practical attempts to understand sexual reproduction and, by extension, to make erotic activity itself intelligible and regulatable.[52] The social ascription of the gender woman to the body female (perceived as subject to fertile growth and change)—and the host of demands placed on fertile women that followed from this ascription—was thus hardly arbitrary, nor the immediate expression of an originary power dynamic, but rather a necessary moment in our efforts at explaining the conditions of our existence.

Without the gendered distinction of woman from men, and other gender distinctions, nothing else could be made intelligible. Power dynamics of the highest order resulted from this explanatory effort, to be sure; but these dynamics had to draw their energy *from* (before they could give energy *to*) such explanatory exertions.[53] Put another way, power dynamics are not intelligible *as* power dynamics unless sense is being made of the conditions whereby we exist—even if knowledge can only take hold by being socially powerful.[54]

Likewise, large-scale normative collapses can only be explained if such historical shifts can be seen to result not just from the perception of 'new' realities that do not fit the earlier explanatory paradigm, but from the way the *emergence of those new realities themselves* comes to threaten the overall sense we make of our worldly conditions.[55] In other words, profound power shifts reflect deep threats to sense-making—accompanied by the realization that those threats must be overcome, not just for the sake of maintaining of a particular social hierarchy or social 'discipline,' but so that anything at all can be intelligible. This, I think, helps us explain one puzzle with which I began: the world-historical importance of *gender* as social norm.

And I am suggesting, further, that strict enforcement of restrictions on the activities of fertile females was a requirement for the normative foundations, and the self-understanding, of our ancestors' societies. Consequently, these restrictions must have been rooted so deeply as to determine the regulative ascription of other genders and gendered roles: not just fertile female, but also wife, daughter, virgin, mother, older woman, concubine, son, young man, older man, eunuch, hermaphrodite or intersex individual. Those 'roles' are formed and delineated in practice—by carrying out activities intelligibly undertaken at different stages of life, in view of the self-conception under discussion here: sexual reproduction.

At the same time, regulations on fertile women (as socially gendering beings) must have been the basis on which 'subjective' experiences of sexual activity could first take shape, and develop in the direction of other possibilities. The desire *for*, and the desirability *of*, different individual bodies as a basis or reason for sexual activity could have been compelling only *after* the intelligibility of such as desire as specifically 'erotic' was established—thus only after the regulation of fertile women was in force, since only on the basis of a shared reason for that regulation was erotic activity even discernable as such, or so I am arguing.

This is a long-winded way of saying that sexual practices and *ars erotica* in their astonishing variety first took a self-aware shape—began to develop new practical possibilities, discursive articulations and social consequences— only in virtue of the force of those sexual regulations that were required for the intelligibility of our lives together. The whole field of what we mistakenly call sexualities or sexual orientations is not originary—one is no more 'born' heterosexual than one is 'born' a man. But in addition to this claim, already made by Foucault and others,[56] I want to say that sexual acts and possibilities, including our fantasy lives, develop over time on the basis of social restrictions, without which we could not make sense of our shared conditions in the world.

The earliest such restrictions concerned fertile women, I am suggesting, since fertile women—those individuals whose growth can portend pregnancy and birth—must have been the most unavoidable threat to the intelligibility of human life, its temporal dimension and its reproducibility. Multiplicity and fruitfulness in human life could not have made sense if sexual reproduction could not be grasped. And reproduction, in turn, could not be grasped unless procreative bodies could be known and their actions collectively disciplined and regulated.

Only on the basis of such sexual regulations could a number of more complex norms and social institutions *then* take shape as possible ways of living out those earlier restrictions. These include various exogamous kinship structures, the incest taboo, the formation of economic relations whose bedrock 'value' was the arrangement of sexual 'partnering' for fertile women, matrilineal ties and other kinship formations whose intelligibility was structured in terms of proximity to a fertile woman or women. This would also include many patrilineal kinship formations, inasmuch as these are practiced in terms of external control over the sexual activities of fertile women.[57] Without wading into the thickets of comparative anthropology, it is enough for now to bear these divergent possibilities in mind.

Pregnancy and Childbirth

Let me pick up the story, then, by considering what must have been the next threat to sense: the extent to which pregnancy and childbirth must also have been experienced as a mysterious or natural (not *fully* regulatable, not even fully perceptible) process, even though pregnancy was known to be the practical result of a regulatable sexual act.

There must have been a significant divergence between what was known about sexual reproduction at this point—namely, that we can and do regulate sex acts—and how childbearing was actually lived and experienced. Miscarriages, or so-called natural abortions, for one thing, must have been bewildering. Indeed, they still are—inasmuch as they are explicable only as 'events,' rather than as the result of any regulatable human action. The stopping and starting of the menstrual cycle, the throes of labor, the frailty of the newborn, multiple births from one pregnancy, the onset of pain or discomfort, nausea, infant mortality, maternal mortality, breech births, stillbirths, anatomical variations in newborns, birth defects—all these must have been experienced as, must have been *explicable* only as, occurrences that were unintelligibly connected to any regulatable sexual act. I do not mean that explanations were not attempted—of course they were. However, none of these explanations was able to gain broad normative authority over our social interactions, because they did not manage to adequately mitigate these threats to sense.

At this stage, then, the lived experience of pregnancy and childbirth could yield no further insight into our erotic practices. Indeed, these felt experiences threatened to make many other aspects of our worldly conditions inscrutable to us—and hence could not form the basis for any new, socially authoritative self-conception. The authority of sexual reproduction in human affairs was thereby reified and reinforced, in light of the ongoing threats to sense-making posed by the vicissitudes of pregnancy and childbirth. At best these 'felt realities' could be regulated only by the crude cordoning of young women as sexual agents, for instance, through the enforcement of female chastity or monogamy. Whence the origins of the social value attached to female 'virginity.' To the extent that fertile women achieved sexual agency at all, at this stage, it was only within these limited confines.

If childbirth and pregnancy remained fundamentally inscrutable, for reasons just mentioned, then those sexual acts that were 'known' to be procreative had to be practically 'bracketed' as yielding relatively little else in the way of further sense-making. For the time being, our ancestors believed that they knew all that they *could* know about what sexual activity between fertile men and women could fundamentally teach.[58] In other words, because sex acts between potentially fertile men and women were, at this stage, fundamentally governed by the 'knowledge' of their connection to reproduction and procreation, these acts remained limited—even blocked—as practical ways to generate further self-understanding or explanatory yields.

It would be difficult to overestimate the immense consequences of this impediment—which reverberate to this day in the sexual practices and self-understanding of numerous social formations and countless individuals across the globe. I do not mean, of course, to suggest that nonprocreative sex acts between men and women were not practiced and cultivated as such. I mean to

say that the *explanatory* force of such practices was limited by their entanglement with Eve's knowledge: reproduction as the possible upshot of sex acts between fertile males and females. Possibilities for interactions between men and
women thus remained stunted, self-understanding obscured.

In later sections of this book, I will suggest that this state of affairs has only
been loosened by the historical achievement of lovemaking—perceptible, first,
in the sexual exertions of fertile men and women trying to come to grips with
what *else* they might be making sense of when engaging one another sexually
besides reproductive knowledge (and social hierarchies and gender roles rooted
in that knowledge), and then, only later, acknowledged as a viable and immensely significant basis for social life. However, prior to the hard-won achievement of lovemaking—both its necessary individual exertions, and the achieving
of broad social recognition for its significance—the explanatory yield of sexual
activities between fertile men and women remained, for generations, limited.

Think of it this way: the cultivation and development of erotic practices between fertile men and women—as a significant *explanatory* effort—continued
to orbit around the regulatory business of determining when and where fertile men and women were permitted to copulate, in view of the reproductive
potential of the act. Whence the duration of institutions already mentioned:
of exogamous marriage, of economic arrangements whose value rested on
the social authority of sexual reproduction, of kinship terms whose intelligibility structured what was then known about sexual activity between fertile
men and women. Where the development of these institutions displays variances between cultures or social groups, these can be largely attributed to local
knowledges or ancient wisdoms. According to some of these variances, for
instance, worldly goods and prerogatives were made inheritable in virtue of
one's mother—according to others, matters turned on who one's father was. The
very existence of such variances, after all, can be explained by the *particularity* of the wisdoms from which they drew their authority. However, broad social authority—transcultural, nonlocal knowledge—only comes into the world
when fundamentally *new* explanations authoritatively emerge, such that these
become necessary for the intelligibility of anything at all. For the time being,
however, the only such world-transforming knowledge birthed in the sexual
education between men and women remained the procreative knowledge
whose origins I have been tracing: reproduction and sexual agency.

In short, the inscrutability of pregnancy and childbirth—the fact that our
explanations for its as-yet unregulatable aspects could not yet become *broadly*

authoritative for much else we do—threw our ancestors back on the question already posed: How could we explain what we were doing sexually when we were *not* procreating, since on such occasions we seemed to be doing something intelligibly related (however vaguely) to procreating, and yet we were not producing offspring?

The question is immense. How to explain erotic practices, in their vast, manifest sociality? What might our erotic practices *themselves* help us to make intelligible?

Providing answers to these questions—answers that could generate broad social-institutional authority—required the intentional articulation and development of *other* sexual practices that might yield further insight into our worldly conditions. Where to turn, then, for the practical achievement of new knowledge?

Again, because it was clear that new explorations must be based on the cordoning and restricting of sexual activity between fertile men and fertile women, our ancestors turned to sexual activity between *others*—between men (young and old), women (young and postmenopausal), eunuchs, concubines, hermaphrodites or intersex individuals—for further socially significant explanations. This is not a chronological claim. Doubtless, sex acts between all kinds of individuals have been going on since time immemorial. Rather, I am suggesting that the threat to sense posed by pregnancy and childbirth required, in light of Eve's knowledge, the social regulation of, and explicit reflection upon, what could be learned by sex acts between those sexual partnerings which were known to be incapable of giving birth.

The inventions and developments of sexual identities, practices and possibilities that resulted from this stage of our sexual self-education are, to say the least, vast and varied. On the one hand, we can survey the variety of sexual practices across cultures and over history in light of the particular societies whose local wisdoms, beliefs and values these practices reflect. As reflections of the sheer scope and range of sexual possibilities, whose future developments have hardly been exhausted, these are not insignificant. To the extent that we today remain sexually *active*—meaning not just that we perform acts which we understand to be 'sexual,' but insofar as we continue to learn, explore and invent new possibilities and acts sexually—we cannot proceed without such local knowledges, without continuing to cultivate them.

On the other hand, it is important to remember that not all local practices or beliefs turn out to be anything other than local flourishings, blossomings of sexual identities or cultures that take root only in a particular knowledge or wisdom, and that turn out to be unnecessary for the self-understanding of human life broadly—that turn out, in other words, to be necessary only for the internal coherence of a particular way of life or culture. Likewise, if local cultures can come to end—if particular practices or ways of life cease—then that cessation raises the question of whether those *practices* were, finally, necessary for the rest of us in our efforts to make sense of the world; or whether, instead, sense could only be made of the world if those practices *ceased* to be necessary for the internal coherence of any society.

Because I am trying to answer *that* question, I am trying to track broad social-historical transformations in our self-conceptions, in view of the historical achievement of lovemaking arising out of prior sexual practices, whose origins I am trying to illuminate. Given this aim, I do not mean to undertake a comparative analysis of sexual practices whose specificity, from my vantage today, appear local. I will not compare, say, details of ancient Taoist doctrine concerning sexual activity between men and cultural analyses of pederasty in ancient Greece.[59] Instead, I will try to say something about what I think is at stake in broad social transformations in view of which we might begin to grasp that which, in those local *ars erotica*, turns out to be necessary for our overall self-understanding and that which, over time, might simply come to an end.

Giving Birth in Wisdom

Love [*erōs*] must be a lover of wisdom [*philosophos*, "philosopher"], and, as such, in between being wise and being without understanding.

Plato, *Symposium*

East and west, north and south, the cultivation of the various *ars erotica* requires time and energy, space and resources. Some well-known ingredients are the consumption of food and drink, alcohol or other intoxicants, the gathering of potential sexual partners, the possibility of lying horizontally, perhaps even facilities for sleep and rest. The Greek *symposion* (drinking together) offered one such recipe: food, followed by heavy drinking, musical and sexual entertainment, usually supplied by flute-girls (*aulētrides*), ending in exhausted collapse on the couches on which the evening had been spent.[60] This is, of course, the context for Plato's *Symposium* (416 BCE)—a text which reports a conversation about *erōs* overheard "a very long time ago," in Athens, at the House of Agathon.[61]

This historical remove, coupled with the fact that the dialogue reports a conversation in praise of *erōs*—it reports a *conversation*, that is, not erotic acts or practices as such—suggests that Plato's aim was to get *erōs* into view as a topic for praise, reflection and discussion, not simply to describe or defend the specifically erotic character of the symposia.[62] Not only, as Alexander Nehamas put it, does Plato's *Symposium* look to us today like "the first explicit discussion of love in western literature and philosophy," but Plato himself also presents the reported conversation as a manifestly *discursive* reflection on sexual love and its significance, as a discourse that emerges out of socially specific erotic rituals (the symposia) for the sake of reflecting *on* sexual acts without being reducible *to* them.[63] Though education and civic discourse were certainly central to symposia in this historical period, Plato's dialogue appears to be the first extant text to explicitly pose the questions we are following here: What are we *doing* in our erotic practices? What *sense* are we to make of sexual activity, and what does that activity make sense of?

As if to make this clearer, we are told at the beginning of the dialogue that the guests assembled at Agathon's house are suffering from a hangover after the previous night's symposium. The consumption of wine, therefore, is to be voluntary rather than obligatory—and the flute-girl is sent away, "to let her flute for herself, or, if she wants, for the women within" (176a–e). In the place of excessive drinking and musical-sexual entertainment, there will be a conversation, or series of speeches, about *erōs* (176e–177e). The dismissal of the flute-girl, and the consequent bracketing of sexual activity between fertile men and women, is presented as a necessary precondition, in this context, for this task of reflection—as if the sexual interactions between men and maidens were seen as antithetical to, counterproductive with respect to, making any sense of sexual activity.

A moment ago, I indicated the central reason for this bracketing. To the extent that sex between men and women was 'grasped' as part of sexual reproduction, *that* sexual practice could do little to help us fundamentally understand anything else. Aristophanes' famous story about the "invention" of sexual reproduction, for instance, makes this clear by noting the procreative consequences of sex between fertile males and females, by emphasizing this difference with respect to other gender configurations. It remains unclear, to Aristophanes, what *else* men and women might be making sense of with one another, sexually or otherwise.

> Zeus . . . rearranges their genitals toward the front—for up till then they had them on the outside, and they generated and gave birth not in one another but in the earth, like cicadas—and for this purpose, he changed this part of them

toward the front, and by this means made generation possible in one another, by means of the male in the female; so that in embracing, if a man meets with a woman, they might generate and the race continue . . . (191c–d)

Note that as with Eve's knowledge, so too, Zeus' "invention" of sexual reproduction brings sex into view as a distinctly human activity (before that, we are told, human beings had cast their seed and made offspring in the earth). In Aristophanes' account, sexual reproduction provides the explanation according to which sexual practices *tout court* could be articulated—minimally, by allowing reproductive sex to be identified and isolated. However, once sexual activity emerges as a practical possibility, *erōs* between other genders—because such *erōs* was known to sequester procreative consequences while remaining perceptibly erotic—opens new practical possibilities, greater freedom, and indeed satisfaction *as* a sexual act.[64] So, Aristophanes continues:

and if male meets with male they might at least find satiety in their being together; and after which they might pause and turn to work and attend to the rest of their livelihood. So it is really from such early times that human beings have had inborn in themselves Eros for one another. (191d)

The practical cultivation of erotic *satisfaction*—the source of our desire to love each other—develops in those sexual interactions whose meaning is not saturated by procreation, but which are nevertheless made intelligible and regulatable *in view of* sexual reproduction. For, without a division of sexual acts into the procreative and the nonprocreative—as in the two passages just cited— sexual practices would have lost (at this historical moment) the formal distinction on whose basis they were intelligible and regulatable at all.

By the same token, sexual acts that remained unentangled with the production of children acquired the chance to develop a kind of practical autonomy, the chance to seek out specifically *erotic* satisfactions. As I have been arguing, in this way sexual activity—*erōs*—wins for itself a practical autonomy; it can start to understand and regulate itself according to 'rules' other than the sheer fact of procreation. This explains, at least in part, the social significance acquired by same-sex relations and by pederasty in ancient Greece, as well as the way in which other ancient *ars erotica* began to be cultivated and regulated as distinctly 'sexual' satisfactions (not just as procreative acts). It also explains the corresponding social 'devaluation' of sex between men and women in this historical period.[65] Indeed, sexual acts between men and women were often thought to be undertaken, like eating and drinking, in the service of a "vulgar" appetite—as Pausanias suggests.[66] If the men harbor deep doubts about the intellectual parity of women with respect to men—as in Pausanias' speech—and hence see no reason to include women in a conversation devoted to these questions, then these doubts expressed not only a culturally ingrained misogynism but, more fundamentally, the view that interactions between men and women had nothing further to *contribute* to the task of *making sense* of sexual activity, or figuring out what sense sexual activity makes of anything else.[67]

The speakers in Plato's *Symposium* are charged with speaking "in praise of *Erōs*" (180d), and their speeches have routinely been interpreted as competing efforts to say something about what *erōs* is: as if Plato were merely staging a definitory exercise.[68] I will take a different approach to the dialogue, which seems to me to stage an attempt, not to explain *erōs*, but to see what *erōs* helps us to explain.[69]

Consider that each speech, in turn, invokes *erōs* in terms that try to clarify or explain something *else*—as if the aim were not just to make *erōs* intelligible, but also to grasp what *erōs* (understood not just as desire, but as specific erotic practices) makes intelligible. Phaedrus, for instance, sees *erōs* as praiseworthy not only because of its connection to the virtue of courage or self-sacrifice, but also because *erōs* is a primary activity through which courageous acts are apprehended as such (179b). Pausanias' speech, as already intimated, suggests that the difference between vulgar and noble erotic acts is explained by, rather than being an explanation for, *erōs*.[70] Eryximachus' pedantic speech turns to *erōs* to make sense of medicine (Eryximachus' own area of expertise), as well as music and meteorology. Aristophanes' tour de force suggests that *erōs* (as love of individuals) explains the origins of sexual identities, gender roles, sexual differentiation, sexual reproduction, and indeed sexual activity itself. Although Aristophanes' discourse proceeds, as it were, in the inverse direction to the one I am taking in the present work, it is nevertheless clear that Aristophanes, too, wants not just to explain *erōs* but to understand what *erōs* explains. Agathon's speech, perhaps the most parodic, makes this same point about the explanatory ambitions of the speeches.[71]

Socrates' own speech is particularly interesting in this respect. By shifting the focus from a discussion of the qualities of the beloved to those of the lover (204c), Socrates suggests that wisdom is not something offered by one lover to another, as a teacher to a student, but that wisdom is itself one of the beautiful things that lovers desire. In other words, for Socrates, *erōs* not only makes sense of *other* things that we might also want explained—such as those issues just mentioned; *erōs* is also what grips those people who crave wisdom as such, those who want knowledge for its own sake: philosophers. Philosophy, or the desire for wisdom, is a form of love, according to Socrates. Indeed, philosophy is the highest expression of *erōs*.

In Diotima's famous 'ascent,' recall, *erōs* is not just the pursuit of a beautiful body.[72] More fundamentally, *erōs* is a pursuit of the continual possession of good things (201a–d), a pursuit she attributes to our desire to "give birth in beauty" (206b–e). "All human beings" says Diotima, "conceive both in terms of the body and in terms of the soul, and whenever they are at a certain age, their natures desire to give birth" (206c). This striving for reproduction—which she also characterizes as a striving for immortality—can occur through physical offspring, or in the doing of glorious deeds, or in anything that will outlive the individual in question. For my purposes, what matters is that this striving springs from the fact that philosophers learn *through sexual activity* that bodily life is fleeting, that experiences are irremediably temporal. *Erōs* turns out not just to be an accompaniment to the (non-erotic) educative discourses that the symposia of Plato's day also provided. For Socrates, *erōs* is itself educative, formative, knowledge-generating. In *erōs*, for instance, we learn that the beautiful body we 'loved' will eventually cease to be beautiful, which leads us to desire more permanent goods and, ultimately, beauty itself as the highest good (211d). *Only* through this inherent frustration of erotic love, according to Diotima, do we come to see what *else* we might be doing erotically: making offspring, performing virtuous deeds, and finally pursuing beauty as such. Only if the philosopher learns *sexually* that the beauty of the soul is higher than the beauty of bodies, can he focus on those "ideas that will make young men better," having realized along the way that "ideas" are "beautiful" as such and, hence, that he seeks knowledge above all: "unstinting love of wisdom [*philosophia*]" (210e).

Although *erōs* is unintelligible to Socrates as a mere physical event, sexual activity remains a necessary moment in the 'ascent' of *erōs*—the initial way that philosophical *erōs* is experienced and provisionally understood. It is not that Socrates devalues bodily experiences, but rather that he regards unreflective, unthinking *erōs* as impossible. Being a sexual lover entails, minimally, something like the reflective awareness of being a sexual lover, or at least the 'positive' desire to not be ignorant of what being a lover amounts to (207c). At the same time, in virtue of the dissatisfactions that sexual activity inevitably generates in self-aware lovers—above all, the threat to sense-making posed by the temporal changes inherent in bodily life, and the way that sexual cravings haul us back and forth across the keel of lack and temporary fulfillment—*erōs* gets revealed as a fundamentally philosophical passion. For Socrates, indelible aspects of felt sexual experience are *themselves* attempts to try to understand certain phenomena: lust, temporary satiety, bodily change and growth, temporality and finitude (207e). So this desire to understand is not somehow separate from sensuous *erōs*; since one cannot be a sexual lover without also being gripped by some desire for such understanding. (208a–b) Precisely because *erōs* cannot be severed from this craving for understanding, philosophy itself turns out to be a profound form of erotic satisfaction. (Readers of Plato will remember that this is a conclusion reached time and again in the dialogues, not just in the *Symposium*.[73]) *Erōs*—and this is the point I want to underscore—turns out to be the practice under investigation, as well as the subjective experience of the investigation: the phenomenon to be made sense of, *and* the desire to make sense.

When Nietzsche, as part of his critique of Platonism, referred to philosophers as "clumsy" (*linkisch*) lovers, he seemed to be objecting to basic assumptions in this passage.[74] On the one hand, Nietzsche saw no reason to think that erotic experiences are inherently dissatisfying, or that sexual affairs necessarily entail the threat to sense-making just mentioned, or that erotic acts had to somehow promise permanence or immortality. If philosophers demand 'knowledge' or eternal possession, then they look like clumsy or inexperienced lovers. "They can seem like young lovers who must constantly demand from each other pledges of eternal love, as opposed to more 'experienced' lovers, who can love passionately, and not cynically, without such delusory hopes."[75] That said, such love can seem less immature if we consider that part of what it is to love one's children is to fervently desire not to outlive them; this also belongs to Socrates' considerations (208e).[76]

On the other hand, Nietzsche's broader suggestion seems to be that this "Platonic" desire for permanence and transcendence cannot be explained by anything inherently 'dissatisfying' in temporal, bodily sexual practices, or by any desire to leave 'ignorance' behind. Here, I think, Nietzsche actually agrees with what he takes to be a crucial insight of Plato's, even if he thinks that it remains somewhat undermined by the letter of Socrates' and Diotima's teachings. Like Socrates, Nietzsche is convinced that philosophers do indeed "love their truths."[77] Nietzsche is not being cynical, or derogatory when he says this. Like Socrates, he is intensely attuned to a connection between philosophical love (of wisdom, knowledge) and sexual practices. What makes philosophy erotic? What does this say about the kind of (free) life we might lead?

For Nietzsche, the desire to understand is not just about striving to ameliorate those 'ignorances' that, according to Socrates, attend erotic experience—such as those caused by the temporal finitude of bodily life, mentioned above. Nietzsche does not think that learning to be a lover/philosopher, or "mastering the art of love" (as Socrates puts it), is just a matter of overcoming ignorance, or of replacing blindness with insight. What makes *erōs* philosophical, and what makes philosophy erotic, is that sexual lovers and philosophers strive for something that they want *in itself*. The lover/philosopher desires what he desires irrespective of any other good it brings or privation it cancels. The lover/philosopher wants what he wants, such that he is characterized by that wanting. As Nietzsche puts it, he "does not want to be misunderstood or mistaken for anything else."[78]

Recall my discussion of Eve's plucking of the forbidden fruit, her becoming Adam's lover. Eve sought not just to alleviate the pain of her ignorance by attaining knowledge; instead, she offered her self-conception to Adam, desirously, as in Johann Carl Loth's painting "Eve Tempting Adam" (c. 1655–1698). To act as a lover/philosopher, Nietzsche wants to say, is likewise to express that whatever we want is not only lovable in our eyes—it is not merely lovable because 'we judge it so,' or because it helps us avoid something bad (like hunger, or ignorance). It *is* something fundamentally lovable to which we attach ourselves, an intrinsic value on the basis of which we act, a 'good' the desire for which determines who we are. Beauty is not just in the eye of the beholder, say lovers/philosophers; nor do we love what we love just because we are driven (by nature or instinct) to love in such-and-such a way, or to fulfill lacks (to convert hunger to satiety, ignorance to knowledge). Our loves are neither caused (by anything in nature) nor deduced (inferentially, or reflectively, the way we might select an apple on the basis of its qualities). Our love-affairs express who we think we are. Philosophical eros thus at least points to a free life that we might *lead*, a self-expressive life, not merely a well-fed existence.[79] Freedom—the possibility of living one's life—requires erotic investment. Only the life lived erotically on the basis of positive desires for something lovable—rather than just in 'negative' avoidance of hunger, pain or discomfort—can be free in the sense under discussion in these pages. ("They will be free, *very* free spirits, these philosophers of the future," enthuses Nietzsche.[80])

Such an erotically charged life is, Nietzsche wants to insist, the only kind of existence to which we can *attach* ourselves. Indeed, Nietzsche was convinced that the biggest obstacle to freedom faced by these "philosophers of

the future" (namely us) is a dearth of this kind of erotic investment, the per-
vasiveness of "un-free" life.[81] These "philosophers of the future" point toward
"something more, higher, greater, and fundamentally different, something
that does not want to be misunderstood or mistaken for anything else."[82]
Nietzsche's insistence, while perhaps the loudest, is hardly unique among
modern philosophers. In her discussion of love in Augustine, Hannah Arendt
asserted the same when she wrote that erotic attachments amount to claiming one's life as one's own: "the lover is never isolated from what he loves; he
belongs to it . . . the question of who he is can only be resolved by the object
of his desire and not, as the Stoics thought, by the suppression of the impulse
of desire itself."[83]

Now, if our love-affairs are to express who we think we are, then they must
be socially *accepted* as such, recognized as a way of life. Eve's knowledge could
not be shared until Adam, too, partook. Only when our erotic activities manifest and articulate a *shared* self-conception—in light of which certain *kinds* of
love-affairs become possible—can individuals act erotically and self-expressively. If Nietzsche is right to worry about the viability of this kind of erotic life
in the modern era, then it is because, like Socrates, he worried that such eroticism is not now a shared *way* of life—what we might call a *bios erotike*. Did not
Socrates' condemnation at the hands of his fellow Athenians also signal the lack
of such a shared self-conception?

To live erotically in this robust Nietzschean sense—although Nietzsche
himself seems not to have made this point—requires that our erotic deeds also
be bids to articulate a shared self-conception, to put in play whatever we think
we 'know' about ourselves and each other in a given moment. We cannot act
erotically—we cannot act *self-expressively*—unless we are also putting into play
some 'knowledge,' disprovable knowledge about ourselves and the conditions
of our existence. Or so I am claiming (though Nietzsche himself is not).

What new knowledge can we offer or articulate in our sexual acts? How
do we 'comprehend our own time in thought' in our love-affairs?[84] How do
our love-affairs—from Heloise and Abelard to Sartre and Beauvoir—manifest
historical self-conceptions? These are the sorts of questions I will be trying to
foreground next.

Let me, once again, pull together some conclusions reached thus far.

At this stage, *all* self-aware sexual acts—if they are to be self-expressive
in the sense under discussion—require, at a minimum, our ancestral 'knowledge' of sexual reproduction, the recognition of the institutional authority of

sexual reproduction for sexual practices. Of course, if the social authority of sexual reproduction is *all* one knows—if its authority is unquestioned—then one's self-expressive capacities as a lover remain correspondingly limited. Let me say this more forcefully: *if sexual reproduction is all one knows about erōs, then the lives we lead as lovers and philosophers remain correspondingly stunted.* As already indicated, if the 'knowledge' of sexual reproduction appeared (in Plato's day) to be 'all that one could know' about erotic acts between men and women, then such acts remained limited in terms of how free and self-expressive they could be. This stunting of *erōs* was as intolerable to Socrates as it was to Nietzsche.

In light of this, then, Socrates and Plato were seeking to consolidate further 'knowledge' gained from those erotic practices whose cultivation required and expressed the bracketing of procreative sex—above all, pederasty (in their case). Nietzsche's 'clumsiness' critique notwithstanding, Socrates and Plato clearly knew that sexual love meant the love of bodies, in all their temporal, fleeting beauty.[85] The author of the *Symposium* was no inexperienced, clumsy lover, much less a Stoic. But then—to ask the familiar question—*why* does Plato talk of 'love of souls' over 'love of bodies'? Of the 'birth of ideas' over physical offspring? Of the midwifing of ideas out of pederastic sex? Of philosophy as the highest form of *erōs*? What knowledge was Plato seeking to consolidate out of the erotic practices of his day?

This, I think: erotic lovers and philosophers are self-expressive, provisionally 'free' agents not only because they act on the basis of something other than rational deliberation or natural instinct, but also inasmuch as they manage to make new sense of our worldly conditions in a shared self-conception. To "give birth . . . to many beautiful speeches and thoughts; until . . . he may discern a certain single philosophical science."[86] Our ancestors began such sense-making, sexually, in response to those threats to sense that I have been following throughout these last pages: reproduction, individual mortality, bodily transformation, temporal change and the cultivatable satisfactions of nonprocreative sex. Plato was not wrong, I think, to see *erōs* and its vicissitudes—the generation of discourse as well as offspring—as a fundamental activity by which we strive to make sense of all these phenomena.

In love, we not only act self-expressively, we give birth to new collective self-conceptions. At the same time, we can now say, by *erotically achieving* new, hard-won self-conceptions—new understandings of ourselves and our worldly conditions—we also lead freer, more erotically charged lives.

"Suppose that truth is a woman":
On Gender-based Social Standing

Suppose that truth is a woman—and why not? Aren't there reasons for suspecting that all philosophers, to the extent that they have been dogmatists, have not really understood women? That the grotesque seriousness of their approach toward the truth and the clumsy advances they have made so far are unsuitable ways of pressing their suit with a woman?

                    Friedrich Nietzsche, *Beyond Good and Evil* (1886)

Socrates and Nietzsche have helped us to see how freedom—self-expressive deeds and normative autonomy—entails, minimally, leading an erotic life in the sense just discussed. However, it is important to remember that Socrates' conclusions were not reachable simply by detached intellection or 'aha' moments. Instead, Socrates' philosophical reflections arise directly out of a specific history of erotic practices—in this case, the love of men for boys—and as an effort to make sense of what we do as *lovers*. If Socrates' love of truth points to an actively erotic desire to know or understand, then this desire had to be distinguishable from needful appetite, from negative-reactive passions driven by some claim of nature, or engaged in for the sake of lessening some pain or void. And I am suggesting that, without the sexual self-education that brought such 'positive' wanting into view, this 'higher' sort of erotic-free-leadable life to which Socrates and Nietzsche are pointing would not have seemed possible.

   What did this sexual self-education entail? Minimally, I have been suggesting, its historical-practical development must have entailed the practical sequestering of sexual affairs between men and women as the initial, decisive step. Such a Socratic sexual self-education could *only* have been cultivated between women and girls, eunuchs and women, men and hermaphrodites, men and boys and so forth—*not* between men and women.[87] This is not to deny the patently obvious—namely, that men and women *also* engaged one another sexually, and that the consequences and vicissitudes of such engagements were also the source of intense cultural reflection and regulation. However, so long as the 'known' and observed connection between sex and the arrival of offspring remained shrouded in opacity—subject to the threats to sense I mentioned earlier (miscarriages, birth defects, menopause, multiple births, confusions over paternity and so forth)—it had to remain unclear whether any purported eroticism concerned the relation between man and woman, or whether it actually revolved around the prospect of a child whose arrival remained to a large ex-

tent inscrutable, unknowable, unregulatable. In short, so long as sexual reproduction remained the unrivalled matrix through which it was made culturally
intelligible and governable, sex between men and women could not be practiced or experienced 'freely' in the sense under discussion—nor even, I now
want to say, as 'loving.'

This is the impetus, I think, for Nietzsche's riddle, "Suppose that truth is a
woman." For the 'free' life envisioned by Socrates and endorsed by Nietzsche
could only have emerged through erotic practices which were discerned, regulated and predicated upon the devaluation of sex between men and women as
*un*free, not erotic enough.

To avoid one common confusion: this devaluation had nothing to do with
the so-called sexuality (or sexual orientation) of our ancestors—an innate or
socially induced taste for boys, say. Although, as just mentioned, Socrates saw
erōs as self-expressive—as putting into play the stakes of one's attachment to
whatever one finds desirable as such—the ancient Greek world did not see *erōs*
as the manifestation of the sexual orientation of the lovers. As Foucault and
others have amply demonstrated, the notion that sexual practices manifest
the supposedly true sexuality of particular subjects belongs to a quite different (much more recent) historical self-conception than the one under consideration here.[88] The Greeks, instead, "believed that the same desire attached
to anything that was desirable—boy or girl—subject to the condition that the
appetite was nobler that inclined toward what was more beautiful and more
honorable."[89]

In other words, the cultivation of erotic acts as distinctly *erotic*—and not just
as expressions of natural appetite (*orexis*) or procreative demands—entailed
seeing love-affairs as expressing distinct and articulatable *values*, not just biological events or processes.[90] Indeed, the "noble" appetite was distinguished
from the "vulgar" appetite precisely by virtue of an erotic self-disentanglement
from procreative demands. In this way, erotic attachments came to articulate
and express social 'goods' that could be venerated and loved as such, as occasions for self-expressive deeds.[91] These 'goods' are not just the 'good' and
the 'beautiful' in Plato's otherworldly sense (although we can begin to see the
practical circumstances in which talk of a supersensible realm of Ideas starts
to seem plausible), but also social goods, or "fragile goods" as Martha Nussbaum has called them.[92] Goods, that is, whose worth is measurable by the love
they inspire, the bonds and self-expressive ways of life that such values institute
and sustain. Is this not why the interlocutors in Plato's *Symposium* considered

erōs in light of these kinds of fragile goods whose veneration 'love' helps to explain—courage, medicine, friendship, beauty?

In sum, erotic freedom took root in the bracketing of sex between men and women, since it was this bracketing that allowed for the development of erotic practices between *other* genders—that is, for a practical experience of the *erotically loving* as such (as distinct from procreating and appetite).

However, to turn to the next issue, precisely because it had to be predicated on a bracketing of sex between men and women—on a gender-based division rooted in the social authority of sexual reproduction—this practical cultivation of erotic love necessarily developed as the articulation of a social-gendered power structure. And the development of erotic love as freedom was—inescapably, at this historical moment—*also* the articulation of a hierarchical, gendered power dynamic.

To avoid confusion on this point, let me repeat—contra Foucault—that I do not take this to signal that the explanatory authority of sexual reproduction was inseparable from, or was *nothing other than*, the set of social hierarchies and power dynamics that it instituted. As I said earlier, I understand the explanatory authority of sexual reproduction—Eve's knowledge—to have been a historically nonoptional way that our ancestors were compelled (on pain of senselessness) to make themselves and their worldly conditions intelligible. The *explanatory* power of sexual reproduction—the sense it made of fundamental threats to the intelligibility of our lives (temporal change, birth, bodily transformation, pregnancy)—remained the source of its social authority. However, I am arguing further, one immensely significant, historically downstream result of this authority was the way in which it made distinctly *erotic* activity possible, via the social sequestration of procreative sex, and in this way brought into view erotic freedom and Socratic, self-expressive attachment to the 'good'— *but* at a cost. The cost was that erotic love *had* now to develop practically—for reasons just given—through the articulation of a social-gendered power structure: minimally, a certain privileging of social relations between men or between women over relations between men and women. Erotic love as freedom thus became entangled with, even indistinguishable from, the articulation of a social-gendered hierarchy—necessarily, at this stage.

The implications are, of course, immense. What I have in mind, after all, is the emergence and articulation of gender-based social standing—the fundamental underpinnings and rationale for a gender-based division of activities. Wherever a socially gendered individual (boy, girl, woman, man, matron, eunuch,

widow, concubine) is recognized or refused recognition in view of a social hierarchy, then the rationale lies—to a much larger degree than has ever been recognized—in the erotic self-education under discussion. Or so I now wish to claim.

How to Act Sexually?

Inasmuch as one essential aim of the sex act was to disprove its being merely
wrung out of us—something 'undergone,' as a 'passive' reaction to a natural appetite or biological demand—the act itself had to somehow demonstrate its being expressive of an agent. For if all that was known was that sex between men
and women could *not* (yet) be erotically free in this way, it must have seemed
unclear just how sexual *activity* itself was to be carried out as an activity, 'freely'
lived, other than as entangled with procreation.

One provisional solution to this problem has already presented itself. My
suggestion above was that the social regulation of fertile female bodies made
possible the articulation and understanding of further social gender ascriptions
(older woman, virgin, young man, eunuch and so forth). This also made acts between other erotic gender configurations intelligible *as* erotic. Erotic encounters
between alternative erotic gender-configurations—other, that is, than between
men and women—could now be practiced as distinctly cultivatable, potentially
regulatable acts.

However it still had to be demonstrated that these practices, this *ars erotica*,
really amounted to sexual *activity*, expressive of sexual *agents*. In other words,
it had to be demonstrated that such acts were not distinct *merely* in virtue of
bracketing or avoiding the potentially procreative (passive, unfree) dimension of male-female sex. After all, such bracketing amounted only to a kind
of negative freedom, or agency as an avoidance of procreative demands. It still
remained to be shown that these were genuinely erotic, positive, free acts.

Thus, I now want to say, the demonstration of *sexual agency* became a fundamental aim of sexual practices at this stage.

Such demonstrations, however, faced an immediate and profound problem.
Inasmuch as the cultivation of further erotic practices had to be predicated, for
reasons just given, upon a social-gendered distinction—minimally, the cordoning of male-female procreative sex from all other possible erotic gender-
configurations—this cultivation threatened to *remain* determined by the external
demands of sexual reproduction. In other words, at this stage, it threatened to appear as though the fundamental difference between an *active* and *passive* sexual

act depended—not on anything the lovers themselves performed sexually—but only on whether their sexual encounter was potentially procreative or not. The difference between activity and passivity, and gendered distinctions, would still be determined by a natural fact rather than by an act for which an agent could be held accountable. Genuinely free *activity* thus remained doubtful.

In order for genuine *agency to be positively achieved*, then, it had to be shown that sexual acts *as such* could express an agent who really *acts sexually*, with rights and responsibilities, such that the difference between activity and passivity is determined by a recognizably human, social-institutional achievement rather than by a blind natural process. This required something more than Eve's knowledge about the potentially procreative or nonprocreative status of that type of act. It required a demonstration—a new acquired knowledge—that one is really acting sexually, that a distinctly sexual agency can be socially and institutionally acknowledged.

But *how* to socially establish that we achieve agency through the sexual act itself, rather than on the basis of what we think we know about ourselves as sexually reproducing (Eve's knowledge)? How, that is, can one 'know' that one has *acted* in having sex, and is thereby institutionally accountable to others for such acts, and is not just the passive subject of biological demands or natural processes?

Sexual Domination

At this point, there could only have been one way to achieve such knowledge: the institutionalized, repeated sexual domination of some by others. Agency and accountability had to be recognizably demonstrated and achieved *through* repetitive, institutionalized sexual domination, by an iterated division of certain individuals into active and passive roles by the collective bestowal of sexual prerogatives upon some at the expense of others. This meant that some had to dominate others *not* merely by physically overpowering them, nor by outwitting them, nor merely by exercising a prerogative or 'right' already bestowed via some other nonsexual social recognition or standing. The active sexual domination of another—the achievement of *this* form of sexual agency, of human agency—had to be a *sexually realized, institutionalized* domination, a socially sustainable prerogative or right to use another sexually.

In the starkest terms, at issue is the sexual realization of a provisional human 'freedom' for some through the use of another's body: the limiting of another's sexual agency through the repeatable exercise of one's own, the sub-jugation of another's desire to one's own—the sexual realization of another's passivity or unfreedom. Sexual domination is achieved here by blocking what sense the other might make of her life or the world, sexually, *other than the fact of her own subjugation.*

The social legitimation of such sexual prerogatives was undertaken, then, for the sake of realizing a truly sexual *act*, at least by some—not just a deed ex-pressing physical prowess, nonsexual social prerogative or some other nonsex-ually acquired form of social recognition (military, economic, political). After all, by acting merely on the basis of a natural, physical or nonsexual authority, one demonstrates nothing *sexually*. Sexual engagements themselves would still appear unfree—reflections of social authorities or natural processes, perhaps, but not intelligibly connected to individual agents as their deed. And, I am sug-gesting, the institutionalization of sexual domination did not just reflect power regimes of a nonsexual sort—economic, military, political or other. Sexual domination is a way that a distinct power regime, and a provisional agency for some, was achieved and sustained over time.

But how, exactly, is institutionalized sexual domination to be upheld over long periods of history, and across cultures—as something other than the mere expression of physical or social forces, as something other than a temporary 'reign of terror'?

My suggestion is this: institutionalized sexual domination could have been upheld over time—intergenerationally and across cultures throughout history—only through the eventual reification of a *social-gendered hierarchy*, in which the subjugated's life can be put at risk, and which served to articulate a gender-based distinction between active and passive sexual beings. The sociopolitical institution of a gendered hierarchy—the *living out* of gendered hierarchies as an objective way of life—is the result of the need to institutionalize sexual domina-tion over time, to demonstrate again and again that a provisional sexual agency is real, at least for some, in virtue of their sexual domination of others.

At a certain stage of human history—one that, collectively, we have not left behind—the installment and sustaining of a social-gendered hierarchy was the only way to make sexual *agency* intelligible as an institutional achievement over long durations of time, rather than as the expression of some other social or natural force (like procreation). The reification of social-gendered power dy-namics between active agent and passive subject (sexually subjugated) mani-fests and results from 'successful' institutionalizations of sexual domination over time. Gender-based hierarchies are the upshot of this institutionalization of sexual domination.

Without something like the transcendental account of sexual domination that I am offering here, it is hard to see how gender-based hierarchies could have gotten their traction.[93] The hardening of gender-based power relations—or gendered 'roles' (active, passive)—resulted from the distinct institutionalization of sexual domination over time, even if other forms of domination (economic, political, physical) were also brought to bear. One has to state the point carefully to avoid being exculpatory. However wrong, institutionalized sexual domination was, at the historical moment under investigation, the only way for some to *act* erotically freely.

Counterintuitive though it may be, then, my suggestion is therefore that social gender-based hierarchies were not just the basis for the intelligibility or regulation of sexual interactions. Again, this is my difference from the structuralist position. Rather, gender-based hierarchies, and the forms of sociopolitical recognition they made possible—man, boy, woman, concubine, maiden, virgin, eunuch—furnished the 'demonstration' that institutionalized sexual domination had been achieved for the long haul. Recall, my argument throughout has been that gendered-social roles are formed in sexual practices, that they are one result of our sexual self-education over time—that gender hierarchies (like the gender-based division of labor) are not just the expressions of 'contingent' power norms. We can now see that this means that power dynamics in gender roles were forged through institutionalized sexual domination. Equally, gender-based roles and activities are a demonstration that power relations have been sexually achieved, institutionalized. The social authority of gender roles is a fundamental way in which societies recognize sexual agency as a non-natural achievement, as a form of sociopolitical domination.

Furthermore, at this stage of our sexual self-education, self-aware, erotic (non-appetite-driven) acts took the form of articulating an explicit, socially recognizable distinction between an active agent and a passive or inactive other. Here, we come upon an issue that was of intense interest to Foucault in his study of sex in the ancient world—one that, so far as I can tell, he never quite resolved or explained: namely, the pervasive privileging of "activity over passivity" not just in social roles generally (military life, education, politics) but also in the *experience of sexual activity*.[94] But if we take a step back from Foucault, and think for a moment about the sheer range and variety of sexual acts and rituals, across history and cultures, then we can get some sense of the immense and ongoing impact of this stage of erotic freedom, which still explains many contemporary sexual affairs. Moreover, because at this stage, it remains unclear what *else* human beings might be doing with one another sexually—we have not yet arrived at the historical realization of courtship or lovemaking. Thus, sexual activity remained *either* a matter of natural-procreative processes—hence, less free, or even "vulgar"—*or* a form of active domination, with the one-sided 'freedom' for a few that this afforded. Given these two alternatives, then, sexual domination had to realize itself as institutional if it was to be a self-expressive human *activity* at all. This is why it could only become 'known' in manifestly social-gendered, institutional, intergenerational ways of life.

After all, our intergenerational ways of life just *are* society-wide efforts to make the transmission of 'human' life belong to social deeds and practices, rather than to given facts or processes. Sexual domination, too, should be seen as a fundamental way in which entire forms of life, whole societies, came to understand themselves as communities of the living and the dead. Sexual domination can even function as a fundamental basis on which one can be 'born into,' 'initiated into,' inculcated into a human world. Let me make this point as bluntly as I can: institutionalized sexual domination and the intergenerational gender-based hierarchies that resulted, should be understood—alongside care for the dead, the naming of the young, or the transmission of property—as a fundamental way in which human societies have understood themselves to be *ways* of life, as a way human societies have made themselves transmissible and intelligible as human cultures.

The mind reels when we consider the countless 'initiations,' the deep and lasting ways in which human beings have lived this out, physically and psychically.

This one-sided sexual 'freedom' (domination) means instituting the systematic abuse of boys and girls, concubines and prostitutes, wives and mistresses. Again, at issue is not just a prerogative exercised on the basis of some other form of social authority, but rather the institutionalization of sexual domination as itself constitutive of agency for some through the abuse of others. This means enshrining such abuse at the foundations of intergenerational human sociality, such that entire social-historical forms of life could not understand themselves as 'human,' as lived out by agents, without the institutionalization of sexual domination. The litany of such institutional forms is all too familiar; they survive and flourish to this day. As I will argue later, only in recent centuries have the subjective sufferings inflicted by this practice come to be heard or to resonate with significant force.[95] We have already mentioned *paiderastia*. Is it any wonder that Plato's Socrates sought to extract his vision of love as freedom from the vicissitudes of pederasty, however "clumsily"?

But there is also prostitution, the 'oldest profession'—whereby the 'client' or 'brothel' achieves status as "active" agent by determining the limits and conditions of a prostitute's sexual agency. This may occur through financial, social or physical coercion, but we should remember that in prostitution the power dynamics are ultimately confirmed and accomplished only through sex acts—not merely through financial transactions, social placement or other forms of physical treatment. Prostitution in fact distinguishes itself as an institution by virtue of the distinctly sexual domination through which it sustains itself *as* an institutional practice: namely, the condemnation of the one who is prostituted to unfree sexual interactions.[96] And then there are institutions like traditional marriage, wherein (in many settings) one partner is denied the right to refuse the other's advances, or perhaps, where the wife's social legitimacy is reduced to her reproductive capacity or domestic service, the husband's to his patriarchal or paternal claims. Following the work of structuralist anthropologists and sociologists, and after Marx and Engels, we tend to think of traditional marriage as a fundamentally economic arrangement, as an "exchange," or a means for the transference of social legitimacy.[97] But we should also recall the extent to which marriages have also made themselves intelligible as an intergenerational social institution by sheltering acts of sexual domination.[98] This sheltering of abuse is not incidental nor an aberration; it belongs to the structure of the practice. And this list of institutions could be extended considerably to include many other intergenerational modes of life predicated upon sexual domination and subjugation—harems, palaces and courts, libertinism, the various other domains of what we now call sex trafficking, rites of initiation, genital mutilation, and the myriad age-old institutions of sexual objectification that serve to limit the sexual agency of some by realizing, 'making real,' the hierarchically sustained, gender-based activity of others.[99] The technical innovations involved, still today, in the perpetuation of such practices might blind us to their historical depth. But we should understand them as profoundly foundational for the historical intelligibility of human cultures and the realization of human freedom. We and our ancestors have done awful things to one another in our efforts to make our lives, our freedom and world intelligible.

At the same time, the erosion of such practices—which is relatively recent, confined to certain parts of the world, and still fragile and halting—does not result from the discovery of a moral fact that our ancestors had somehow missed. Rather, such practices can only come under critique from the point of view of a 'way of life' that no longer depends on such practices for its own intelligibility, or in order to make sense of the world and ourselves (some of us) as agents. And the achievement of that point of view is precisely what is under discussion and still open to question.

In the pages ahead, then, I want to more fully explain these institutional practices of domination, and to bring our understanding of them into what I think is the proper horizon for thinking about them: sexual love as a provisional, hard-won achievement of freedom in human affairs.

Consider the sheer variety of the institutional forms taken by sexual domination—their persistent and continued flourishing, the innovations in their variations, their stubborn durability in the face of *other* shared values and priorities that should halt them. This alone should make clear that we are not dealing just with the rise and fall of local mores and customs, but with a fundamental way in which we human beings have come to see ourselves as agents in the world, part of a fundamental way we came to *understand* ourselves and our worldly conditions.

I will try to say more about this. What is important to note, for the moment, is that sexual acts not only express or reflect nonsexual power relations that might be operating in a society more broadly—as the usual 'ideological' critique would have it. We are not, put differently, dealing just with institutional power and its sadistic manifestations or the helplessness of certain subjects before the law, of victims of the 'system.' More deeply, sexual acts have also been one fundamental matrix through which power relations are themselves articulated, the activity through which some difference between active agent and passive subject gets established or achieved.

Some of us continue to be more immediately impacted than others by this, and in unequal and uneven ways. But we are all implicated.

Courtly Love and Chastity

One cultural moment where the dynamics of sexual domination get crystallized and subject to critical scrutiny is the advent of courtly or chivalric love.

As most commentators on this institution are at pains to emphasize, courtly love has identifiable literary origins in the twelfth century, but it radiates practical and explanatory implications that continue to this day, in many parts of the world. Courtship, as I will discuss the practice, has flourished and continues in various forms around the world—Shakespeare called it "wooing." Nowadays we might call it "dating"—so, when I speak of courtship in the following pages, this term should be understood to designate this range of practices, which of course continue to this day. The point is that courtly love is a historical practice — it was not always 'there'—one which matters not only for the understanding of certain historical eras, such as medieval Europe, but as a matrix for human self-understanding broadly.

In courtly love, recall, sexual acts and erotic gestures do not merely reflect the extant social-hierarchical positions of the lovers—the Knight and the Lady, to use the traditional names, or 'man' and 'woman.' Rather, courtship is a practice through which a certain hierarchy works itself out, in the lovers' interactions. For instance, the Knight does not merely claim sexual prerogatives as a social privilege —and the Lady, conversely, does not withhold any 'favors'—on the basis of some other, non-erotic social hierarchy, such as the monarchy or feudalism. Courtly love thus demonstrates that extant institutional power-relations (economic, religious, political) do not fully determine the kind of sexual practices that might develop between particular human beings, even though sexual interactions can have no other context of origin. At the same time, erotic courtship confounds non-erotic social structures—like marriage, for instance, insofar as the affair is adulterous; or like feudalism, through the use of ostensibly economic terms (vassal, or *midons*, "my lady") to articulate an erotic code.

In this way, courtships managed to develop with a relative erotic autonomy, within the walls of sexual domination, and other institutional power structures. In courtship, gender-based roles of passivity and activity can be improvisationally self-determined or worked out in ways which might confound or interrupt institutionalized forms of sexual domination. Think of the way a client might 'fall for' a courtesan, and begins to court her in ways which were initially facilitated by her sexual subjugation, but which might also unfold in ways which call his domination of her into question.

The concrete practical possibilities for human interactions opened by this development are immense: love-letters and poems, new literary and musical conventions, and then, as anyone who has ever tried to find a poetic way to say 'I love you' knows, there are the tokens, rings and vows; initials carved into trees; locks fixed to iron bridges; new clothing; terms of endearment; and so on.

Here too, of course, sexual domination as the articulation of activity and passivity lives on—but the point is that it starts to become, in these practices, ever more aware of itself as such. Courtly love, we might say, is a practically achieved reflection on the implications of the agency achieved by some, in circumscribing another's sexual activities and experiences. In one sense, courtship is self-aware reckoning with the implications of drawing an active-passive distinction along gender-based lines.

The point of the courtship, unlike that of sexual domination, is not just to decide who will *play* the passive role. The goal is not to figure out whether, say, the woman will 'play' the Damsel in Distress or the High Lady, or whether the Knight will be on 'top' or on 'bottom.' What we see is a self-ritualized eroticism, conceived through innovative feats of courtship to determine who will write the script and direct the action. The lovers 'court,' in other words, so that it might become clear *to them*, first of all, who will determine, sexually, the bounds of the other's agency. If, for instance, the Knight manages to somehow stage his own servitude, then he demonstrates that *he* and not the Lady sets the scene—even if he 'serves' her and even if she plays her role with verve.[100] This is not a battle of the sexes waged erotically, nor is it a 'war through courtship.'[101] Contrary to a common misinterpretation of such wooing, sex is not merely wielded as a weapon in a broader struggle between the genders.[102] The lovers do not play to conquer or subjugate the other, even if they sometimes mistakenly think that is what they are doing—as in the rivalry between the Marquise de Merteuil and the Vicomte de Valmont in *Les Liaisons dangereuses*.[103]

Courtship is instead the articulation, or practical working out, of a subjective, normative bond between the lovers—a passionate 'way of life' (*their* way of life) that is to be the *result* of their courtship.[104] The "game of love," as it was already called in medieval times, was not oriented toward any final victory or annihilation of the other, as in the Hegelian struggle to the death. Instead, the game aimed, by means of an extended courtship, toward the achievement of a subjective, practical bond that could endure over time between the lovers.

In Hegel's *Phenomenology of Spirit*, the parallel to courtly love is not (as Beauvoir thought) the struggle to the death, but rather the subsequent moment in Hegel's text—namely, installment of the lord-bondsman relationship as a historical-institutional way of life.[105] However, to better reveal the transcendental genesis of courtship that I am proposing, let me also draw attention to some limitations of this parallel.

Two of these should be immediately mentioned. First, unlike Hegel's "bondsman" who submits to the "lord" only inasmuch as he fears death (the "absolute lord"), the one who 'submits' to his sexual lover—by carrying out an objective way of life on the basis of that submission—does not do so because he fears death (his life is not directly threatened by his lover) but rather on the basis of a sexually-achieved, institutionalized, gendered-hierarchical distinction between an active and a passive lover in the course of the courtship, insofar as the courtship serves to articulate for the lovers themselves who is active and who is passive.[106] Second, Hegel's bondsman embodies the lord's "desire," disciplining himself and negating his own desire because he cannot negate his own bodily existence (his life). However, sexual courtship allows for a different kind of *Bildung*, one whose implications Hegel seems not to have fully considered. For in courtship, one participant "tames" the other without threatening the other's life, such that the *courtship*—rather than the natural boundary between life and death—occasions the articulation of activity and passivity.[107]

How does this happen?

■ ■ ■

Let us consider courtship in more detail.

Remember: in order for the sexual act to be seen as an *act*, institutional forms of *sexual* domination had to be objectively established, lived out as intergenerational, gender-based hierarchies. However, these institutions of sexual domination and gender-based hierarchies also *had* to be subjectively practiced and experienced through *sexual* acts—even if they were also supported by, and intertwined with, other forms of social domination (political, economic, military, paternal, maternal). After all, as already discussed, unless the domination was carried out sexually, the practical autonomy or freedom that was sought would not have been proven.

And herein lies the rub. The actual practice of such sexual acts over time must have led, here and there, to the realization that not *all* sexual acts can be intelligibly felt, subjectively lived or experienced as either expressions of inherited gender-based power hierarchies (the institutionalized domination of one by another), or as manifestations of natural demands for procreation. Not all sexual acts, in other words, can be intelligibly *lived* as either institutional forms of domination or as acts determined by the demands of procreation. Again, consider the client at the brothel who falls for the courtesan who falls for him in turn—or, at least, both of them discover that they cannot make sense of what they find themselves doing together as being *merely* the subjugation of one by the other. Certain moments of sexual domination must have tumbled into the experience of a provisional, passionately subjective, way of life—a courtship, precisely—that could not be intelligibly experienced as either the institution of a gendered power structure, or as a moment in a natural process of procreative demands.

Lovers must have discovered—in the very act of courting, from within institutions of sexual domination—that their courtship need not even be recognized as legitimate, as socially real, in order for it to be real and actual for the lovers, somehow binding *for them*.[108] Is this not why so many courtships remain secret and clandestine—proceeding through pledges, secret contracts, elopements, exchanges of rings, and other forms of wooing? Here, then, another powerful threat to sense-making arises in certain experiences of sexual engagement. In courtship, sexual activity itself can turn out to be unintelligible in terms of the alternative self-conceptions it has produced: natural-procreative or dominating-subjugating. This is the first new subjective self-awareness achieved in courtly love.

A second realization follows in its train. If the achievement of a provisional agency is given symbolic reality in a ring or a secretly whispered pledge—and not just in the instituting of a broad, objective, social form of domination—then such agency ceases to be identified fully with 'strong' institutional sexual domination, and becomes a kind of improvised form of mutual sexual recognition.[109] And this is so, even when such improvisation itself becomes a 'weak' institution of a sort—as when lovers 'go steady' or 'remain faithful' or 'chaste.' At first, the mutuality of such courtships may of course be socially unreal, or at least socially marginal to the point of near irrelevance. One sign of this marginality is that it was first detected poetically, as if by a kind of whispered secret passed from poet to poet, from the troubadours to Ariosto to Shakespeare to Goethe and so forth.

Third, then, the eroticism of courtly love was often achieved through practices of chastity or sexual fidelity. Abstinence from sexual intercourse was integral to the cultivation of courtship.

The point of this chastity was not just to flaunt one's ability to reflectively evaluate the force of one's desire, or to stoically prove that one was not merely subject *to* lustful appetites. To be sure, that may be one reason for the significance given to chastity in ascetic religious orders and philosophical schools, in certain Cynic or Stoic traditions. Like fasting or other regimes, vows of chastity can signal an evaluation of desire, hence the demonstration that one is not subject *to* desire. However, in courtly love, chastity is not a vow made to oneself, as the condition of belonging to an institutional order, but a mode of contractual allegiance to another individual for the sake of passionately binding oneself to that person.

Why should chastity of this sort have become a form of erotic activity? What was chastity trying to explain?

Recall that the initial 'freeing' of erotic activity from its entanglement in appetite, or from natural processes of procreation, entailed the bracketing of sexual relations between men and women (especially young, fertile men and women) as unfree, less noble. Nothing explained thus far has yet budged potentially fertile male-female sexual affairs from this position of relative 'vulgarity' (vulgar, because 'instinctively procreative' or 'appetite-bound'). Even the forms of courtship currently under discussion did nothing to liberate the conception of sexual relations between men and women *sexually* from the vicissitudes of sexual reproduction.

If men and woman are to be sexually free with one another—hence, if men and women are to be free sexually at all—then they must still manage to *sexually* disentangle procreation from eros. (I will return to this.) Minimally, this requires the cultivation of erotic acts that manage to distinguish *themselves* from natural-procreative processes—as opposed to merely avoiding or bracketing procreative demands, as we saw in Greek pederasty. Put another way, the difference between lovemaking and reproduction should be determined by the lovers' own acts, and not by gendered configurations which remain determined by the external demands of biological reproduction.

This, I believe, explains the rising importance attributed to sexual relations between fertile men and women in this period, as definitions of courtly love from this period attest: "Love is a certain inborn suffering derived from the sight of and excessive meditation upon the beauty of the *opposite sex*," wrote Andreas Capellanus in the late twelfth century in *De amore*.[110] Moreover, where reliable means of contraception are lacking or unavailable, the cultivation of abstinence and sexual fidelity *as* erotic *must* play a part in the courtship. Is this not why Tristan and Iseult were discovered asleep, lying in the forest, their bodies separated by Tristan's sword?

The self-disentangling of sex between men and women from procreative processes, from what were perceived as "vulgar" appetites, has been a long, arduous historical achievement. It continues well into our own era, at least until the widespread use of reliable contraception by individual lovers—an achievement that is now hardly one generation old, and which adheres only in certain parts of the world. I will have more to say about this at a later point. For the moment, I want to underscore that the cultivation of erotic acts which manage to make their distinction from natural-procreative processes *belong to the sexual practice itself* brings about a radical shift in the reality, and self-perception, of what human beings do with one another sexually.

For by liberating—even if only provisionally—sexual activity between men and women from its entanglement in procreation, sexual activity is also made *unintelligible* as the manifestation of mere species-level appetite. And once that occurs, then the need to demonstrate—through sexual domination—that appetite and procreation are *not* the only basis for sexual activity is thereby overcome. This, I am suggesting, is also what lovers' courtships have been achieving over the past centuries.

Once sexual activity between men and women is seen as cultivatable and practicable independently of the demands of procreation and the claims of a natural appetite, then sexual freedom no longer needs to be achieved as *domination*. For it turns out that one can *act* sexually, freely, without dominating the other. And this is precisely what the chaste character of courtly love allowed to come into view.

With this, the demands of mutuality and reciprocity are unleashed by lovemaking.

"Each kiss, better than wine"

Kiss me with the kisses of his mouth:
for thy love is better than wine.

The Song of Songs

Just as lovers have long believed themselves to be in the grip of some appetite or erotic urge, struck by Cupid's dart, so, too, it seems reasonable to think that at least *some* fertile lovers must have felt that this urge had something to do with the reciprocal satisfactions of lovemaking itself—that they were not *just* in the grip of some divine power, species-level impulse or procreative urge. The view that men and women can love reciprocally, actively, was in fact formulated in one of the earliest and strongest defenses of mutual love between men and women, Plutarch's *Erotikos* (*Dialogue on Love*).[111] "O Hercules!" cries Pisias, one of the interlocutors in Plutarch's dialogue, "What levity and audacity for men to state that they are tied to women as dogs to bitches, and to banish the god of Love from the gymnasiums and public walks, and light of day and open intercourse, and to restrict him to brothels."[112]

In *The History of Sexuality*, Foucault suggests that Plutarch's text marks a discursive turning point, away from an earlier Greek conception of *erōs* as active or passive and as noble or vulgar and toward a conception of love as a reciprocal activity between two agents.[113] Some classicists have criticized Foucault's use of textual evidence. But surely Foucault is pointing us the right direction by indicating that something in sexual experience itself—to which Plutarch's dialogue testifies—must have given rise to grave doubts about the then-available 'explanations' for sex in the Greek world: procreation or sexual domination (some articulation between active and passive). The participants in Plutarch's dialogue defend the subjective 'feeling' that lovemaking is reciprocal, occurring between two agents and not just the activity of one (the lover) at the expense of another (the beloved), and not just a natural-procreative process. Given the historical context in which he writes, Plutarch ties this defense of reciprocity to a critique of the privileging of pederastic love over male-female love, and of the notion (expressed by Protogenes in Plutarch's text) that procreative appetites aptly characterize male-female relations.[114]

Of course, this is simply an assertion—as part of a dialogue—that there is genuine reciprocity between two people in lovemaking. And, anyway, the *feeling* that lovemaking offers satisfactions of its own probably took root in lived sexual experiences where such reciprocity was felt. Or in the examples of 'good' male-female marriages of equals, of which Plutarch's dialogue speaks.[115] As Plutarch's dialogue attests, if love was to be seen as genuinely reciprocal, then lovemaking had to distinguish itself from raw appetite, from institutionalized forms of sexual domination, and, in the end, become part of an objective way of life.

First, let me consider how lovemaking distinguishes itself from species-level impulses and appetites.

In order for our ancestors to 'know,' rather than just 'feel,' that they were not merely gripped by some species-level impulse to reproduce, they had to make an objective distinction between love and appetite *belong to the loving practice itself*—rather than making an objective distinction between 'types' of love (potentially procreative versus not potentially procreative). Somehow, lovemaking between potentially fertile men and women had to accomplish its own separation from species-level instinct and procreative demands.

This required at least two things: first, it required a special, intense, cultural preoccupation with love-affairs between fertile men and women. Plutarch had already detected this, but it becomes patently obvious when we consider the preoccupation with fertile male-female couples in the poetics of romantic love ever since Ovid's and Plutarch's time. This preoccupation with male-female affairs, at least in Roman-era and post-Roman-era poetics of love, has far less to do with homophobia or heteronormative prejudices than with the task of liberating lovemaking from the social authority of sexual reproduction. Or so I am arguing. Lovemaking, rather, finally had to confront the real possibility of offspring in order to distinguish *itself* from procreative demands.

Second, in order to 'know' that lovemaking between men and women really *is* something other than the result of the desire to perpetuate the species, procreation had to be blocked as part of the act of lovemaking itself. Hence, contraception, or the cultivation of abstinence and chastity *as* 'loving,' must play a central part in love-affairs. These are issues to which I will return in later pages, in my discussion of the modern novel. But, to repeat, we can get already get a sense of the importance of both issues, in the post-Roman and troubadour traditions, just by remembering that Tristan and Iseult were discovered asleep, in the wood of Morois, their bodies chastely divided from one another by Tristan's sword—their lovemaking neatly cleaved, at certain times of the month at least, from the production of offspring.

The Tristan and Iseult myth, in fact, presents a remarkable image of the transcendental genesis of lovemaking as the self-distinction of male-female sexual love from appetitive processes. This occurs in the episode of the *philtre*, which leads to aphrodisiacal lovemaking.[116] Let me recount the adventure and its implications for our discussion, before moving on.

Having set sail to take Iseult to marry King Mark, Tristan and Iseult find themselves adrift at sea, daydreaming and surveying the waves. Their minds wander, as their bodies bob up and down on the waves. Soon, however, both are driven by an oppressive heat to quench their thirst in whatever they find at hand. Anything potable to humans will do. On the one hand, the drink itself (wine) seems incidental to the urgency of the desire, since it is just there to be consumed. On the other hand, to *really* want a drink in the most urgent, elemental way is to discover that what might appear incidental is something on which one's existence depends. In this way, at any rate, Tristan and Iseult are yanked out of their daydreams and are thrown back on their desperate appetites and thirsts.

Hegel identified experiencing these two sides of appetite (*Begierde*) as the starting point or "genus" of self-consciousness. Not only are Tristan and Iseult simply alive in a basic biological sense, immersed in what Hegel calls the "sphere of life," but they are also conscious of themselves *as* living, by virtue of being thirsty. They are at once alive, and aware of wanting to *stay* alive. Each is "a living self-consciousness"—self-consciously immersed in, and also estranged from, the process of living.[117] In his discussion of these issues, Hegel could have followed earlier philosophers in attributing this immersion and estrangement to a split between the mind and the body, soul and matter. Instead, Hegel saw something more animalistic is at work. If the mind's separation from the body depends, as Descartes proposed, upon the mind's negation of sensuous experience, then—Hegel averred—the mind's distinction from the body belongs not to the 'thinking ego' alone but to appetite. After all, the negation of the sensuous world is simply what hungry creatures do all the time. "Not even the animals are excluded from this wisdom," wrote Hegel in the pithiest response to Descartes ever written, "for they do not stand before sensuous things as though these were in-itself; they despair of this reality and, absolutely convinced of the nothingness of sensuous things, they grab them without further ado and consume them."[118]

To make better sense of our immersion in and estrangement from the sphere of life—without the help of a mind-body dualism and on the basis of appetite alone—Hegel's ingenious approach was to flip the question right around: how is the sphere of life both immersed in and estranged from self-consciousness?

One answer to this question is that the sphere of life is estranged from self-consciousness when and where living does not appear to require another living self-consciousness.[119] Wine, for example, does not need to be self-conscious in order to be desired; wine is thirsted after whether or not the wine is aware of this. Moreover, if *all* we did was drink, then we would be nothing more than "a minutely set, ingenious machine for turning, with infinite artfulness, the red wine of Shiraz into urine."[120] In short, estrangement of the sphere of life from self-consciousness amounts to an inability to distinguish one's *own* desire from mechanistic causality, impersonal biological processes.

So how, from within the sphere of life, is one to distinguish oneself from a biological process, from a mere machine for transforming wine into urine? We saw one traditional answer to this problem in Plato's *Symposium*: namely, the doing of glorious deeds or the having of children, the quest for transcendence and immortality. Other religious traditions speak of the immortality of the soul or of a life beyond life. However, whereas such answers aim at something beyond the sphere of one's own life, we are trying to understand how a living self-consciousness distinguishes *himself* from biological necessity from *within* "the sphere of (his) life." So, we have to ask: What within the sphere of life is not estranged from a living self-consciousness?

In the Tristan and Iseult myth, we already have our answer: another living self-consciousness, another desiring ("negating") being.[121]

With this, we can begin to explain the 'magic' of the aphrodisiacal wine in the Tristan myth. On the surface, of course, the mystery is how two individuals' thirst for wine could be transformed into a burning desire for one another. But we can now see that the legend is doing no more than depicting how satisfaction comes to be sought in another person, from within the sphere of living (routine appetites and thirsts). At the same time, we can also answer another traditional source of puzzlement regarding the Tristan legend: if Tristan *really* loved Iseult and vice versa, then why should the philtre have been necessary? Why should the romance look like intoxication?

In response, we can say—with the legend, as Richard Wagner's opera also understood—that love can have no other source than the desires proper to the sphere of life from which it springs.[122] To imagine otherwise is to imagine that Tristan's and Iseult's lovemaking has some otherworldly origin—that they are meant for each other, fated to be together by some 'higher power.' Conversely, love is not just sensuous inebriation, an aftereffect of alcohol under the hot sun. For that, ordinary wine would have been enough. Instead, as the legend explains, "she had found not wine—but Passion and Joy most sharp."

Lovemaking leaves behind the opposition between drunken sensuousness and supersensible 'fate,' stepping away from appetites and one-sided domination in the mutual recognition of sexual lovers. "Each kiss, / better than wine" (1.4)[123] If it feels magical, then this is because there is no higher source of enchantment.

Lovemaking

To make love, we can now say, is to experience our inability to 'live out'—to carry out sexually—the social authority of sexual reproduction and of sexual domination. To make love is to 'feel' the insufficiency of natural appetite, procreation, or institutional domination to explain what we are feeling, experiencing. Lovemaking and courtship enact the collapse of the explanatory authority of sexual reproduction and sexual domination, at least for the subjects involved.

Those who make love—or even fantasize that it might be possible to make love—thus confront a new threat to sense: the inability to understand what we are doing sexually as being either a moment of procreation or natural appetite or an act of domination or subjugation.

At the same time, this does not yet guarantee that any *other* sense of lovemaking has been made.

Lovemaking must have been 'felt' long before poets reported on it; the Tristan myth and the Song of Songs drew their legitimacy from these subjective feelings, as did Plutarch's dialogue and early Hindu works. But if the feeling of love gained intense lyrical expression in the works of these poets, then this was because lovemaking had 'reality' in the world *only* as a passionate, subjective experience—not yet as an objective practice that might orient and authorize a way of life. Even the voluptuousness of the Song of Songs took root in a context in which "sex [was] sanctioned only in marriage; on this point the Old Testament laws are unequivocal."[124] Lovemaking could only be shown as permitted by institutionalized powers that were forged in sexual domination, for instance in the marriage of man and woman in the Old Testament, or as occurring behind the back of these institutional powers, as in the Tristan myth.

This does not mean that medieval lovers like Tristan and Iseult were "adulterous," in the sense of not being authorized to make love by the social powers that be (the church, a court, God, or feudal society).[125] If troubadour poets could depict extramarital sex whereas the Old Testament could not, then this was not because "love is adulterous" or constitutively "heretical" or traitorous—as Denis de Rougement and Tony Tanner have claimed.[126] It was because sexual practices had finally been cultivated, over time to the point where *sexual activity* itself had become clamorously unintelligible as either the manifestation of base appetite or as institutional domination (as in traditional marriage). Hence, the emergent significance attached to lovemaking, or so I have been arguing. Lovemaking is 'felt' to have occurred as soon as sexual interactions cannot (or can no longer) understand *themselves*—cannot be intelligibly *experienced*—as either a natural demand (appetite, procreation) or a social obligation (traditional marriage, adherence to command). Lovemaking—lovers themselves—had thus to be perceived as a challenge to the normative authority of sexual reproduction and sexual domination. (As occurs in Shakespeare's *Romeo and Juliet*, too.)

That said, lovemaking itself had not yet achieved any social-historical or institutional reality at this stage. Lovemaking may have been achieved as 'real' *by the lovers*; indeed, it must have been intensely 'real' to anyone who had made love. But this reality had not yet established itself as socially authoritative, capable of organizing a broad way of life. Love's 'reality' was not yet recognized as a value around which a way of life might be constructed.

At best, lovemaking was recognized through its exclusion from institutional forms of life. This, again, is why lovemaking had to be portrayed as unreal or magical, immersed in subjective sensuousness and intoxication, expressed lyrically or in song. Medieval poets were not being coy when they couched love-affairs within tales of fantastical quests for grails; exchanges of rings and swords; and sorcery, unicorns and magical settings. Like the troubadours who sang their tales, lovers themselves did not fully know what they were doing, for they had no way of seeing it as socially real or valuable. Lovemaking was necessarily presented as a moment of intoxication, of blind nature, or worldly fate, or as the working of some other social or divine mechanism behind the back of the protagonists.[127] Lovemaking may have made the collapse of the normative authority of sexual reproduction and sexual domination *felt*—but it could not yet become the basis for a way of life, a rationale for the organization of an intergenerational social world. From Tristan and Iseult to seventeenth-century Japanese love-suicides—lovers appeared doomed by a passion that engulfed their lives, by a magical spell or pact to the death: a *liebestod*.[128]

What I want to consider next, then, is *how* lovemaking became socially real and normatively authoritative, not just subjectively felt or lived.

Lovemaking, after all, is far more socially real to us today than it was to Tristan and Iseult. Indeed, love—*sexual love*—has achieved an unprecedented normative authority in our own world. Lovemaking and courtship are the very basis of the modern family in both traditional-bourgeois and nontraditional forms—an issue to which I shall return. Love is also the practical reason, I want to argue, for any number of laws and regulations that *limit* institutionalized forms of sexual domination. It is not simply, as is often claimed, that sex is now incorporated into 'love-based' partnerships or marriages, whereas marriage had once been a cold arrangement designed to achieve economic ends (sexual pleasure being sought elsewhere). Sex actually *became* lovemaking, at least for some. And this development has led over time, I want to claim, to courtship, and lovemaking itself acquiring an unprecedented institutional authority—to its fundamentally altering our practices and our self-conception. Or so I will to try to show in the coming pages of this book.

I do not mean that lovemaking acquired such authority *on its own*, independent of any other practical domains. I mean, rather, that we have lived through a number of important historical changes which cannot be understood *unless* we see lovemaking as central to any account we want to give of them. Consider: over the past four centuries or so, we have witnessed, in certain parts of the world, a sharp decrease in arranged or enforced marriages; the widening and enforcing of laws limiting the sexual trafficking of children; sexual 'liberation' and the increasing acceptance of *public*, individual acts of love (kissing on the street, holding hands, open declarations of mutual sexual attaction[129]); the articulation of moral and legal codes according to which individuals can *refuse* the sexual advances of others, including, importantly, those to whom one is subjected through other institutional, political or economic power; expanded possibilities for divorce and separation which render marriage unions freer; the right of women to own property; and growing economic equality. The list goes on to include increased access to birth control and abortion by individuals, a radical shift in what it means to have children, the rise of feminism and the disappearance of a gender-based division of labor. These issues will occupy my attention in the closing pages of this book.

So, again, the question is, *How* did lovemaking go from being just the subjectively *felt* or 'lived' explanatory inadequacy of natural appetites or institutionalized forms of domination, to acquiring this kind of normative authority? How are we to explain the world-historical significance of lovemaking, as a human achievement both subjectively felt and objectively consequential for our way of life?

At the same time, it is important that we not underestimate the extent to which sexual reproduction and sexual domination retain their authority in many social contexts around the world. Obviously, prostitution, the subjection of women, the systematic abuse of children, sex trafficking, enforced marriages, entrenched opposition to contraception or abortion, and a host of other practices whose 'legitimacy' is derived from the social authority of sexual reproduction and sexual domination all continue to this day. But it is also important not to underestimate the challenges to the legitimacy or rationality of these practices mounted over the past several centuries, starting with the *experiential* failure of sexual reproduction or sexual domination to explain what we are doing as lovers. Indeed, I want to try to explain these challenges in order to understand their legitimacy.

To this end, let me make a few methodological points before continuing. First, I want to repeat my conviction that none of these historical developments can be explained as the discovery of any moral facts that our ancestors somehow failed to uncover. We cannot, for example, explain the abolition of the slave trade or of public torture simply by attributing it to the discovery of the moral fact that "all men are created equal," or that the "individual body is morally inviolable," as if these 'truths' had lain hidden for millennia under layers of bad theologies and incorrect moral philosophies and were just waiting to be discovered, or as if moral progress were an "expanding circle," ever more inclusive of those who had been excluded.[130] It is of course true that certain practices that have been occasions for communal festivity—executions, punishments, lynchings, gang rapes, torture—can and have become repugnant and horrifying, at least in certain parts of the world. But the historical novelty of such revulsion and the legal fact of abolition do not explain, or make intelligible, the criminalization of the practices that provoke such horror. After all, such practices were not always and everywhere felt to be horrific; on the contrary, they have been essential to the self-understanding of certain communities. So, how do we explain large-scale normative transformations? My suggestion is that we stand to learn much from better grasping how lovemaking challenges institutions and practices that take sexual domination and sexual reproduction to be socially authoritative.

It can be tempting, of course, to answer such questions by relying on a version of the adage that 'times change'—by saying, in effect, that new social-institutional conditions, such as mercantilism or capitalism or colonialism, demand the emergence of new practices and the cessation of other old practices. The problem with that kind of answer is not its falsity, but its explanatory insufficiency. For what we are trying to understand is how essential features of our own forms of social organization—love-based partnerships, contraception, laws against sex trafficking, legal protections against sexual assault and sexual harassment—came to *be* as central as they are. We want to understand how and *why* (not just assert *that*) we could not be 'who we are' without those kinds of commitments. And we want an account that does some actual sense-making, not just a "one damn thing after another" account, as Robert Pippin succinctly put it.[131]

In order for such an account to have robust explanatory force, it has to do more than offer one plausible story about how we 'got to be us.' We have to offer a story, I think, *without which* no other story that we tell about how we got to be us could make much sense; an explanation upon which other explanations can thereby also hang, and cohere with whatever other sense we can make of our activities and commitments, past and present. So, although my aim here is not to offer *the* story or the 'last word' on how the gender-based division of labor has been eroded, or how love and freedom became such paramount values, neither am I offering one of any number of possible stories. I want to offer a particular account of love and freedom that also sets criteria for how others might think about these issues. One criterion is this: unless we understand *how* lovemaking gained normative authority, we will not be able to understand fundamental features and values of contemporary societies.

Behind this claim lies a methodological suggestion: there are self-induced developments in our practices, internal to our practical attempts to make sense of the world, and their retrospective illumination can help us make (further) sense of how we came to think and act as we do. Not all self-induced transformations in our practices are highly explanatory—sometimes we just stop doing something because the reason for doing it goes away. But the *way* we undertake a certain activity can also change, over time, in ways that might explain not just that activity but lots else besides. One such activity—one that has not been adequately considered *as* sense-making in this way—is sex, as it turns into lovemaking both 'subjectively' (passionately) and 'objectively' (as normatively authoritative) over the course of history. So, I am suggesting that we see lovemaking as an activity that arises out of human attempts to make sense, sexually, of our lives and the conditions of our existence. At the most general level, I am arguing that we simply cannot understand a number of features of our contemporary world, our ways of living, without the story I am telling about love and freedom.

How, then, did lovers come to *know* themselves as making love? How did lovemaking become real in the world, as the basis for a way of life lived among others—not just a felt subjective reality?

Of course, not everything human beings feel or perceive as initially unintelligible turns out to be capable of—or worthy of—being the basis for any other experience, of any further attempt to make sense of anything. Not all of our feelings (pleasures, joys, sufferings, miseries) turn out to be capable of telling us whether anything *else* is true or false, important or unimportant. Rare are those indelible experiences that force us to see not just *that* experience, but our whole world, our whole existence, differently. And yet there are profound traumas, moments of getting knocked off our horses, of epochal upheavals to entire ways of life (the industrial revolution, say, or Attic tragedy) that would seem to qualify as inducing felt threats to the entire way we make sense of the world. I think lovemaking rises to this level of trauma, both in the lives of individual lovers and over the course of human history: Nothing could ever be the same for human beings once it became clear that people were making love, that we can make love.

But *how* do certain indelible experiences *force* us to confront or resolve the threats to sense that they pose? Moreover, how can such experiences turn out to be capable of installing a new way of life—of changing the way we human beings organize our lives at the most fundamental level?

Hegel, like Thomas Hobbes before him, thought that one such experience was a fight to the death with another human being. Hegel thought that the experience of fighting another person in a battle of life and death could so radically reconfigure the self-conceptions of the participants as to install a fundamental institution, on the basis of which other institutions could historically develop and through which they could understand themselves: that institution was slavery. Here, again, a contrast between my understanding of lovemaking's normative authority and Hegel's presentation of slavery, out of the life-and-death battle, might be instructive for what I have to say next.

For Hegel, recall, the mutual recognition of two desiring people occurs in the life-and-death battle. And when that struggle does not lead directly to the death of one or both combatants, it leads subsequently to the objective installation of an institutional way of life (master and slave). As already mentioned, one limitation of Hegel's account of this transition in *Phenomenology of Spirit*, is that it makes it difficult (if not impossible) to conceive of an objective institutional form of life that might be installed subsequent to acts of 'mutual recognition,' unless normative authority is attributed to some external, universal power: in this case death, "the absolute lord." (The bondsman recognizes life itself, *his* life, as that which he cannot negate without giving up the 'freedom' for whose sake he risked his life in the first place. Dead people are not free.)

But what happens if we shift—as I am proposing—the primary scene of the mutual recognition of two independent desires from the struggle to the death to lovemaking, from a duel to something like the episode from the Tristan myth, just discussed? Can lovemaking become normatively authoritative, 'objectified' as a value in our rituals and practices, just as life and death remain authoritative for Hegel's bondsman or for the Capulet family?

Consider: the mutual recognition of independent self-conscious beings need not only determinately negate the sphere of life, in the transformation of animal appetite into human desire depicted by Hegel and Hobbes. Mutual recognition might also determinately negate the sphere of history and culture, refute something in that history. What I mean is: in order to 'make love,' as a matter of practical necessity, an individual needs not only to see his lover as capable of denying him and his desire, to recognize her as a 'true,' independent being in the horizon of the sphere of life and its demands. He must *also* see his lover, socially and historically, as not sexually dominated by him or anyone else—as somehow distinguishing herself as 'independent' within a historical-institutional way of life sustained by gender-based distinctions and sexual domination. If he is to *know* that they are making love—that she makes love with him, and he with her—then she must be knowable not only as 'free' from appetites and natural processes, but also as 'free' from the socially institutionalized sexual domination and gender-based hierarchies we inherit.

At this point, then, to bring the discussion into more concrete focus, let me assume that, arguably, the most pervasive and historically powerful social-historical institution of sexual domination is what we tend to call patriarchy. I shall assume that one feature of sexual interactions between men and women under patriarchal conditions is this: sexual engagement *feels*, to the lovers themselves, forced. Sex under conditions of patriarchal domination and gender-based hierarchies can feel experientially indistinguishable from—unintelligible apart from—the circumscription of female sexual agency by men. This circumscription can, of course, take many forms: in demands for virginity and honor, virtue and chastity, or in displays of obedience and permissiveness, submission and obsequence, and 'feminized' behavior. The mechanisms are well-known: physical and psychological coercion, social and economic pressure, the enforcement of political and legal restrictions. And as already emphasized, the domination at issue in patriarchy is fundamentally sexual—affirmed in sexual activities and in the gender-based division of labor, and expressed in sexual behavior.

All of this makes it difficult to *know* 'objectively' that one is making love to another, even if that may be what one is doing. Again, this is why medieval romance was filled with scenes of lovemaking grasped only as magic or as wild twists of fate. At the same time, the Tristan myth and other romances show us how sexual domination and its institutional manifestations were, like sexual reproduction, increasingly unable to make sexual experience itself intelligible: hence the 'magic' of lovemaking.

Consider the problem from a practical point of view, as a historical impasse: How is an entitled man living under patriarchal conditions to *know* a female lover as one who makes love to him, rather than as one who merely enacts her subjugation or provokes 'appetite'? How can such a man *know*, sexually, that he does not dominate his lover, or that he and she are not just swept away by appetitive impulses?

Or, if one is a woman, living under patriarchal conditions—severely limited in her agency, above all in her *sexual* agency—then how is she to become active as a lover? Can she give up on it entirely? Wait for rights to be granted her by men, to be 'awakened' like Sleeping Beauty? How might she *know* herself as one who can make love, as provisionally free in that way? Might lovemaking be one practice, to recall Beauvoir's question, through which women might achieve freedom "in the feminine condition," under the rule of patriarchy?[132]

Imagine, even more concretely: a powerful, socially venerated man, wants to *know* that he loves his wife, that she loves him. Seeking proof he can accept, he demands that she await him in bed. She complies, wedding sheets draped across her body. Now, the man enters. Almost in spite of himself, he is aroused by the sight; bending over her, he inhales her scent and kisses her.

In medieval romance, we know how this would go. When Chrétien's Parsifal encounters a beautiful woman sleeping alone in a tent, the boy, "innocent fool that he was," simply kissed her ("as my mother taught me I should") and spent the night with her. They knew not what they did, nor did they stop to wonder.[133]

But when Shakespeare imagined such a scene, he supposed the man would have entered the room racked by self-doubt, and that he would have whispered to his wife: "Be thus when thou are dead, and I will kill thee / And love thee after" (5.2.18–19).[134]

Othello and Desdemona

Lie with her? Lie on her?

Shakespeare, *Othello* (1602–03)

Over the following pages, I want to pursue the questions just raised with the help of Shakespeare's *Othello*, whose denouement turns on the hair's breadth difference between lovemaking and murder. I see *Othello* as tracking the promise of lovemaking, as well as its failure to become actual and real, at the dawn of the modern age.

To set the stage for what I have to say, let me briefly recall some reflections offered by the philosopher Stanley Cavell in his book *The Claim of Reason*, which not only concludes with a well-known interpretation of *Othello*, but also raises many of the same issues I am raising here under the heading of what Cavell calls "the truth of skepticism."[135] Following Wittgenstein (and, before him, David Hume), Cavell claims that the real issue in skepticism is not the limitations of our knowledge of the world out there—the confines of our senses, say, or the finitude of our intellect. Descartes notwithstanding, we pretty much accept that there are sidewalk curbs on which we might trip, trains and planes we might catch or miss. As Hume drily put it, "the great subverter of . . . excessive scepticisme is . . . the occupation of life."[136] At the same time, Cavell claims (again following Hume and Wittgenstein), skepticism is not just a matter of *self*-knowledge—if by self-knowledge we mean some sort of boot-strapping, solipsistic circuitry in which I take myself to be both the subject and object of my thinking.

Instead, for Cavell, the primary issue raised by skepticism is an abiding uncertainty concerning *other people*—doubts about who they are, how to deal with them, or how to live with the worry that we can probably never know them fully. Some philosophers call this the 'problem of other minds.' Othello, too, says, "Men should be what they seem;/Or those that be not, would they might seem none!" (3.3.126–27). Because this problem can never be overcome by amassing knowledge or evidence about other people, getting to know an-other person is shot through with skepticism. By the same token, skepticism is especially pressing wherever our exposure to one another is heightened, as in intimate relationships like love-affairs.[137] Further, if we can never fully know another person, then it does not take much for the skeptic to begin questioning whether others are truly as they seem to be. Is this other person *really* another person—independent, desiring, and self-aware as I think I am? How can I know that she is real, authentic? And, if so, how? These are issues, I will suggest, that explain Othello's violence against Desdemona.

Cavell also suggests that this uncertainty about others cannot be separated from a deep anxiety about ourselves: Do *I* exist? Am *I* true, authentic and real—and how can I be sure? If my own self-certainty is bound up with my doubts about other people, then "the integrity of *my* existence . . . may depend on the fact and on the idea of another being's existence, and on the possibility of prov-ing that existence."[138] Which means—to put it the other way around—finding another authentic, true human being amounts to discovering whether anyone really *knows or understands me*. (Am I just a walking shadow? "Does any here know me?"—to borrow King Lear's succinct question—"Who is it that can tell me who I am?" (1.4.216–17). And this anxiety tumbles into other problems pur-sued by Cavell as well.[139] Shouldn't *I* be in the best position to judge whether someone else really knows *me*? Shouldn't I know myself—what it is like being me—better than (or, at least, in a different way than) anyone else does? After all, if I am *fully* knowable by someone else—if the gap between how others might know me and how I know myself were erased—then the difference between myself and others starts to break down: I lose myself. When Othello says to Iago, "I'll know thy thoughts," Iago tells him, "You cannot, if my heart were in your hand, / Nor shall not, whilst 'tis in my custody" (3.3.162–64). At any rate, Cavell's intriguing suggestion is that the achievement of first-personal experience—the feeling of 'leading one's life'—arises from objective efforts to know or understand others, from my concrete efforts to make others know or understand me (to "say what I mean," in Cavell's phrasing).[140] All this is worth bearing in mind.

Now, in his reading of *Othello*, Cavell argues that Othello "avoids acknowledging" Desdemona's independence, her desires and vitality, by murdering her.[141] While suffocating one's lover in bed may seem an extreme manifestation of such failure, nevertheless its possibility belongs, according to Cavell, to "the way human sexuality is the field in which the fantasy of finitude, of its acceptance and its repetitious overcoming, is worked out; the way human separateness is turned equally toward splendor and toward horror."[142] According to Cavell, Desdemona confronts Othello with something he cannot tolerate—the independence of her vitality, of her desire, awaiting him stretched upon the bed. "O curse of marriage, / That we can call these delicate creatures ours / And not their appetites" (3.3.272–74). She presents Othello with his limits: both *her* desire and, perhaps worse, the urgings of *his own* desire. In Cavell's words, Othello is "surprised by [Desdemona], at what he has elicited from her; at, so to speak, a success rather than a failure."[143] In some respects, Cavell's interpretation is helpful, not least because it counters a common misunderstanding of the play according to which Othello is a kind of a puppet or "credulous fool" (4.1.42) whose strings are pulled by Iago.[144] To return to the terms of my discussion, we could say that if Desdemona *wants* to make love to him—to *him*, Othello (not just to him as 'male' or as 'general')—then Othello cannot make sense of his sexual interactions with Desdemona as *either* his sexual domination of her, or as their entanglement with the demands of natural appetite and procreation. Shakespeare's play begins, then, with lovemaking's profound threat to sense: the *prior self-conceptions* in our sexual self-education—that human beings sexually reproduce, and that human beings 'act' by sexually dominating other human beings—start to lose their explanatory force.

However, Cavell points not only to Othello's "surprise" at eliciting Desdemona's desire. Cavell also sees Othello's surprise as that which renders him murderous, as the reason Othello accepts the idea of Desdemona's infidelity and smothers her in their bed.[145] Here, I am left with questions about Cavell's interpretation. How can Othello apprehend—that is, how can he even identify, and thus be surprised by—the independence of Desdemona's desire as something that he elicits, unless he is already engaged sexually with Desdemona in a nondomineering, nonappetitive way? If Othello has had no experience—however fleeting, however preliminary—of making love with Desdemona, or at least of imagining it, then how could Othello be surprised, in the way Cavell suggests, by a "success rather than a failure?"[146]

Moreover, why should the "surprise" of lovemaking—of a genuine seduction—lead Othello to murderously "avoid acknowledging" that surprise, and to take refuge instead in the "convenient" "idea" that Desdemona is "an adulterous whore" by, ultimately, smothering her in their bed?[147] Cavell's answer to this is that Othello "is rendered impotent and murderous by aroused, or by having aroused, female sexuality—or let us say . . . horrified by human sexuality, in himself and in others."[148] But then why should the experience of lovemaking—or the experience of imagining it—lead to impotence, or arouse murderousness? Whence this horror in the face of "human sexuality" in general, or in response to "female sexuality" in particular? In discussing *Hamlet*, Cavell seems to see this as kind of ahistorical, psychic necessity: "Human sexuality" or "female sexuality" can be horror-inducing, to the point of arousing murderousness, Cavell thinks, because "accepting one's individuality or individuation" involves "the necessity of a double acceptance"—accepting "one's mother as an independent sexual being" and accepting "one's father as a dependent sexual being."[149] If I understand Cavell here, to be "horrified" by "human" or "female sexuality" is part of the challenge of accepting one's separateness from others, a work of mourning and, in particular, of acknowledging male dependence on female sexual independence.[150]

I confess that it is easier for me to see sexual disgust (or the work of mourning) as an explanation for, say, Hamlet's behavior toward Gertrude than as an explanation for Othello's murder of Desdemona. In *Othello*, Shakespeare seems to have had a different dynamic in mind, another dramatic stake. Othello does not seem horrified by sex as such, the way that Hamlet seems to be when he speaks of Gertrude and Claudius, "In the rank sweat of an enseamèd bed, / Stewed in corruption, honeying and making love / Over the nasty sty" (3.4.92–93). If Othello is unsettled by Iago's image of Desdemona and Cassio "as prime as goats, as hot as monkeys" (3.3.406), then this has less to do with Othello's 'acceptance' of Desdemona's independence than with his efforts at proving her independence.

And in the murder scene are we not tempted by Shakespeare to imagine Othello doing something else with Desdemona in bed, besides smothering her? Moreover, what was Desdemona thinking, as she lay in bed under Othello, as he put his hands on her? Desdemona did not try to escape, or scream for help—as Gertrude did, crying out "Help, help, ho!" when Hamlet sat her down in her bedchamber. Does not Desdemona play a role in this, beyond the one Cavell assigns to her?

Let me, then, look again at Shakespeare's drama to see what else the play might help us to explain and understand.

First, consider that Othello's early courtship of Desdemona required Othello to question a deep-seated conception of himself as 'master.'[151] As a high-ranking officer, Othello was of course accustomed to exerting mastery over his own bodily life as well the bodies of others; institutional domination and the satisfaction of his desires had gone hand in hand. Indeed, Othello thinks that Desdemona loves him for this very reason: "She loved me for the dangers I had passed, / And I loved her that she did pity them" (1.3.166–67). Given this, it is striking that Othello does not simply look upon Desdemona the way he regards his soldiers—as a body to be commanded, as the instrument for the fulfillment of his orders, as his property or chattel.[152]

Having won Desdemona with his tales and displays of mastery in the world, Othello discovers that he does not want be *her* master. Not that Othello is physically or socially or economically incapable of coercing Desdemona. Sexual domination is just not what he desires with her. It matters to him—quite a lot, in fact—that Desdemona turn out to be an independent being, acting on her own desires. He finds that *his* desire for her is not indifferent to *her* desires, whatever they may be. He cares about what she wants, because he also wants to know that *he* has seduced *her*—that each is acting freely. Indeed, by courting Desdemona, Othello has learned that institutionalized forms of sexual domination cannot provide the freedom (the love) he seeks. He has absorbed the lessons of courtship discussed above.

Othello would rather see Desdemona dead at his feet than bent before him on her knees.

If this is not wrong, then at least a few things follow.

First, although it is true that Othello is concerned with Desdemona's sexual fidelity or "honor," to the extent that this touches on his own social standing, this is not his primary concern.[153] Contrary to a common misunderstanding about the play, it is not the objective *fact* of Desdemona's behavior—her

supposed sexual infidelity—that most disturbs Othello. Nor is cuckolding beyond bearing.[154] It is rather Othello's first-personal experience of her sexual adventures that upsets him. He makes this clear:

> I swear 'tis better to be much abused
> Than but to know't a little.
>
> . . .
>
> What sense had *I* of her stol'n hours of lust?
> *I* saw't not, thought it not; it harmed not *me*.
> *I* slept the next night well, fed well, was free and merry.
> *I* found not Cassio's kisses on her lips.
> He that is robbed, not wanting what is stol'n,
> Let him not know't and he's not robbed at all.
>
> . . .
>
> *I* had been happy if the general camp,
> Pioneers and all, had tasted her sweet body,
> So *I* had nothing known." (3.3.338–52; my emphasis)

Or, as Iago says, "if it touch not you, it comes near nobody" (4.1.189). But why
should such first-personal knowledge unsettle Othello if whatever is known
(objectively, as it were) is not disturbing in itself, if it is disturbing only because
it is known *by him*? What is the difference between facts being known and
knowing the facts?

Consider—as a way of providing an answer—the difference between Iago's
and Othello's preoccupations. From Iago's perspective, jealousy—the "green-
eyed monster" (3.3.170)—expresses a lack of certainty about the way things
stand 'out there' in the world, a nagging sense that one is ignorant about
some objective reality that touches directly upon one's own standing before
others. Put in terms of this discussion thus far, Iago thinks that jealousy
targets clandestine lovers (the "adulterous" lovers I discussed above, whose
only 'reality' is their passionate lovemaking), those whose affairs threaten or
undermine institutionalized forms of sexual domination, and hence require
stamping out.

Precisely because cuckolding or passionate, adulterous affairs have so little
objective standing in the world, for reasons I gave earlier, Iago can goad Othello
with his sheer lack of concrete evidence. This is why Iago tempts Othello with
(semi)concrete evidence of a passion that cannot be objectively proven from
the outside: lovemaking. And it is why Iago thinks he can manipulate Othello

with the promise of further testimony that "speaks against [Desdemona] with the other proofs" (3.3.446):

> That cuckold lives in bliss
> Who, certain of his fate, loves not his wronger.
> But O, what damnèd minutes tells he o'er
> Who dotes yet doubts, suspects yet fondly loves! (3.3.171–74)

Or, again, as he later says to Othello:

> O, 'tis the spite of hell, the fiend's arch-mock,
> To lip a wanton in a secure couch
> And to suppose her chaste! No, let me know,
> And knowing what I am, I know what she shall be. (4.1.68–71)

For Iago, then, it is clear that "love" amounts to what I have been calling "sexual domination." Othello's sexual agency (for Iago) hinges on the objective "proof" of, the institutional demand for, Desdemona's chastity and subjugation—just as Othello's standing as an officer demands his soldier's loyalty, just as a daughter's obedience demonstrates a father's ability to command. "Love," for Iago, names a bond or fidelity that must be publically demonstrated through sexual dominance—and hence that would be publically undone when such fidelity cannot be demonstrated.[155] Love and jealousy are mutually exclusive; for Iago, it would be a straightforward contradiction to love jealously.[156]

And yet—to repeat—the objective facts of Desdemona's interactions with Cassio are not what ultimately unsettle Othello. It is Othello's subjective viewpoint—the unavoidability of his first-personal stance (*knowing* the facts)—that upsets him. If this is right, then Othello does not interrogate Iago because he craves the sort of evidence that might convince a jury, or to establish Desdemona's sexual fidelity to him. Just as no one could ever convince Othello of Desdemona's innocence, so too, no one could convince him of her guilt. Which is to say, no one can demonstrate to him Desdemona's love—any more than he can objectively prove to others his love of her. This should be obvious; otherwise, all we are witnessing is the depressing soap opera of a jealous husband who enlists a devious detective to do the work of deciding for him whether his love is merited, whether his wife has been subjugated to him.

But if, for Othello, "love" does not mean sexual domination, or a publically verifiable bond rooted in objective evidence, then what does he mean when he says he "loves" Desdemona? What does he mean when he says things like "My life upon her faith" (1.3.293), if he does not mean that he prizes her obedience of fidelity above all?

Well, he clarifies somewhat when he says things like, "Perdition catch my soul / But I do love thee, and when I love thee not, / Chaos is come again" (3.3.91–93). By "chaos," Othello seems to mean a profound threat to any sense he might make of his life and its conditions. Hence, it is not his honor, but the intelligibility of anything at all that he sets upon Desdemona's faith and his love for her. "If she be false, O then heaven mocks itself!" (3.3.282). The question, then, is how did the intelligibility of Othello's life and worldly conditions come—for him—to depend upon the fate of his courtship of Desdemona?

We have already identified one reason. Because mastery and sexual domination are not what Othello wants with Desdemona, it is not her disobedience—but rather the cessation of his love—that would render his actions unintelligible, that would mean "chaos is come again." Othello intuits that his freedom *is* his love of Desdemona. Without mutual recognition, without genuine seduction between two independent beings, what is there? If before Desdemona came into his life, Othello could reassure himself that the life he was leading was 'his' by means of conquering and subduing—military life, sexual domination—here such reassurance is not possible: he cannot love Desdemona by conquering her because, to repeat, he is not indifferent to what she wants. If his desire is thus entangled with hers, then his self-conception as 'free' depends upon demonstrating *her* independence. In order to be sure that he is living his life, realizing his desires, Othello now needs to be certain that Desdemona is doing the same. This is his predicament, the meaning of his jealousy.

Othello aims to demonstrate the independence and vitality of Desdemona's desire—not, as Cavell has it, to "avoid" or "deny" that independent vitality.

But why should this demonstration turn out to be murderous?

I am not suggesting that Othello is fully aware of all the thoughts and feelings I am describing here. I understand Othello to be finding out what he wants as he goes along—especially, through the slow discovery of the difference between Iago's offered evidence and the 'proof' he really seeks. This is the stuff of their well-known exchanges, during which Iago and Othello talk past each other. Iago, for example, admonishes Othello to "beware . . . of jealousy" (3.3.169), meaning, again, that Othello should seek public proof of his sexual domination of Desdemona.

Othello, however, hears Iago to be suggesting that he, Othello, should take care to be sure of what *he himself* is doing. Othello hears a warning not to doubt *himself*. Here is the exchange:

> Iago.   That cuckold lives in bliss
> Who, certain of his fate, loves not his wronger.
> But O, what damnèd minutes tells he o'er
> Who dotes yet doubts, suspects yet fondly loves!
>   . . .
>
> Good God the souls of all my tribe defend
> From jealousy!
> Othello.   Why, why is this?
> Think'st thou I'd make a life of jealousy,
> To follow still the changes of the moon
> With fresh suspicions? No, to be once in doubt
> Is once to be resolved.
>   . . .
>
>   No, Iago,
> I'll see before I doubt; when I doubt, prove;
> And on the proof, there is no more but this:
> Away at once with love or jealousy. (3.3.171–96)

I hear Othello to be saying that the sense he makes of the world will come from what *he himself* demonstrates to his own satisfaction, from what *he* accepts as proof or knowledge. While Othello will listen to Iago's counsel, he will think and decide for himself on the worth of that counsel; Iago may give him evidence, but it is evidence whose meaning Othello will adjudicate. Jealousy, for Othello, means the search for proof that *he* accepts.

For the time being, however, Othello fails to see that there is no objective evidence or proof that can furnish for him this first personal certainty. Getting proof—and *accepting* that proof—is going to be a lot more wrenching than merely looking upon this or that bit of evidence and making a detached judgment. Nevertheless, for the moment, Othello continues to hope that Iago might at least furnish him with the evidence to be judged. And this, of course, tumbles directly into the farcical exchange in which Iago is all too happy to participate. "Villain!" cries Othello, taking Iago by the throat, "be sure thou prove my love a whore. / Be sure of it. Give me the ocular proof. . . . Make me to see't" (3.3.364–69).

"You would be satisfied?" taunts Iago.

"Would? Nay, and I will," bellows Othello, setting the ball on the tee for Iago.

And may. But how, how satisfied, my lord?
Would you, the supervisor, grossly gape on,
Behold her topped?

   . . .

It were a tedious difficulty, I think,
To bring them to that prospect. Damn them then
If ever mortal eyes do see them bolster
More than their own! What then, how then?
What shall I say? Where's satisfaction?
It is impossible you should see this,
Were they as prime as goats, as hot as monkeys,
As salt as wolves in pride, and fools as gross
As ignorance made drunk. (3.3.398–410)

The image of this farce—or of any other bedroom farce, probably—is the perfect depiction of Othello's impasse. For even if he were to "behold her topped," he would still not have the proof he seeks—an objective demonstration of Desdemona's independence (and hence of his own). Moreover, the extant institutions of patriarchal, sexual domination would leave Othello with an empty choice: either deny the reality before his eyes by proclaiming the lovers innocent (as King Mark did, when he found Tristan and Iseult in the woods); or deny the reality through violent punishment (as the Sultan does in a murderous rage in *The Thousand and One Nights*). Either option would leave Othello's love of Desdemona, his desire to have *her* independence demonstrated, unrealized.

Why, then, does Shakespeare ask us to imagine the farce? Not to furnish, once and for all, concrete evidence of who is having sex with whom.[157] The image of the farce, rather, places the cuckold on the spot; it requires him to perform a self-expressive deed, to make clear through his action or response how he sees himself and others, to express his understanding of the situation in which he finds himself.

So, Othello finds himself pressed.

The question is no longer what Desdemona and Cassio objectively did, but what Othello himself will do with them. Which means that Othello's search for external evidence itself—for a wholly third-personal, institutional perspective that might remove the need for first-personal experience and second-personal intimacy—must grind to a halt. This, I think, explains why the circumstantial evidence of the handkerchief, and not concrete proof, finally concludes Othello's interrogations of Iago. Because the insinuations around the handkerchief require Othello himself to take action, to take up the matter with Desdemona, he has no further need of Iago. Which is also to say, Othello never needed Iago for the reasons Iago believed—to decide on Desdemona's guilt or innocence. The proof Othello seeks—of the independence and vitality of Desdemona's desire, that she is not merely an extension of *his* desire—is something that he cannot furnish unless he engages her. He must somehow confront Desdemona. But how?

I understand Othello's shift into the first-personal hot seat to be signaled in the play by the trance or "fit" into which he falls at precisely this moment. ("Lie with her? Lie on her?") According to Cavell, Othello's trance expresses not "conviction in a piece of knowledge" but "an effort to stave the knowledge off."[158] But again, I do not think the only issue here is Othello's difficulty in accepting Desdemona's literal innocence—his failure to "acknowledge" Desdemona's adoration of him.

At issue is the moral imagination required of Othello, subjectively, if he is to acknowledge Desdemona as an independent being. In order to perceive (or imagine) Cassio and Desdemona in an intimate embrace, Othello must also perceive (or imagine) such intimacy *for himself.* Iago cannot do *that* for him—no matter how carefully he sets or describes the scene. Even as spectator—indeed, precisely as ideal spectator—Othello simply cannot remove himself from the picture. He cannot let Iago's perspective replace his own. His fantasies must take over (or not), as is suggested by the exchange preceding the trance:

> Othello.   What hath [Cassio] said?
> Iago. Faith, that he did—I know not what he did.
> Othello. What, what?
> Iago.   Lie—
> Othello.   With her?
> Iago.   With her, on her,
> *what you will.* (4.1.31–33; my emphasis)

At which point, Othello's own sense-making is engaged. Is Othello envisioning himself with Desdemona when he says the following?

> Lie with her? Lie on her? We say 'lie on her' when they belie her. Lie with her?
> 'Swounds, that's fulsome! Handkerchief—confession—handkerchief. To confess
> and be hanged for his labour. First to be hanged and then to confess! I tremble
> at it. Nature would not invest herself in such shadowing passion without some

instruction. It is not words that shakes me thus. Pish! Noses, ears, and lips! Is't possible? Confess? Handkerchief? O devil! (4.1.34–41)

Where might such fantasies lead? What would it be to live out the sense Othello is making of things?

In the next scene, then, Othello externalizes his fantasies. He strikes Desdemona, using the same word, "devil," repeatedly—as if literally acting out the subjective fantasies expressed in his trance.[159] Because we often forget this moment of naked aggression—which presages, and might help explain, the final tableau—let me recall the exchange, in which Othello makes violent remarks as he overhears Desdemona's conversation with Lodovico, remarks that are assumed by Desdemona and Lodovico to be his reaction to the contents of a letter from Venice, which has just been delivered to him by Lodovico:

Lodovico.   How does Lieutenant Cassio?

     . . .

Desdemona. Cousin, there's fall'n between him and my lord
    An unkind breach. But you shall make all well.
Othello. Are you sure of that?
Desdemona. My lord?
Othello. [*reads*] 'This fail you not to do, as you will'—
Lodovico. He did not call; he's busy in the paper.
    Is there division 'twixt my lord and Cassio?
Desdemona. A most unhappy one: I would do much
    T'atone them, for the love I bear to Cassio.
Othello. Fire and brimstone!
Desdemona.   My lord?
Othello.   Are you wise?
Desdemona. What, is he angry?
Lodovico.   Maybe the letter moved him;
    For, as I think, they do command him home,
    Deputing Cassio in his government.
Desdemona. Trust me, I am glad on't.
Othello. Indeed!
Desdemona. My lord?
Othello. I am glad to see you mad.
Desdemona. Why, sweet Othello!
Othello. Devil! [*He strikes her*] (4.1.217–235)

As I see it, Othello's actions might be made intelligible along the lines I suggested earlier—as Othello's attempt to know whether Desdemona acts independently.[160] Othello, I am suggesting, wants to know that he has seduced, not mastered, Desdemona; that this is a love-affair, not military life. Striking and debasing one's lover in front of others might seem a counterintuitive—if not counterproductive—way to demonstrate her independence. But perhaps it looks less mysterious if we remember that lovers' quarrels are often nothing more than bald-faced provocations—attempts to 'get a rise' out of one another, to bring one another back to life, to achieve a confrontation between two independent, living, desiring people.[161] Of course, on the one hand, if the provocation continues to be merely abusive, then there remains only straightforward opposition or contempt, or the domination of one by the other. On the other hand, the conflict could lead to reconciliation *with* the other's independence—which might be why such provocations and squabbles can lead so immediately to kissing and making up. As everyone knows, lovemaking can result from—even accomplish, or finish—a quarrel.[162]

At any rate, by slapping and berating Desdemona, I understand Othello to be testing her independence—to be looking for objective proof of her independence that he can accept.

She responds evasively—"I have not deserved this," she says tearfully (4.1.236).

Othello tries again, this time mocking her tears as false:

> O, devil, devil!
> If that the earth could teem with woman's tears,
> Each drop she falls would prove a crocodile.
> Out of my sight! (4.1.239–242)

Desdemona complies, slinking away. "I will not stay to offend you," she says. "Truly, an obedient lady," says Lodovico—unaware that it is precisely such servility that Othello wishes to disprove. Hence, Othello tests her again, demanding that Desdemona return—"Mistress!"

"My lord?" she repeats for the fourth time in the exchange, obedient as ever.

"What would you with her, sir?" says Othello to Lodovico—underscoring that Desdemona's obedience makes her attachment to him, Othello, interchangeable with her attachment to any master or man:

> you did wish that I would have her turn.
> Sir, she can turn and turn, and yet go on

And turn again, and she can weep, sir, weep,

And she's obedient, as you say, obedient,

Very obedient. (4.1.243–53)

Desdemona shows herself to be obedient, dominated sexually and otherwise.[163] Where the others see in this a virtue, Othello sees vacuity. (*Anything but your obedience! Your obedience makes me interchangeable, one of many possible masters in a game of sexual domination. Unless you demonstrate that your actions are not extensions of my authority, of sexual domination, then we are not lovers.*)

This is the thrust of Othello's pursuit, when he next confronts Desdemona.

In the face of her confusion—"I understand a fury in your words, / But not the words"—he demands to know: "Why, *what art thou?*" (my emphasis).

"Your wife, my lord, your true and loyal wife," comes the (to Othello) maddeningly routine response.

Othello tries again:

Othello. Come, swear it, damn thyself,

    Lest, being like one of heaven, the devils themselves

    Should fear to seize thee. Therefore be double-damned:

    Swear thou are honest.

Desdemona.   Heaven doth truly know it.

Othello. Heaven truly knows that thou are false as hell. (4.2.33–41)

How he jabs at her!—declaring her as honest "as summer flies are in the shambles, / That quicken even with blowing" (4.2.68–69).[164] Just as Hamlet accuses Ophelia of making "wantonness [her] ignorance" (3.1.147–48), so Othello musters his considerable eloquence in order to call Desdemona a whore.[165]

Was this fair paper, this most goodly book,

Made to write 'whore' upon? What committed?

Committed? O thou public commoner,

I should make very forges of my cheeks,

That would to cinders burn up modesty,

Did I but speak thy deeds. What committed?

Heaven stops the nose at it, and the moon winks;

The bawdy wind, that kisses all it meets,

Is hushed within the hollow mine of earth

And will not hear't. What committed?

    . . .

Are you not a strumpet?

. . .

What, not a whore? (4.2.73–88)

Why does Othello prod Desdemona thus? "A beggar in his drink / Could not have laid such terms upon his callet," says Emilia (4.2.119–120).

I agree with Cavell when he says that Othello knows Desdemona to be innocent of Iago's slander. But, unlike Cavell, I do not hear Othello trying to "avoid" this knowledge. Rather, I hear him *testing* or challenging Desdemona's innocence, trying to make sense of it as something other than obedience and fidelity to command.[166] How better (he thinks) to upend the institution of sexual domination than to call one's innocent, obedient wife a whore, a strumpet? How better to find out if she is anything more than obedient? How better, that is, to see if and how *she* reacts?

You are a whore, aren't you? insists Othello.

> Desdemona.   No, as I am a Christian.
>   If to preserve this vessel for my lord
>   From any other foul unlawful touch
>   Be not to be a strumpet, I am none. (4.2.84–87)

"What, not a whore?" Othello tries one last time. "No, as I shall be saved," affirms Desdemona piously.

"Is't possible?" Othello throws up his hands in frustration, leaving with her one last zinger: "I cry you mercy, then. / I took you for that cunning whore of Venice / That married with Othello" (4.2.89–94).

Am I alone in sensing Othello's disappointment at not having had his volley returned?

If Othello fails to incite her with words and blows—if he perceives only obedience ("My lord")—then *how* to know the independence of Desdemona's desire? How to demonstrate that he has seduced and not mastered her? This is why her obedience is unnerving—her acquiescence effaces her, it makes her (and him) interchangeable parts of a social hierarchy. If she merely obeys, then he has mastered, not seduced, her.

And that is not all. Othello also finds Desdemona irresistibly attractive, intoxicating. But her beauty and his arousal only leave him asking: *By whom or what am I seduced?* If it is just her feminine beauty and sensuous charm, then *she*—Desdemona—has no independent existence: there is only 'woman,' witchcraft, voluptuousness, impersonal appetites. Seduction starts to look like compulsion or impulse, not freedom. The threats to sense mount. But how to prove that she is not a witch? How to know that he desires her—Desdemona, the real live person, someone who might accept or refuse him? There is, Othello concludes, only one way to find out: "Get you to bed on th'instant. I will be returned forthwith. Dismiss your attendant there. Look't be done" (4.3.7–8).

With this, let me return to the questions with which my discussion of *Othello* began. Can a seduction be known? Can we *know* that we are lovers? Can the achievement of such knowledge be something other than its sexual consummation, a subjectively felt passion?

Othello enters their bedroom and gazes upon Desdemona, "that whiter skin of hers than snow / And smooth as monumental alabaster," inhaling her "balmy breath" (5.2.4–5, 16).[167] Othello is surely self-aware enough to know that there is no use denying his sexual desire for Desdemona, that even killing Desdemona will not free him from wanting her.[168] He even says so—"Be thus when thou art dead, and I will kill thee / And love thee after" (5.2.18–19). So, I cannot believe that Othello does not want to get into bed; I also cannot believe that he does not know that this is what he wants. Yet he fights the urge.[169]

In part, this is because he seeks to prove to himself that he is not driven by desire alone, that he is not merely attracted by a sensuous body that feeds and stokes his appetite. However if Othello *only* wanted to prove that he is not driven by blind desire, then it would have been enough to reject her advances— "Will you come to bed, my lord?" (5.2. 25)—or to leave the room, or to practice some other form of chaste restraint. So, what else is he trying to prove?

Othello, I think, wants *objective* proof that lovemaking is being achieved, that there is genuine, 'subjective' seduction between two independent people. Indeed, he will refrain from making love with her until the independence of her desire is demonstrated. But this leaves Othello with the impossible task of parsing his own arousal while gauging the risks of intimacy with Desdemona. On the one hand, because he seeks an objective demonstration that *he* can accept, he must remain on the bed next to her—tarrying with his own arousal, searching her eyes for evidence. On the other hand, because he will not accept lovemaking itself (that subjective act) as objective proof, he must not let himself get *into* bed with her.

Let me shine a light on this moment to make an important claim before going on. The untenability of Othello's position—the internal contradiction just described—*is* the historical impasse under consideration at this point in my broader account of love and freedom.

The subjective act of lovemaking—the mutual recognition of two independent people, achieved by lovers like Tristan and Iseult—has not yet made itself socially real, for reasons already explained. And, I now want to say, lovemaking *cannot* make itself real unless it becomes 'objective'—demonstrable, proven. Othello is not wrong to need a worldly demonstration of Desdemona's love, of his love—not of obedience, but of *love*. For, without objective proof that they are lovers, what do they have? Domination and subjugation, perhaps, or blind appetites, or at best, fantastical lovemaking and exchanges of tokens (handkerchiefs, rings) that remain, like medieval romance, fantasies by the lights of Venice's reality. Othello cannot be satisfied with such unreality.

For Othello also sees himself as central to Venetian life, just as Venice is essential to him. He wants his marriage to be real in the world—which is to say that he needs lovemaking to be at the *core* of his *whole* existence, a source of its meaning and value: both his subjective passions and his objective commitments to a way of life. This is not an idle need or pleasant daydream. Othello cannot make sense of anything he is doing with Desdemona unless he gets this objectivity. And if he cannot make sense of what he is doing with her, then of what *can* he make sense? Merely that he has objectively "done the state some service, and they know't" (5.2.348), which is where he, suicidally, ends up. Leading a desirable, intelligible life as something other than a cog in a social machine or natural process *requires* lovemaking to be achieved as real, both to the lovers and objectively in the world.

Othello, thus, cannot make love to Desdemona unless their lovemaking gives him, not just assurance of their mutual recognition, but proof that this mutual recognition is the value on which their lives, their social existence, can be demonstrably based. But Desdemona cannot give him that proof. How could she? Publically and objectively, and hence privately and subjectively, she can only offer to Othello that which Venice recognizes in her: obedience, sensuousness, willingness, desirability, impossible beauty. She can make love to Othello, even offer him her life, but she cannot—by making love to him, or by dying—give Othello a world in which lovemaking could have objective standing, demonstrable normative authority.

What, then, is required for the achievement of such a world? What does a *demonstration* that we are, really, lovers—truly free, independent desiring agents—require? We are, I think, today still working out the answer to that question, in our social practices and revised collective values. But I have already mentioned some of what is required. Recall the list of social commitments re-

cited above: a sharp decrease in arranged or enforced marriages; sexual 'liberation' and the increasing acceptance of public, individual displays of affection;
moral and legal codes according to which individuals can *refuse* the sexual advances of others; expanded possibilities for divorce and separation which render
marriage unions freer; the right of women to own property; economic equality;
increased access to birth control and abortion by individuals; a total reconception
of what it means to have children; the erosion of a gender-based division of labor.

Is it too much to consider each of these immense social-historical transformations, and others beside—whose significance and many implications cannot
be overestimated—as *rendered necessary* by the need to make lovemaking objective, real? I do not think so.

I do not think so, because each of these social changes answers directly the
challenges, the threats to sense, faced by Desdemona and Othello. Othello and
Desdemona cannot make their lives and actions intelligible—to themselves, to
one another, to the world—unless they manage to be lovers, subjectively-pas-
sionately and objectively in their shared way of life.

So, we watch Othello on the edge of the bed—struggling to get the objective
proof he seeks without making love. Because he must avoid accepting subjective passion for objective proof, he must resist Desdemona's entreaties. "I hope
you will not kill me" (5.2.37)[170] "O, banish me, my lord, but kill me not" (5.2.85).

> Desdemona. Kill me tomorrow; let me live tonight.
> Othello. Nay, an you strive—
> Desdemona. But half an hour.
> Othello. Being done, there is no pause.
> Desdemona. But while I say one prayer. (5.2.87–91)

But in a world in which lovemaking has not yet achieved objective standing
or normative authority, what could Othello hope to prove?

At most, Othello can have objective evidence that Desdemona wants him
more than she wants to stay alive, that she wants him no matter what. He can
sever her desire for him from both her impersonal appetite and her social obedience. To prove that she loves him, she can let him put his hands around her
neck. It is a logic with which seducers are not unfamiliar: physical surrender is
necessary in order to demonstrate independence and the freedom of love.

Here the seducer's logic reaches its apotheosis. Desdemona's dead body is
the only objective proof of freedom, of their love, that Othello will have. No
shedding of blood, no ruining of the flesh. So as to kill her and love her after.

. . .

To accept a world in which lovemaking has no social authority, no demonstrable standing in our practices—at the heart of our way of life—is to accept a world in which Desdemona can live only as the embodiment of procreative demands and sensuous appetites or as a subjugated, obedient woman. Either that, or accept the necessity of her death.

Shakespeare, I take it, is tallying the precise cost of a world in which lovemaking remains a subjective, passionate possibility, but not yet a social reality. The cost is a world in which killing one's lover, being killed by one's lover, is perhaps the only way to prove that one loves truly. Love is 'externalized' in this world through the lover's dead body. To fully weigh the cost, moreover, Shakespeare also needs to show Desdemona's experience of what happens to her. That is, Shakespeare needs to show us what Othello—and we—are *missing* if we accept the necessity of Desdemona's destruction, or if we accept her reduction to procreative being or subjugated woman. Put another way, Shakespeare must show us that Desdemona might have lived freely *not* just in virtue of being recognized or treasured by 'us' (or by Othello or the men in her life)—but because she herself is capable of realizing a free life, of being Othello's lover, of *earning* her freedom.

What freedom does Desdemona earn "in the feminine condition," to borrow Beauvoir's formulation?

So far as we perceive, Desdemona speaks only when addressing another. Shakespeare hears her only in dialogue. Not unlike Juliet, Desdemona was "bound" by duty to her father "for life and education" (1.3.181). What life she had, she owed to Brabantio and her family—in whose patriarchal bosom the independence of her desires had remained invisible. What was unthinkable to Brabantio was not a union between Othello and his daughter, but that his "quiet" daughter should be the one to want it.[171] Not, of course, because Othello was thought disagreeable, but because Desdemona was seen as obedient, sexually dominated by patriarchy. If Othello "won" Desdemona—thinks Brabantio— then it must have been "with some mixtures powerful o'er the blood, / Or with some dram, conjured to this effect, / He wrought upon her" (1.3.104–106).[172]

Of course, just as Juliet encountered Romeo at the Capulet masque, so, too, Desdemona came to know Othello within the family's routines without needing to relate to Othello as family. This offered Desdemona the chance to claim the independence of her desire before her father, without having to oppose him (1.3.173–96). Although circumstances required drastic actions from Juliet, all that Desdemona needed do in order to leave her family—as far as Brabantio and cosmopolitan Venice were concerned—was to indicate that she knew what she wanted.

> That I did love the Moor to live with him,
> My downright violence, and storm of fortunes
> May trumpet to the world. (1.3.243–45)

Once her desire came into view before all of Venice, Desdemona could no longer stay in her father's home (1.3.237–39). Not because Desdemona's desires were seen as illegitimate, but because the cloister of patriarchy could no longer offer a context in which these desires might flourish. Brabantio was not expressing bitterness at having been "deceived" by Desdemona when he told Othello—"Look to her, Moor, if thou hast eyes to see; / She has deceived her father, and may thee" (1.3.287–88). He was merely advising Othello to attend to Desdemona's independence. As I have been claiming, Othello tried to do precisely this.

Some suspect that Desdemona wanted to die all along, that she sought death at Othello's hands.[173] More often, she is seen as "helplessly passive" or as a psychological "type."[174] Yet Desdemona is an individual, hence in a concrete historical predicament; and as she prepares to go to bed with Othello, she articulates her sexual desires against Emilia's disproval. Othello has abused her publically. He has called her a 'whore' and has thrown money at her (4.2.92). And now he is demanding that she await him, alone.

"Am I that name . . . ?" "I am sure I am none such" (4.2.117, 122). Desdemona does not understand Othello's accusations; but she tries to understand his meaning. On the one hand, she cannot simply accept Othello's accusations, since she does not take herself to be a "whore."[175] His words and actions sting her because they are at odds with her self-conception; she cannot just *be* (or become) what he calls her. On the other hand, what Othello calls her, how he treats her, these things matter deeply to her. She is not immune to his gaze or accusations. She is not at all sure, then, either of herself or of Othello.[176]

In her exchange with Emilia, Desdemona weighs her own desires—and tries to arrive at *her* view of the meaning of sexual engagement with Othello. When she asks Emilia whether she—or "any such woman"—would "do such a deed for all the world," she is asking *for what reason* a woman has sex with men: For material gain? To satisfy an urge? For "sport"? Out of "frailty?" As part of a power struggle with one's partner—as a way of trying to control his behavior?

Each of these is named by Emilia (4.3.80–98), and if none of these 'reasons' satisfy Desdemona, then it is because she sees them all as institutionalized forms of what I have been calling sexual domination, gendered hierarchy. And she is trying to understand what her dissatisfaction with sexual domination says about *her*—what *she* or any woman in her position, under patriarchal conditions, might reasonably seek by craving a different form of sexual engagement with a powerful man. (*Why should I make love with Othello, rather than someone else? What satisfaction can lovemaking afford me—given the risks involved, given institutionalized sexual domination?*)

I am not suggesting that Desdemona (or that any of us) finally arrives at *the* final answer to these questions—only that Desdemona's dissatisfaction with the available answers spurs her onward: "Heaven me such uses send, / Not to pick bad from bad, but by bad mend" (4.3.106–8). Thus, having been commanded to await Othello in bed, Desdemona prepares herself. Not that she mechanically follows instructions. Desdemona wants to know whether she can make love with Othello, in this particular setting—given his rage and his abusive behavior; given Emilia's doubts; given her own excitement and misgivings; given the patriarchal institutions of sexual domination. Desdemona takes up these questions by undressing, by looking in the mirror. She is young and beautiful, and she knows it; she sees the evidence reflected in the mirror and feels it in her bones. The experience of her own body—of her anatomy, of the way her flesh betrays her excitement and desires, the way her voluptuousness signals her desirability—all this belongs to the sense she makes of herself and her conditions. "Shall I go fetch your nightgown?" asks Emilia. "No," answers Desdemona, "Unpin me here" (4.3.33).

In order to know whether she can make love—negate natural impulses and sexual domination—she will give Othello the right to make love to her, or to take her life. To have her own way, she will let him have his way with her. Is this freedom?

I hear one response in Giuseppe Verdi's arrangement—when the harsh, relentless strings of Othello's violence give way to Desdemona's voice, hanging in the air: *Nessuno . . . io stessa* (Nobody . . . I myself). Not even respiration is involuntary, if she can let it be stopped by another.

Verdi was right to hear the source of opera's "undoing of women" in Shakespeare's play—echoes of which had already begun to reverberate in Monteverdi's aria "Lasciatemi morire" (in *Ariana*, 1607–08), and which resound in every subsequent opera in which a woman "dies" at the hands of her lover. But if "on the opera stage women perpetually sing their own undoing," as Catherine Clément memorably put it, then this is not because opera stages the subjugation of women in a sequential plot or story.[177] Shakespeare and Verdi present not merely Desdemona's murder, but also the way Desdemona lives it out. The operatic voice [the *melo*] stages how the woman *feels* or experiences what is happening to her [the *drama*, or story]—it gives that subjective experience an objective, clamorous, undeniable reality.[178]

Desdemona's death is not experienced by her as sexual subjugation or obedience. She has given another the right to destroy her. Under the circumstances, it is the only action she can make sense of as her own.

How to Marry

[A]s I have often said, I cannot live without you; and I would divide, with all my
soul, my estate with you, to make you mine upon my own terms . . . how, then, with
the distance between us, in the world's judgment, can I think of making *you* my wife?

Samuel Richardson, *Pamela* (1740)

Just over a century after *Othello*, in arguably the most popular and influential book of the seventeenth century, we read the story of an aristocratic landowner and erstwhile libertine, Mr. B, who finds himself attracted to his servant girl, Pamela. Readers of Samuel Richardson's novel will recall that Mr. B also assaults Pamela, with the help of another servant woman; that Pamela grows desperate in her condition of subjugation; and that she later finds herself seduced by Mr. B, following his expressions of remorse at his treatment of her. They eventually marry.[179]

Told from Pamela's point of view, Richardson's epistolary novel drew upon the relaxing of legal strictures on nonmarital sex and, above all, on the growing influence of female viewpoints on men, on sexual subjugation, and on the pitfalls and promises of love—not only audible in operatic arias from Italy, but also legible in the steady stream of publications, 'conduct books' and dramas by groundbreaking English women writers in the generations following Shakespeare's death: Aphra Behn, Penelope Aubin, Delarivier Manley, Eliza Haywood, Elizabeth Rowe and many more.[180] Several features of these writings bear discussion here.

First, we are confronted with the rapacity of men.[181] In numerous first-personal accounts, told by women, we learn what enforced "seduction" (the term here, of course, is a euphemism for sexual subjugation) or entrapment into prostitution *feels* like.[182] In *Clarissa*, to mention only the most well-known example, Richardson draws upon such accounts to recount how Robert Lovelace ("a man of birth and fortune") preys upon Clarissa Harlowe: he lies to her, imprisons her in London, tricks her into entering a brothel, drugs her, rapes her. Beyond Richardson's novels and Defoe's *Moll Flanders* and beyond England, first-personal experiences of men's rapacity and women's ruin also had immense cultural impact, as is evidenced in subsequent works by Rousseau, Diderot, Laclos, Goethe, Kleist, Pushkin, Sade and others.[183] This history is well-documented. The point I wish to make here is that these first-personal accounts laid bare, undeniably and for the first time, the inner practical workings of what I have been calling institutions of sexual domination and gender-based hierarchies: what it feels like to be sexually subjugated, or reduced to a bearer of children.[184] These voices attune us, in the starkest tones, to the way that gender-based hierarchies were sustained, not merely through physical force, nor through tricks and schemes, nor through the exercise of social or political or economic prerogatives—but precisely through sexual domination, the use of another's body, the limiting of another's sexual agency through the exercise of one's own. If other forms of coercion—physical, economic, social, intellectual (that is, efforts to outwit)—were brought to bear by men like Mr. B and Lovelace, then they were brought to bear in order to achieve and demonstrate sexual domination, by reifying a gender-based hierarchy.

Familiar accounts of this period often claim something like the inverse, of course—namely, that sexual domination (rape, enforced prostitution, 'ruinous' subjugation, marriage contracts that subordinate women to men) were essentially a physical *means* for achieving or sustaining or confirming some other form of social power: patriarchal, economic, political.[185] It is true that socially entitled men could often 'have their way' with poorer women like Pamela, in part because they possessed the means (economic, physical, material) to facilitate taking advantage of them, sexually.[186] But we should hesitate before conceding that male privilege is, on its own, the *explanation* for sexual domination. We should, that is to say, not be too quick to share the view of Mrs. Jewkes, the servant woman who helps Mr. B pin Pamela to the bed: "Are not the two sexes made for one another?" she says, "And is it not natural for a gentleman to love a pretty woman? And suppose he can obtain his desires, is that so bad?" (111).[187] The view that men rape women or force them into prostitution in order to demonstrate and maintain social, economic or physical standing can hardly make intelligible the sheer scope of the rapacity under examination here, much less the breadth of the suffering being recorded. To say that patriarchal power structures are partly upheld (as they no doubt are) through ritualized acts of sexual terror—gang rape, enforced prostitution, 'secret initiations,' genital mutilation—is not the same as concluding that such power structures (or for that matter, instinctual-evolutionary forces) fully explain these actions. Unless, of course, we want to take Mrs. Jewkes' word as final. I, for one, do not.[188]

And the question being forced is, *Why* the rapacity? Was it really necessary? Is it still necessary? How are we to explain it?

Another familiar answer to these questions, versions of which have linked Marxist critique to feminism since the mid-nineteenth century, is that socio-economic and political interests, and changing modes of production, explain the sexual domination of women—prostitution, domestic servitude and the articulation of a gender-based hierarchy such as patriarchy or the bourgeois family.[189] However, if sexual domination is fully explained by economic necessity, by *homo economicus*, or by the power dynamics of social and class-based interests—rather than just 'made possible by' ongoing economic or social or physical hierarchies—then we ought to be able to fully account for this. That is, we ought to be able to explain why the domination *must* be carried out sexually (not just economically, or politically, or socially). And we ought to be able to explain why "women are (sexually) oppressed in societies which can by no stretch of the imagination be described as capitalist"—why, in New Guinea, women are said to be "tamed with the banana."[190] As I have discussed at several points, I know of no such *convincing* account.

In my discussion earlier, I tried to provide a transcendental genesis for sexual domination by arguing that, at a certain stage of human history, the agency of some had to be realized through the use of others' bodies, in the circumscription of others' sexual agency, in their sexual ruination. Institutionalized sexual domination is, however awful, a practice through which some human beings have realized a provisional agency, and made sense of their lives and their world, one that can be critiqued and overcome only when that sense-making *fails*. If sexual acts are merely taken to express and articulate some other non-sexual physical or social authority—economic interests, political clout, social prerogatives, physical strength or natural impulses—then we would have been left with no way to explain ourselves as *acting* self-expressively, as doing anything sexually other than expressing or embodying social or physical forces that course 'through' us. Lovelace, Mr. B, Pamela, Clarissa and the rest of us would not be human agents—we would not be leading lives for which we are answerable, or on which we could meaningfully report; we would be merely bearers of impersonal forces working behind our backs. This kind of indeterminacy, I argued, turns out to be *practically* unintelligible. That is, it turns out to be extremely difficult to *experience* or 'live out,' sexually, the indeterminacy of economic or social forces that are purportedly coursing through one's body. *We* (or some of our ancestors) committed acts of sexual domination, and those who have carried out those acts understood themselves as agents in the world by doing so.

And, I now want to add, it becomes downright impossible to accept notions of such indeterminacy when one hears, first-personally, what a young woman (often of low social standing) *feels* as she is raped, sold, or subjugated. For, if *she* can express what it feels like—what her life and fate amount to, in her own eyes—then her 'subjectivity' is not illusory. She is not just waiting around to see how she will react once market interests or male privilege or evolutionary-natural-social forces start to take over her life (in the shape of a man named Lovelace, say). Rather, she is *reporting*, after the fact, that she cannot make any sense of her life whatsoever unless she can see herself—her first-personal stance on the world, and any sense she can make of *that*—as having been violated at the hands of particular human beings, with names and faces. To conclude that Lovelace *must* 'have his way' with Clarissa, lest an entire social order collapse or be rendered unintelligible, requires that we *not listen* to Clarissa—that we not take seriously her 'subjective' viewpoint on Lovelace's actions.

So, to pick up my argument, sexual domination is only explicable as a set of particular acts performed by particular agents—it means the enacted use of another's body, the sexual articulation of active and subjugated beings, such that a connection between agent and 'act' comes into view through the circumscription of another's agency. Sexual domination should be understood as one, awful moment in the achievement of human freedom—one that, I am arguing, *can only be overcome or subjected to critique from a historical standpoint in which lovemaking has been achieved, subjectively and objectively.* We are still working out, historically, what that achievement implies and requires—as I will go on to argue in the remaining pages of this book, while also providing a sense of how crucial the modern novel, as an art form, has been to its realization.

I realize that this is a highly counterintuitive claim, and that it will seem outlandish to many. At this point in my argument, however, I want to emphasize again that social, gender-based hierarchies and institutions (like patriarchal prerogative) are sustained and instituted by sexual domination. Not the other way around. The economic, social, gender-based, physical hierarchies that make sexual domination manifest and real are not explanations *for* sexual domination: they can be explained *by* sexual domination once sexual domination comes into view as only a (necessary) stage in the achievement of love as human freedom.

The first-personal *experiences* of rapacity and sexual domination that were finally being heard and read by the turn of the eighteenth century—and which have only been amplified around the world in the years since—bring sexual domination into view, in precisely this way. For these voices made it impossible to explain away acts of sexual domination as 'justified' by obligations adherent to existing social structures. Put bluntly, nothing that English society could intelligibly be said to require for its proper functioning was detectable in the extreme lengths to which Lovelace and others go in order to 'undo' their victims. As *Clarissa*, for example, makes clear, sexual domination is to be achieved not only in the physical contact itself, but in the social 'ruin' of the woman. Moreover, as anyone who has made his or her way through the pages of Richardson's novels knows, the questions that repeatedly issue from Clarissa or Pamela are *Why? Why is he pursuing me? Why me?*

If such questions increase in volume and intensity, then it must because the answer is no longer intelligible *at the practical level*. The libertine's pursuit is indeed one of sexual domination, in all the ways that I have been arguing—a necessary institutional moment in the sexual achievement of human freedom. *But* something of libertinism's routineness, or cultural normalcy, is here being disrupted and registered as such. Not only because we hear, finally, from the subjugated, but *also* because the libertine's pursuit appears perversely single-minded, given the intensity with which Lovelace pursues Clarissa, and with which Mr. B pursues Pamela. ("By my soul," says Lovelace, "I can neither eat, drink, nor sleep; nor, what's still worse, love any woman in the world but her."[191]) We seem to have reached a moment at which rapacity and sexual domination entail, at the practical level, not just ritual forms of violation but a single-minded domineering pursuit and an intense presentation of what it feels like to be subjugated.[192] But why? Indeed, the depiction of the victim's point of view and the pursuer's single-mindedness are connected by the questions they raise: Why the rapacious pursuit of *these women*? Why do these men dedicate so much thought, time, energy and resources to their singular pursuit of *them*?

Richardson's novels—and the period's dominant discourse—suggest that the answer somehow lies in the women's "virtue." But what is meant by that?[193]

Mr. B's pursuit of Pamela leads to an attempted rape: the point at which his sexual domination of Pamela is to be realized in his use of her body. And what he finds, as a matter of practical fact, when he finally pins Pamela down and puts his hands and mouth on her, and declares her to be in his "power" is that she screams: No!

> I screamed out in such a manner, as never anybody heard the like. But there was nobody to help me: and both my hands were secured, as I said. Sure never poor soul was in such agonies as I. . . . O God! my God! this time! this one time! deliver me from this distress! or strike me dead this moment! And then I screamed again and again. (213)

Pamela's scream is her virtue. It is *her* felt experience of sexual domination, her resistance to being used in this way, her inability to alienate herself from what is happening to her. When Clarissa says, "I know not my own heart, if it not be absolutely free" (90), she is crying out the same thing.

As everyone remembers, Mr. B takes his hands off Pamela. Indeed, he later apologizes. Of course, Pamela's scream, on its own, need not have compelled Mr. B to stop. His rape of her could have continued, unheeding. Pamela was neither the first nor the last to scream in horror at what was happening to her. (Is not this the *first* thing that Richardson wants us to remember?) Likewise, it seems reasonable to think that Mr. B was not the first man to give up his pursuit—for whatever reason (pity, fondness, loss of stomach). Richardson's fiercest critics—Henry Fielding first among them—may have found it unrealistic to think that an individual like Mr. B would, or should, have stopped. However, the point, which Fielding missed, is not whether a particular person's actions are plausible or reasonable or defensible in circumstances such those as depicted by Richardson.[194] The question, I want to say, is unavoidably moral: not just for this character or individual, but for an entire way of life. Richardson, I think, is asking his readers—his *legions* of readers, cultivated by stories of women's ruin—whether *they* think Mr. B *ought* to stop.[195] And if so, then what would stopping require and entail?[196] Richardson, I think, is not just depicting the intimate lives of these people. He is presenting the genuine normative dilemma of his time. Are we *listening* to these women, or not?

Now, I want to claim further, *if* that dilemma is heard as a genuine moral dilemma—independent of the responses of particular men (some may heed the screams, some may plunge ahead)—then the practice of sexual domination has entered a crisis of legitimacy, and will start to seem *unnecessary* for the realization of human agency. Moreover, the institutional-objective way of life that makes sexual domination 'real' and 'legitimate' will start to look unnecessary, intelligible only as having once been necessary. Let me try to explain further, since this is a crucial turning point in my account.

Consider, again, Mr. B's predicament. *If* he hears Pamela's objection (her scream, her "virtue") then he is faced with a choice as an individual agent: proceed anyway, or stop—where 'proceeding anyway' tumbles into the kind of pathologically obsessive libertinism embodied by Lovelace. The immediate problem, however, is that *either* choice still leaves Pamela fully in his power. Having 'mercy' on her, so to speak, does not mean that she is not subjugated; it only underscores the extent to which she remains in his power, at his mercy. She may have been spared "from distress" "this time! this one time!" as she begs, but the fundamental institutions that make her subjugation *real* have not been altered. And if her subjugation remains real and institutional, then in what sense can her objection have been heard?

Mr. B—like the readers of Richardson's novel—thus finds himself in the position of the audience members at the end of Shakespeare's *Othello* or Verdi's *Otello*. That is, they can *hear* Desdemona's claim to sexual agency, to desires of her own, if they listen attentively. And they can also hear her risking of life and limb, the bodily danger in which she places herself in order to make her sexual agency known. If they listen, then they can hear her claim to independence and sexual agency. But the question—as it was for Othello and as discussed above—is, how can this claim for independence be *real*?

If Mr. B is unsettled by his attempted rape of Pamela—and, I take it, he is profoundly unsettled—then this because he is struggling to find a way to *make sense* of Pamela's resistance, to understand what 'reality' it could have for him, what claim it could possibly make on him, besides tugging at his heartstrings or begging for his mercy. After all, if her claim is *merely* a means for him (or for us) to 'decide' whether he is a cad or a decent fellow, then her claim itself has no reality—she is just prop in a morality play of which he is the hero. If she is to be perceived as real, if her resistance to sexual domination is to have any genuine standing in the world, then her resistance to sexual domination must have *institutional, social* reality. Her freedom must be made socially legible, lest she remain unfree.

This is, of course, the question that generates the remaining plot of Richardson's novel. *How* can her freedom be made socially legible? After all, is Pamela not socially inferior? Is she not poor, young, a woman, a servant? Obstacles exist, obviously, but they are not insurmountable. "Consider the pride of my condition," reflects Mr. B, "how, then, with the distance between us, in the world's judgment, can I think of making *you* my wife? Yet I must have you" (251). His proposal of marriage is not merely due—as the secondary literature so often concludes—to some 'inner' change of heart. Rather, he can undergo no meaningful change of heart, and she can have no *real* virtue (beyond screaming) unless they can actively marry as equals—unless *she* accepts his proposal, unless her reciprocal commitment is authoritative for him.[197] This is not just a matter of what they work out 'between them'—although the commitment has no force, no reality, unless *they* also 'work it out' (unless, therefore, the aborted assault comes to be seen by them, in retrospect, as an essential part of that working out). It is *also* a matter of making their reciprocal commitment normatively authoritative for the social-institutional world in which they live. *Others* must not only accept their marriage, but also organize their own lives and values accordingly. Readers of the novel will recall that this is precisely the direction the story takes. Students of history will know, more to the point, that the eighteenth century witnessed the vast expansion of what we now call 'love-based' marriage.

With this, we can finally start to turn to the emergent social authority of sexual love, and the beginning of the erosion of the authority of sexual domination and sexual reproduction.

The State of Being in Love

Among peoples who hold the female sex in scant respect, marriages are arranged by the parents at will without consulting the young people. The latter raise no objection, since at that level of culture the particularity of feeling makes no claims for itself. For the woman it is only a matter of getting a husband, for the man, of getting a wife. In other social conditions, considerations of wealth, connections, political ends, may be the determining factor. In such circumstances, great hardships may arise through making marriage a means to other ends. Nowadays, however, the subjective origin of marriage, the state of being in love, is regarded as the only important originating factor.

Hegel, *Elements of the Philosophy of Right* (1821)

We are now in a position to turn to an account of issues raised in the Prologue, which pivots us toward our own historical moment.

I have been arguing that sexual domination cannot be explained by impersonal economic, natural or patriarchal forces. On the contrary, once we grasp the transcendental genesis of sexual domination, along with the normative authority of sexual reproduction, I propose that we can explain the trajectory of gender-based social hierarchies, including the fate of a gender-based division of labor. Sexual domination and sexual reproduction, I have been saying, are *also* ways our ancestors have made sense of human lives and the conditions of human existence: they are not arbitrary norms or power-formations, but fundamental ways in which we make sense of the world as we encounter it. Sexual domination and sexual reproduction *lose* institutional authority, then, by failing to explain the world as we apprehend it. If my reflections so far are accurate, then we have arrived at a moment when the world as we perceive it—Pamela's scream, Desdemona's last breath—cannot be made intelligible within the explanatory framework offered by sexual reproduction and sexual domination. And before that, lovemaking itself—as a passionate, subjective possibility—was starting to threaten the explanatory power of both sexual reproduction and sexual domination; lovers run up against the practical unintelligibility of both just by making love.

With love-based marriages and partnerships, this crisis in the authority of sexual domination and sexual reproduction becomes institutionally real—not just subjectively felt or passionately lived. Hegel was among the first to see this, and to try to grasp its significance.[198] For Hegel, 'love-based marriage' and the emerging bourgeois, nuclear 'family' are primary ways that the challenges of mutuality and reciprocal recognition are taken up. More importantly, the existence of these institutions teaches us that these challenges *can* be taken up in our revisable ways of life. The demands of mutuality are not bounded by the limits of nature or divine fate, but by the latitude we grant ourselves in our fundamental social practices.

Before we go further, it is important to see what Hegel meant by "love." In one sense, there is something apparently contingent (hence, possibly irrational) about the feeling of being in love: namely, what Hegel calls "the particular inclination" of the people who enter into the relationship, or the contingency of the circumstances through which they came to know one another.[199] Two centuries ago, Hegel could still speak quaintly of the "foresight and initiative of parents, etc." as one such contingency,[200] though nowadays we might think of singles bars or 'hook-up apps' on smartphones. Goethe published *Elective Affinities* in 1809; Schlegel's *Lucinde* had appeared ten years before that; Montaigne had penned *Parce que c'était lui, parce que c'était moi* (Because it was he, because it was I) long before. Hegel, however, is critical of attempts to present love as indifferent to history—as a matter of chemistry, attraction, or happenstance.[201] So, Hegel further suggests that this "feeling" itself has a historical (hence, rational) character. "Love," he writes, "means in general the consciousness of my unity with another, so that I am not isolated on my own [*für mich*], but gain my self-consciousness only through the renunciation of my independent existence [*meines Fürsichseins*] and through knowing myself as the unity of myself with another and of the other in me."[202] This is, I think, one way of expressing something that I have been suggesting throughout: the *feeling* of sexual love is the practical unintelligibility of interacting with another on the basis of ostensibly natural demands (sexual reproduction, appetite) or institutional hierarchies (sexual domination). To put it another way, lovemaking is a historical achievement because it requires the failure of sexual reproduction and sexual domination in order to 'make sense' of the deepest threats to sense.

In a sense, Hegel seems to anticipate the title of this book when he elsewhere defines freedom in these same terms: "For freedom is this, to be with oneself in the other."[203] I say *seems* to anticipate, because I need to say a bit more about how I think we should read these statements of Hegel, and also about where I want to situate these statements in the present overall account of love and freedom.

First, by speaking of a "unity of myself with another and of the other in me"—Hegel is not (nor am I) offering a *definition* of love or freedom, if by 'definition' we mean an account that aims to transcend the historical moment in which one fixes it.[204] Hegel's aim is to apprehend his own time in thought, as he himself says in the Preface to the *Elements of the Philosophy of Right*. Far from defining love, this "unity" names a form of self-awareness that is historically realized *in love* as a matter of ongoing experience and practice. Again, Hegel seems to think that that we might get better at meeting the challenges of mutual reciprocity, and that we take a giant step in that direction just by seeing that we *do* meet those demands in our institutional way of life, over which we have a large measure of control.

The "feeling" of love as mutual recognition—or independence within dependence, "the consciousness of my unity with another"—is not an ahistorical feature or ambition of human life. Lovemaking, I have been arguing, is a practical *response* to the inability to grasp what we do with one another, sexually, in terms of either sexual reproduction or sexual domination. Love is, moreover, an open-ended historical achievement, a result of our human efforts to make sense of our lives and world. And just as the consciousness of being "with oneself in the other" is one of lovemaking's results, so too in lovemaking the challenges of mutuality and reciprocal recognition are unavoidably tackled. With regard to love, therefore, I would prefer to be even more explicit than Hegel, and say that this consciousness of mutuality (Hegel's "unity") was realized over time in lovemaking, out of the practical unintelligibility of sexual domination and sexual reproduction. If consciousness of this "unity" (or, at least, of the potential for achieving it) is *not* achieved in lovemaking, as a matter of historical practice in all the ways I have been suggesting, then I fail to see *how*, as Hegel claims, consciousness of mutuality is realized as sexual-romantic 'love' at all.

Elements of the Philosophy of Right is Hegel's attempt to show how the challenges of mutuality and recognition generally, including love specifically, can now be seen as concretely historical-institutional problems. Thus, Hegel thought, these challenges could be grasped only by making sense of the practical domains that characterized the sociality of his day: family, state, civil society. Hegel's account is particularly interesting because it connects this account of love and family to the fate and structure of explicitly political institutions. In order to pursue my own account of love and freedom, and to bring us closer to issues that resonate with contemporary society, let me borrow a bit from Hegel's discussion.

On the one hand, as noted earlier, Hegel sees "love" or mutual recognition or being "with oneself in the other" as a subjective achievement: I compared his account of the life-and-death battle to (my own account of) lovemaking as the reciprocal acknowledgment of two independent beings. On the other hand, everything I have been saying *since* that discussion has led us to see "mutual recognition" and love as concrete historical problems requiring institutional elaboration. (This was Mr. B's lesson.) The point is not *just* that love had to become 'institutional' in order to become objectively real—as if propelled by some inner, divine force. Rather, lovemaking was *practically* unintelligible *unless* we turned, with heightened self-awareness, to the status and implications of our concrete, institutional forms of life. Lovemaking could only *become* a subjective achievement by being objectively achieved in an institutional form of life. Remember: this is why the poets recounting the tales of Tristan and Iseult or Parsifal could grasp lovemaking only in 'magical' or mystical or deadly terms.

And once we 'turned' toward institutional forms of life—for the sake of shorthand, let me say, in Northern European societies in the years separating Shakespeare's lifetime from Hegel's—we could not but see that many of our practices began to look *unnecessarily* domineering. In the sociopolitical arena, we could no longer grasp why we *had* to subject one another to slavemasters or libertines or kings or God's will, above all in light of the suffering such subjection engendered, in order to make our lives and world intelligible. Hence the way in which Hegel's *Philosophy of Right* responds directly to colonialism, the French Revolution, the Terror, and Napoleon's campaigns.

Conversely, something of that subjective suffering—individual woe and weal, desire and frustration, trauma and triumph—now seemed not only redressable, but also intelligible, only in historical-institutional terms. Individuals had to be acknowledged as historical and institutional creatures, precisely in their subjective dimension.[205] Being "with oneself in the other" is Hegel's way of characterizing that acknowledgment: the different institutional domains of state, civil society and family are ongoing practical arenas in which we try to figure out what living it out requires. These are, put differently, objective domains in which we try to address social problems of mutuality and recognition—*but they are more especially ways we try to make sense of what the challenges of mutuality are.*[206] We take up challenges of social reciprocity (of social welfare and income inequality, of gender inequality, of racial inequality) not just because we already 'know' what challenges need tackling, in other words, but also because by responding practically we identify and make further sense of the challenges themselves. For example, this is why Hegel sees the modern, secular "state" as requiring what he calls separate "moments of rational constitution" (legislative power, executive power, sovereign power) to deal with manifestly political challenges of mutuality and recognition—such as poverty or public misery. At any rate, the first point to be emphasized here is that challenges of reciprocal recognition can finally be seen to be concretely historical-institutional problems. That is the first issue that Hegel helps me to get on the table.

Second, from Hegel's historical-philosophical standpoint or from the standpoint of what he elsewhere calls "Absolute Knowing"—no features of our social existence can intelligibly be said to have been set out in advance, by nature or God. All fundamental features of our sociality, insofar as we apprehend them and can make any sense of them, can now be seen as resulting from things *we* have done, from practical ways we organize our lives and have made sense of the world—from "poetic wisdom," as the philosopher Giambattista Vico called it.

To translate this into the terms of my discussion earlier, *we* can now see—though our ancestors (including Hegel) mostly could not—that sexual difference is not just a fact of nature, handed down by God, but also a way that we once perceptually grasped reproduction and fruitfulness in light of the practices that we then had available: most fundamentally, through sex acts—as discussed above at the beginning of Part III. We now know, too, that sexual difference is not *the* way to explain or understand reproduction and fruitfulness. At the same time, we know that, not just because we later discovered facts of nature that had lain hidden, but because we also achieved through our practices (scientific, sexual, social) a standpoint from which reproduction might be *otherwise* achieved and explained. Not only that, but we also learned along the way that we establish powerful norms that govern our activities—like sexual reproduction—on the basis of their explanatory force; and we learned that we *treat each other* in certain ways, we interact in certain ways, on the basis of those norms and their explanatory force. Lastly, we have learned that no set of norms can definitively declare themselves 'explanatory' once and for all. No set of social norms can be definitively satisfying—or explain every threat to sense, satisfy every demand for recognition, alleviate every conceivable suffering. But we can probably get better at grasping the challenges inherent in mutual recognition in our interactions. We can see, too, that our primary institutions help us *do* this—at least, at this historical moment. Seeing just this much can prevent us from throwing our hands up in despair at never quite getting it right (never fully achieving social justice or a classless society, never making our relationships hum along as we want them to).

Plundering from Hegel, my suggestion is that we see love-based marriage as a self-correcting practice of this kind.[207] As I suggested in the Prologue, I do not even think we are helped by limiting ourselves to the terms of 'marriage'—we can and do, after all, alter our nomenclature when we speak of 'companionship,' 'partnership,' 'commitments,' 'affairs.' So, I think we should borrow from Hegel to suggest that love-based marriage is *one* way—not *the* way—that the demands of mutual recognition, such as those that arise in love and lovemaking (including when offspring result), might be better met by being better understood.[208] Bourgeois marriage is not *the* way to meet and understand the challenges of reciprocity, we are entitled to say, for the simple reason that bourgeois marriage itself has proven to be far from stable—both within the life of any individual couple, and within the broader life of a society. Love and lovemaking address and raise *challenges*—threats to sense—that bourgeois, love-based marriages cannot resolve or even clarify. Love and freedom do not come to rest, subjectively or objectively, in bourgeois marriages or in nuclear families. *But*, bourgeois marriage and family life is one, unavoidable way that we have learned that lesson.

Even Mr. B saw love-based commitment (marriage) as unavoidable, historically and rationally, in precisely this way—albeit from his own personal standpoint. He saw that, unless property and assets were shared with Pamela, unless certain institutional commitments were made, unless certain institutional practices developed in ways that accommodated such commitments, he could make no sense of his interactions with her, or of her interactions with him.

Hegel, too, thought that "the family's resources" were a primary and unavoidable institutionalization of love. Although he does not develop the insight, I understand Hegel to be putting his finger on something of immense significance in his discussion of family property. Namely, the acquisition and alienation of material goods and resources *itself* starts to raise and respond to new challenges of reciprocity in love-based relations.[209] No longer is the need for possession explained just by natural need or material want; nor by kinship and lineage inheritances; nor by state-sanctioned 'rights' to acquire or alienate goods (whether individual or collective); nor by the marketplace. Not because these explanations are flat wrong, but because they start to look highly incomplete as soon as the sharing of wealth between *living* loved ones becomes a fundamental way that the love-relation 'knows itself' to be actual *as loving*. The possession of resources no longer merely expresses (makes sense of) material need, class distinctions, exchange value or social legitimacy alone; shared wealth also gives love objective standing in the world. Without a pooling of resources based on love, the love itself loses reality. Which is also to say that a pooling of resources is, objectively, an act of love. The implication, in short, is that the family or love-relation is not just a financial corporation whose practices are fully governed by natural need, the laws of inheritance, marketplace necessity, transferences of legitimacy and social power; instead, *the 'free love-relation' starts to seem like an authority on which a fundamental instrument of social power—property and material wealth—depends for its distinctly modern 'value.'* This strikes me as an extremely important point for further reflection. Its implications have, I think, not yet been adequately addressed in the tradition that follows Marx's and Engels' responses to Hegel. I have suggested, in another context, that Shakespeare's *King Lear* is a harbinger of this seismic shift in the practical bonds between family love and property, since in that play "loving and being loved are the condition for any worldly rights and entitlements, not the reverse."[210] But I cannot pursue the implications further in this context.

In the same breath, Hegel moves from brief remarks on property to a discussion of "the upbringing of children and the dissolution of the family."[211] At this point, Hegel makes another startling and original observation—one which, so far as I know, had never before been made so explicitly, although it was implicit in earlier reflections.[212] Hegel suggests that children actualize the "unity" of love-based relationships. Let me cite the passage, since it will allow us to crystallize a number of points:

> The relation of love between man and wife is not yet an objective one; for even if this feeling [*Empfindung*] is their substantial unity, this unity does not yet possess objectivity [*Gegenständlichkeit*]. The parents attain this unity *only in their children*, in whom they see the whole of their union before them. In the child . . . they see their love before them.[213]

I do not understand Hegel to mean that, as an ahistorical matter of principle, lovers must become parents lest their relationship fail to "attain unity"—as if the "unity" of the childbearing, or child-loving couple were a timeless ideal toward which all families should strive. Rather, I understand Hegel to be suggesting to us that the loving upbringing of children becomes, at this historical moment, *necessary* if the demands of reciprocity and mutual recognition are to be objectively, institutionally lived in love-based relations. Unless children can be *loved* as the objective result of 'free' love-relations, the challenges of mutual recognition to which the history of love has brought us cannot begin to be addressed, much less met.

Allow me, then, one last remark on Hegel's presentation of what I am tempted to call 'love-based children.'

Calling children "objective" is the German philosopher's way of saying that children are real, independently existing. They have a 'life of their own'; they are not *just* the objective form of (the parents') unity—as is obvious, since children can outlive their parents, or die before them.[214] Less obviously, Hegel is pointing out that children must be *recognized* as independent, separate existences, if they are to be loved.[215] Less obviously still, the child is the objective form of the parents' love *only* if the parents love the child more than the child loves them.[216]

In what sense 'more'? The point is this: parents 'love' their child by regarding the child as *theirs* in a practical sense not adequately captured or explained by seeing the child as a bearer of their name, their social legitimacy, or their material inheritance—and utterly opposed to the notion that children are 'possessions,' slaves or domestic laborers.[217] On the one hand, then, "love" for Hegel here means what he elsewhere calls "the natural depth of feeling" character-istic of representations of Mary's love, as depicted in Christian painting, for instance.[218] On the other hand, if the child is to be loved as the objective exis-tence of the parents' love, then loving treatment of the child is necessary but not enough. Certain institutional commitments must be also made: minimally, children must be protected from exploitation, they must "be brought up and supported at the expense of the family," and receive an education, or *Bildung*, which addresses the challenges of mutual recognition that inhere in the child's own expanding freedom.[219] This is not a prescriptive list of what will *always* be required, nor can we say that this is *all* that will ever be required. Instead, Hegel is diagnosing some of what *his* society required. And he is suggesting something that is now patently clear—namely, that the upbringing of children has become a practice through which the challenges of mutual recognition, in the society at large, must be taken up.

Educating and raising children can no longer be a matter of 'following tra-dition,' but must become an open-ended normative engagement with whatever social transformations we deem necessary in order to love our children (safety laws, nutritional codes, sexual mores, material welfare, architectural modifica-tions, vaccinations, school regulations and so on). If we have no broad agree-ment on a lot of these issues, then this too is one sign that the demand to which Hegel is pointing—love-based children as the freedom of sexual love—is ir-reducibly historical and normative and, hence, not a simple one to meet, insti-tutionally. We are still improvising. And here we make good, too, on an insight already nascent in Adam and Eve—namely, that the future of the human spe-cies is in our hands, not God's.

There is, obviously, plenty more to be said about all of this, but the point I want to underscore is the insight that parents' love of their children—hence, the freedom of their own love-relation—is not achievable, not practicable, un-less certain institutional conditions are also fulfilled: parents must be *able* to materially support their child, and to provide for the child's education and so-cial formation; social regulations must protect the child against exploitation. Again, these are obviously concrete welfare issues with which contemporary societies are still grappling. But this just means that society as a whole must change, prove itself capable of institutional and legal 'improvements'—if we are to be able to love our children, or to see our own love in the world. We might even say that our institutions for child welfare and education just *are* objective manifestations, not only of whether we love our children, but of whether we love each other. The importance of these welfare institutions is measured by the depth of our loving bonds, not the other way around.

Imminent institutional critique of social conditions is essential to the intelligibility of love-affairs *tout court*, hence the tension between lovers and society in love stories.

This brings us to a counterintuitive set of conclusions.

By raising these issues, I am trying to fulfill my promise to offer a novel understanding of immense social-historical transformations—ranging from important educational reforms, in which Hegel himself took part and which have continued since, to the introduction of child labor laws, child welfare laws, transformations in kinship formations, new notions of parental sovereignty, birth control laws and so on. These transformations are *not* just expressions of impersonal economic necessity (the need of capitalist societies to produce more skilled laborers, say), nor can they be merely the expression of sociopolitical power-formations (since societies and political regimes can clearly go on 'functioning' even without broad access to education or healthcare), much less are they the results of moral insights (like the belief that all men are created equal) or natural instincts.[220] Instead, these large-scale institutional transformations are required, historically, if parents are *to be able* to love their children and each other. Again, it is not that these institutional conditions are required according to universal, timeless maxims or laws of nature or capital, but that they are historically necessary ways of bringing institutional reality in line with the threats to sense that love brings to light.

A great many modern institutions—schools, heath insurance for children, vaccinations, custody laws, adoption—belong to realization of sexual love in the world today. Immense, epochal social transformations are required in order for lovemaking to be *intelligibly practiced*—for sexual love, that is, to have both subjective (felt) and objective (institutional) reality. *Explaining* those social transformations, then, means taking account of everything love itself has helped us make sense *of*.

Remember: to *fail* to make lovemaking intelligible, as a practice, has repercussions for the sense we make of everything else that I have been tracking since my discussion of Genesis at the beginning of this section: bodily change, temporal transformations in individuals, reproduction, the provisional achievement of human agency through the domination of another, mutual recognition of independent desire (lovemaking), love-based marriage, the changing significance attached to the having of children, and—I will now go on to argue—the erosion of a gender-based division of labor; the world-historical significance of contraception and abortion and of reproductive technologies; increasing acceptance of same-sex kinship; the emergence of feminism and the women's movement. Indeed, lovemaking and love-based marriages determinately negate sexual domination, in ways that parallel and can help explain challenges to other forms of social domination over the past four centuries (political and economic domination and even slavery)—however tenuous and fragile our achievements remain.

It may seem outlandish to propose that love and lovemaking are fundamental practices in view of which all of these immense, world-changing transformations can be (at least in part) explained over such a large swath of human history—*and* to say that love is a practice with which we continue to work through the challenges of reciprocity and try to make sense of the threats to sense that historical changes throw our way.

But that is precisely what I am proposing.

Refuting Sexual Reproduction

[S]he did not enjoy those preparations that stimulate the tenderness of mothers, and her affection, from the beginning, was perhaps somewhat attenuated. . . .

"It is a girl!" said Charles.

[Emma] turned her head away and fainted.

Gustav Flaubert, *Madame Bovary* (1856)

Some readers may object that, in helping myself to aspects of Hegel's discussion, I am overlooking Hegel's misogyny, or things that Hegel himself had to say about sex or lovemaking. Indeed, Hegel says a number of things, about sex and women especially, that are very much at odds with core aspects of my account thus far.[221] However, because I take Hegel's insight into the significance of love-based children so seriously—indeed, because I think that we cannot explain many of our contemporary social commitments, or immensely important social transformations, unless we grasp this significance—I do want to offer one specific response to Hegel's discussion of sexual love in the *Philosophy of Right*.

In order for anyone to raise love-based children, in this robust Hegelian sense—children who are affectively loved, but also objectively 'cared for' (educated as individuals, fed, treated as free)—then there is another institutional requirement, which Hegel did not recognize but which I see as crucial: lovers must be able to distinguish *their own* lovemaking from the natural process of sexual reproduction. Acts of mutual recognition must be able to see themselves as—know that they are—not reducible to impersonal, biological demands. Hegel could not see this, I think, because he viewed sexual reproduction as a natural process, not a social authority.[222] But we are now in a position to conclude, at long last, that lovemaking must be intelligibly freed from the institutional authority of sexual reproduction.

Recall, I went out of my way in earlier sections of this book to argue that sexual reproduction is socially authoritative, not a natural fact. I did this because we cannot make any sense of love as a historical practice, or of lovemaking as a historical achievement, unless we take full measure of the social-historical authority of sexual reproduction: the extent to which that particular explanation of fruitfulness and multiplicity has determined and governed our interactions, our ways of recognizing one another.

So, at this point, we should remember that lovemaking has not yet *objectively* or institutionally negated the normative authority of sexual reproduction. Yes, I said, Tristan and Iseult found ways to abstain at certain times of the month, by placing the sword between them, and thereby made the difference between lovemaking and sexual reproduction belong to their own erotic practices. But these earlier lovers were not yet able to see their subjectively felt love as real, livable, practicable in the world among others, for reasons already discussed. Likewise, it is of course true that same-sex lovers (or male and female lovers who know themselves to be infertile) can dispense with the authority of sexual reproduction when it comes to their own, subjectively experienced love-affairs. And under the normative authority of sexual reproduction, same-sex lovemaking and other sexual interactions can be objectively grasped by virtue of their difference from potentially procreative sex, as we saw in the discussion of Plato and Greek pederasty. However, so long as the having of children *requires* sexual reproduction—hence, so long as our fundamental social institutions must reckon with reproduction as resulting from acts regulated as sexual—lovemaking cannot be free from the authority of sexual reproduction. Not only does love between men and women lack the worldly, institutional conditions to see itself as free, but so do *all* love-affairs.

The challenges are—at this point—institutional as well as subjective. Unless lovemaking can *institutionalize* a "determinate negation" of the normative authority of sexual reproduction, we cannot love our children as ours, in the sense just discussed. If the social welcoming of children is tied to sexual reproduction—and where sexual reproduction is taken to be an immutable natural process (a 'stork' over whose arrival human ways of loving one another have no control)—then no child can be intelligibly seen, socially and objectively, to come of the lovers' mutual recognition. Indeed, the child appears, finally, as the gift or curse of fate, or of impersonal-biological functions; a potential byproduct of certain sex acts (male-female) irrespective of whether those acts are loving or dominating or whatever. This state of affairs creates intolerable contradictions, which threaten to render lovemaking itself unintelligible. And it creates intolerable contradictions above all for mothers, who find themselves *experiencing*—socially and objectively—the arrival of their child as though it were a gift from the heavens, a fact of biology or a twist of fate, *even when they see themselves as having acted subjectively as lovers.*

Indeed, at the very historical moment when some women are known to have managed to make love—to interact sexually in ways they feel to be neither dominating nor subjugating—many other women find themselves, once again, subject to the normative authority of sexual reproduction, which condemns them to motherhood, to what we might call *the* gender-based division of labor *par excellence*: the decree according to which only women bear (and raise) children.

Consider what happens when lovers (above all, women, in this era) attempt to *live out*—socially and institutionally—the authority of sexual reproduction, once they have *also* come to see themselves historically, as lovers, as capable of mutuality and of falling in love. It turns out, unsurprisingly, that so long as lovemaking is governed by sexual reproduction, its institutional, *lived* reality remains correspondingly restricted. These restrictions turn out to be severe, even unlivable.

Let me mention just a few.

On the one hand, when pre-contraception-era love-affairs 'know' themselves to be nonprocreative—in same-sex or transgender love-affairs, or in love-relations between postmenopausal women and men—the reality of these affairs derives merely from their *not* being fertile or procreative, irrespective of the lovers' own mutual recognition. Correspondingly, *their love* finds limited institutional-objective standing: they cannot have or raise children, or share property and wealth in the same way, for example. My argument will be that same-sex (or nonfertile) love-affairs have gained reality and institutional standing, in our own time, in direct proportion to the *erosion* of the authority of sexual reproduction to structure love-based relations and gendered hierarchies. This new standing accorded same-sex families in certain parts of the world is not merely a result of arbitrary shifts in public opinion, social prejudices, or more relaxed sexual mores.[223] The historical 'lateness' of institutionally sanctioned same-sex marriage, for example, is intelligible only in view of the waning authority of sexual reproduction and the rise of lovemaking. Or so I am arguing. Moreover, the authority of sexual reproduction had, first, to be challenged from within potentially procreative love-affairs—between fertile men and women.

By the same token, potentially procreative love-affairs in the nineteenth century remained determined by the lovers' reckoning with their fertility, whether they wanted children or not. That is, the lovers' *own* interactions—the way in which they recognized one another, treated one another, regarded one another—remained subjected to the impersonal authority of procreative possibility (whether or not children arrived). In a world before individual birth control or abortion rights, male-female lovers *must* deal with one another as lovers *and* as potential (or actual) parents, *in the very same dealings.*

Needless to say, this places tremendous practical and psychic burdens on their interactions—to the point, I am saying, where they can no longer make sense of themselves as *lovers*, since to be a lover is (for them) already to be haunted by parenthood, potential or actual. I will turn, in a moment, to a discussion of the practical intolerableness of this burden—particularly for women who 'marry for love' only to discover that they cannot disentangle love from motherhood. It also turns parenthood, as already noted, into a matter of natural fact or chance—rather than the result of free, mutual recognition.

And the objective burdens remain equally heavy: women's social activities, financial freedoms and creative potential continue to be shackled by the weight of their procreative status—the so-called biological clock. For the sake of space, I will not enumerate these burdens here; I assume they will be familiar to many from virtually every corner of our contemporary literary, visual and popular culture.[224]

It seems to me that these burdens have been most trenchantly grasped and probingly explored—not only in political manifestos and in public debates over abortion rights or gay rights—but in nineteenth- and twentieth-century novels, dramas and films. It is as if this artistic labor became visible *as artistic* by responding so perceptively to these objective, historical concerns. Here I have to mention that Hegel's failure to grasp the importance of the novel and modern drama reveals an inconsistency in his thinking both about art and about politics—and not just the historical fact that he was lecturing in Berlin before Balzac or Flaubert had put pen to paper.[225] If Hegel had been true to his own insight about the historical importance of love-based children, then he could not but have been struck by how this importance *must* be made intelligible precisely by depicting the interpersonal dynamics and lived fates of particular lovers.[226] Nineteenth- and twentieth-century novels (and certain dramas and films), provide our fullest reckoning with the subjective and objective burdens—the practical unintelligibility, individually and collectively—of trying to live as lovers under the social authority of sexual reproduction. Learning from the details of these works is, I think, essential for meeting the challenges to mutual recognition that arrive from the vicissitudes of sexual reproduction.[227]

For one thing, the felt crisis in the social authority of sexual reproduction is, I believe, the reason for the prevalence of adultery as a theme in works of this period.[228] Consider the sheer number of nineteenth-century works, across Europe and North America, which depict unhappy marriages and adulterous affairs that unfold against the demands of parenthood, and especially (through not exclusively) the burdens of motherhood: Honoré de Balzac, *Le Colonel Chabert* (1832), *A Woman of Thirty* (1832–42), *The Muse of the Department* (1843) and *Lily in the Valley* (1835); George Sand, *Jacques* (1834) and *Le dernier amour* (1867); Nathaniel Hawthorne, *The Scarlet Letter* (1850); Ernest Feydeau, *Fanny: étude* (1858); Ellen Wood, *East Lynne* (1861); Henrik Ibsen, *A Doll's House* (1879); Benito Pérez Galdós, *Fortunata and Jacinta: Two Stories of Married Women* (1886), Theodor Fontane, *Effi Briest* (1895); Henry James, *What Maisie Knew* (1897); Kate Chopin, *The Awakening* (1899); Tōson Shimazaki, *New Life* (1912); Edith Wharton, *The Custom of the Country* (1913) and *The Age of Innocence* (1920). This is only the tip of the iceberg—and I have not mentioned the countless films that take up these issues. But this list can give us a sense of the variety and depth of reflections on these issues across national traditions, in both men and women artists. In order to make the reader think about the links between marital and parental love, most nineteenth-century novelists depict the conflict between them. (English novels reflect less on adultery than on the status of illegitimate children—who are seen either as half-cursed, as in Dickens' *Little Dorrit* or *Bleak House*, or as a source of redemption, as in George Eliot's *Silas Marner*.)

Then there are the most influential and widely read novels of the nineteenth century: Flaubert's *Madame Bovary* (1856) and Tolstoy's *Anna Karenina* (1877).[229] On one level, as is obvious to anyone who has read Flaubert's novel, Emma's sexual affairs develop in the wake of the birth of her child, Berthe—for whom her maternal affection had been "somewhat attenuated," and whom she hands over to the wet nurse, Mère Rollet, to be cared for in a filthy hut on the edge of town (77).[230] It can be tempting to see Emma's sexual fantasies, her desire for 'love' outside her marriage to Charles, as standing in opposition to, or in rejection of, her maternity: as if adultery were Emma's attempt to separate procreativity from lovemaking, or sexual freedom from marriage.[231] Certainly, Flaubert goes out of his way to make sure we know that Emma is not the doting madonna that Hegel observes in Christian paintings. However, contrary to the critical consensus which holds that Emma rejects motherhood for sexual freedom, I regard Emma as trying to see the objective 'fact' of Berthe (of her own maternity) as somehow subject to Emma's own free, sexual acts, rather than to the fact of procreation. Indeed, I think it is closer to the truth to say that Emma seeks, not to separate lovemaking from maternity, but to see her daughter as belonging to (*lovable only in view of*) the achievement of a genuine sexual love-affair of reciprocal desire.

One thing Emma knows for sure: her relationship with Charles is hardly one of mutual recognition. Though Charles does not try to dominate Emma—*he* thinks their marriage is love-based—he also does not understand her. He treats her as he would his own mother, or as he would one of his patients, and she comes to regard him with contempt. Yet Berthe exists; and, her existence threatens to reduce Emma's sexual agency to procreation, unless she somehow achieves 'love.' In fact, Flaubert explicitly links the impending demands of maternity to Emma's frantic search for sexual fulfillment: her sexual affair with Léon originates in Mère Rollet's hut, at a moment when the infant Berthe spits up on Emma's collar;[232] she later meets Léon using the alibi of piano lessons (ostensibly, so that she might later teach Berthe to play); Berthe is said to be disconsolate and sobbing when Emma spends the night with Léon; Emma is shown reading about sexual fulfillment in novels, while Berthe looks for her mother at bedtime; Emma even injures Berthe, by inadvertently causing her to fall onto a bureau, during an episode of sexual fantasizing; Emma also signals a desire to take Berthe with her, as she plans her escape with Rudolphe.

I do not mean to suggest that Emma is aware of what she wants, throughout. I mean only that Emma is driven to act as she does, ultimately to her unhappy end, by the practical unintelligibility of family love and lovemaking at this historical juncture. Although Emma cannot see her life with Charles as remotely consistent with her own self-realization, neither can she make sense of herself as sexually subjugated in her marriage. Not only because she manages to "relish

. . . triumphant adultery" (162), but also because "before marriage, she thought herself in love" (133). What is unintelligible to Emma, then, is that she should be so sexually free, so capable of lovemaking *and yet* unfreely procreative, subject to her status as a mother. "The happiness that should have followed this love not having come, she must, she thought, have been mistaken" (133). The damage she causes to herself and others is, I think, one measure of the lengths to which a woman will go to make reproduction and the loving upbringing of children subject to, dependent on, the achievement of sexual freedom.

In *Anna Karenina*, the affair between Anna and Vronsky is colored from the start by Anna's unease about leaving her son, Sergei (Seryozha), alone for the first time. In contrast to Emma Bovary (or to, say, Undine Spragg in Edith Wharton's *Custom of the Country*), Anna is a warm mother—far closer to Raphael's or Leonardo's pictures of the madonna. Indeed, Anna is prompted to confesses her affair to her husband, Karenin, not merely by distress at Vronsky's horse-riding accident, but by the knowledge that she has become pregnant by Vronsky. Karenin, for his part, urges Anna to leave Vronsky and threatens to separate her from Seryozha if she persists in the affair, even as he later appears willing to recognize Anna's (and Vronsky's) daughter, Annie, as his own. Anna refuses him—instead eloping with Vronsky, as if accepting the cost of separation from Seryozha as the price of reciprocity. In this way, Seryozha becomes the image (in photos) or the date (his age when she left) or the weight (his body) that tallies the value of Anna's freedom: her son is the price she is willing to pay for it.

Moreover, Anna, we learn, loves Seryozha, her son, with an intensity that she cannot quite manage to bestow on Annie. She loves him because if Seryozha *is not* precious to her, then she has given up nothing of value to be with Vronsky: so, how special can Vronsky be? And she loves her son in spite of the fact that Seryozha was born "of a man she did not love," whereas Annie is Vronsky's daughter and physical perfection incarnate:

> The plump, well-nourished baby, as always, seeing her mother, turned over her bare arms, which looked as if they had strings tied around them, smiling with a toothless little mouth . . . it was impossible not to smile, not to kiss the little girl, not to give her a finger. . . . And Anna did all this, took [Annie] in her arms, got her to jump, and kissed her fresh cheek and bare little elbows; but the sight of the child made it still clearer that her feeling for her, compared to what she felt for Seryozha, was not even love. Everything about the girl was sweet, but for some reason none of it touched her heart. (538–39)[233]

All this might seem to fly in the face of my suggestions made earlier. After all, is not Annie (rather than Seryozha) the 'real' love-based child? Was she not born from the sexual affair between Anna and Vronsky? Anna herself is disturbed by this—by her lack of love toward Annie, in the face of her enduring love for Seryozha.

Yet, I think, the tyranny of the authority of sexual reproduction in the age of love-affairs is visible precisely in this lack of love for *Annie*—although Anna herself is, I wager, painfully unable to articulate this tyranny, given her inclination to be warm with children. Consider, if Anna could not *prevent* the birth of a child with Vronsky while continuing to make love with him—if *she* could not determine whether motherhood might (or might not) result from their love-affair—then in what sense is Annie really *hers*, really *theirs*? In what sense is *anything* real and objectively theirs?

Anna can, of course, still look upon the baby with a kind of warmth—"it was impossible not to smile, not to kiss the little girl, not to give her a finger." But only with the warmth that anyone inclined to smile upon a chubby-armed infant would radiate—generic human warmth. Not the light-filled love of a mother who can look upon her child as *her* freedom, made flesh.

As it is, baby Annie is Anna's *unfreedom* made real, and brought to life at the very heart of what she *thought* would liberate her: her love-affair with Vronsky.

The World-Historical Significance of Abortion and Birth Control

In the kitchen she took down her largest stewing pot, filled it with water and set it on the stove to boil. From storage cartons in the cellar she got out the other necessary pieces of equipment: the tongs that had once been used for sterilizing formula bottles, and the blue drugstore box containing the two parts of the syringe, rubber bulb and long plastic nozzle.

Richard Yates, Revolutionary Road (1961)

Let me say it all at once, then: For love as freedom to be objectively real, not just subjectively felt, we must be able to avail ourselves of reliable contraception and abortion. We also need revisable regulations for adoption and surrogacy, just as we need emergent reproductive technologies, and sufficient conditions for individual financial independence.[234] Doubtless we need other things, too, if the normative authority of sexual reproduction is to remain a thing of the past. I hope to mention at least a few more of love's needs in these remaining pages.

On the one hand, these social conditions must be *objectively* available to lovers—hence, certain legal-technical regimes are required. Contraceptive techniques have long been known, of course, and abortions were practiced by our ancient ancestors. However, such techniques were—and in some parts of the world, still are—socially justified and objectively regulated only for the sake of demographic selection or population control, or to sustain institutions of sexual domination. Given the long history of contraceptive techniques, it is striking that the birth control pill and the morning-after pill, and safe and legal abortion procedures for individuals (on the basis of 'choice,' and not compulsion) have gained large-scale, social-institutional acceptance only in recent generations, and not without intense resistance. The birth control pill was approved for contraceptive use in the United States in 1960. The U.S. Supreme Court case *Roe v. Wade* was decided in 1973. Condoms (often used to prevent venereal disease and as a rudimentary form of birth control for men) had been used for centuries, of course; but until women could also prevent or abort pregnancy, we could not say that reproductive freedom was fully institutionalized (and not just another form of sexual domination).

How to explain this? That is, how to explain not only the human significance of individual contraception and abortion, as well as new reproductive technologies, but also the late arrival of their social acceptance on the historical scene? *Why* should human beings have determined collectively, at this late date in history, that sexually mature individuals should be able to determine for themselves—irrespective of gender, age, or social standing—whether or when to have and raise children?

We will not get very far, I think, if we imagine that the answer to these questions lies in the discovery of a moral fact, such as female equality. And although contraception and abortion rights, which bear so intimately on sexual practices and erotic freedom, could never have been achieved without overt political action—protest movements, legislation, and the resulting rights and recognitions—the question I am asking is: *Why* the legislation? *Why* the protests, or shifts in public opinion? While knowledge of the evolutionary benefits of longer gestation periods in mammals may teach us important things about healthcare needs for pregnant women, or while knowledge of the mechanisms of free-market capitalism may teach something about suburban life in Connecticut in the 1950s, no scientific or sociological knowledge can answer the moral questions just posed. These kinds of immense social changes—which reflect radical transformations in the sense we make of ourselves and our world—are not the result of ignorance or knowledge about what justice is, or what capital is, or what DNA codes are. Nor can they be explained by crying out that, without same-sex marriage, or without equal pay for equal work, the world would be unjust, or economically unproductive, or somehow less pleasant to live in—as if we were just tending the garden of civilization and nothing more.

Rather, if we are to explain these objective and profound self-induced transformations in the conditions of our loves, we cannot avoid posing the basic moral questions *as* live moral-normative questions: Why would an individual or a couple use birth control? Why would any of us have and raise a child? Why would a woman have an abortion? And—I hope—we are now in a position to see that the *answers* we give to such questions are not abstract formulae but *new practical efforts* to make sense of ourselves and our world, new attempts to address fundamental threats to sense. After all, birth control and abortion are not timeless dilemmas, but rather historical symptoms of a profoundly felt threat to sense: namely, that we cannot be or act like lovers without responding to the demands of sexual reproduction as *authoritative*, as a demand that we *imposed upon ourselves*.

Our love-affairs and their objective, worldly possibilities express our best efforts to make sense of, to deal with, the entire history of our deepest self-imposed demands—since these demands, too, express our ancestors' prior attempts to make sense of their world and their lives.

■ ■ ■

April Wheeler, in Richard Yates' *Revolutionary Road*, aborts her third pregnancy with kitchen utensils, and ends her own life in the effort—after leaving a note instructing her husband, Frank, not to "blame" himself. April's final thought, we are told, is that "to do something absolutely honest, absolutely true, it . . . had to be done alone" (426).[235] It is, however, not the *content* of April's thought, but its *form*—the *fact* of her thinking—that is actual and true. She takes herself to be alone, to be unknown to herself and to Frank: in Socratic terms, we could say that she is acknowledging her ignorance.[236] And she is trying to understand what has *led* to this state of affairs, hence the way the concluding pages narrate her efforts to reflect on her past with Frank—to gather up the 'lessons' she thinks she has learned. She wants, in other words, not just to *have* her experiences, but also to gauge them, see what they might make sense of. So, what has April learned?

One thing that makes the love-affair of April and Frank so different from the adventures of Emma and Charles, or Anna and Karenin, is the Americans' optimistic sense that they can improve the conditions of their relationship from within. April and Frank imagine that they *can* be happier and freer with one another, precisely by *becoming* more satisfied with the objective conditions of their lives as a whole (their location, their income, their house, their diet). For instance, they have the vitality and means to imagine Frank quitting his job, and moving to Paris where they would be supported, financially, by April. Unlike Emma and Charles, then, April and Frank are at least capable of imagining that the terms of their relationship need not rest on a gender-based division of labor or the social authority of sexual reproduction—inasmuch as they might live and raise children under material and geographical conditions that they determine for themselves, under the steam of their own earnings (and not, say, the inherited wealth or privilege of Edith Wharton's American nobility).

At least for awhile, their relation bears some resemblance to what Stanley Cavell has called the comedy of remarriage—the "fact of marriage" under democratic and proto-feminist conditions "subjected to the fact or the threat of divorce."[237] By "threat of divorce," Cavell is not talking about situations when one partner bullies the other with an ultimatum, as when Karenin imperils Anna with social disgrace. He is talking about how modern lovers (re)commit themselves over time by taking seriously reasons for separation, indeed by *trying* to separate, without success.[238] Marriages—or temporally significant relations—are day-to-day tests, carried out over time, of reasons for separating. Love-relations confront the deepest threats to their own sense; lovers face whatever in their social world, or in their subjective lives, makes what they are doing seem irrational, meaningless, unintelligible.

I want to emphasize, in light of everything I have been saying, that this kind of self-testing relationship is itself a historical achievement—impossible to realize without certain material and social conditions, and without historically self-aware individuals capable of upending their lives for the sake of fulfilling each other's desires: whether that means having a child, moving to Paris, remodeling the bathroom, starting a revolution, or making art (April tries, for awhile, to be an actress).

Some no doubt read Yates' presentation of the hopes for this self-testing relationship as having been cynically undermined from the start, by suburban ideology or American capitalism or whatever else. (Sam Mendes, for example— the director of the 2008 film version of *Revolutionary Road*—saw in Yates' novel a sequel to the nihilistic suburb of frustrated desires Mendes had portrayed a decade earlier in the 1998 film *American Beauty*.) If such an undermining has occurred, then desires for mutuality *cannot* be fulfilled and the only 'fun' to be had lies in cruelly spoiling the illusion that things might improve, for oneself or for others. In such a world, things *could not* have been otherwise.

But then, in such a world, no one could experience something like regret or remorse for what might have been.[239] And this flies in the face, I think, of the wrenching self-examination to which April submits herself in the closing pages of *Revolutionary Road*. There, April expresses not just general regret—'oh, if only it had been otherwise.' She asks herself: *Was it worth it?* April's reflections thus lead her to consider how she might have acted differently. At this same time, she quickly realizes that her actions were determined by—they were responses to, as well as provocations of—Frank's actions.[240] It would be too much to say that Frank himself *was* April's primary act—that *he* is sole the target of her regret; for that would amount to blaming Frank for April's having committed to him. "And how could anyone else be blamed for that?" she says (417). However, it would not be too much to conclude that Frank, or the fact of their marriage, names the exact sequence of actions whose worth she now weighs.

This is what separates Yates' novel from any cynical or fatalist reading of it. As April sees it, their love-affair was not doomed from the start by forces beyond their control (capitalism, suburbia, nature, or 'the way things are'). Frank doomed it, by giving up on Paris; and when April writes her final note telling him not to "blame" himself, she is pinning him to his compromise. And *she* doomed it, by acting as if the compromise could be denied—"by telling easy, agreeable lies of her own" (416). Their undertaking failed. What she did, she now finds intolerable—but not because her life with Frank was *always* intolerable. It has, rather, *become* intolerable—and this is the point I want to emphasize—because her actions could only have been redeemed had their self-testing relationship managed to afford her the life she had hoped for. She judges her life and her past from the view of the present moment, but only because she also judges the present in light of those past hopes. "And that was when she'd thought it through" (320). Yates tells us. Her hopes had not just been dashed by the way her life had gone; her hopes had been proven *wrong*.

But this does not mean that April was wrong to have had hopes. That is the fatalist view, to which philosopher Theodor Adorno or film director Sam Mendes, too often tetchily succumb.[241] What April confronts, rather, is just the cost or price of being a hopeful creature. The fullest proof of being a lover in a self-testing relationship is that it can fail, after all, and fail from *within*—on its own terms, so to speak. The most stubborn obstacles to leading a life lie not only in social-institutional subjugations, natural ailments, or circumstantial misfortunes—but also in one's own deepest, truest, most hope-invested commitments.

As I understand it, this realization produces a threat to the intelligibility of the life that one is living—not because one is confused or ignorant about the circumstances in which one is living, although *that* confusion can still happen, too. Rather, one sees that the life to which *one committed oneself* is wrong. Hence, that life cannot continue to be lived other than as irrational or mad. Sanity and sense-making thus demand the undoing of that life, those commitments—not just the dismissal of one's past as a mistake, not the rejection of one life-path for another, but the direct refutation of one's own committed *action*.

I asked earlier: Why would an individual, or couple, use birth control? Why would any of us have and raise a child? Why would a woman have an abortion? One reason, already noted, is the need to liberate lovemaking from sexual reproduction.

But another reason is that mistakes can be made, regrettable events can happen—just as glad tidings and luck might also come our way. And we need human ways of acknowledging that, otherwise that luck or misfortune is not ours, not part of our world. And a further reason—the one I want to emphasize here—is that we (individually and collectively) must be able to undo and refute, not just dismiss or wave away, even our deepest commitments, in order to be able to assess whether our activities have been worth it at all. This is why the real threat of divorce is the condition of possibility for any happy marriage. Safe and legal abortion—our final refutation not just of the authority of sexual reproduction but of our having allowed that authority into our lives—is one historical condition of possibility for loving our children and each other.

Love as Freedom

There was some open space between what he knew and what he tried to believe, but nothing could be done about it, and if you can't fix the problem, you've got to stand it.
Annie Proulx, "Brokeback Mountain" (1999)

Because the social world in which April lived did not guarantee her a safe abortion, her death, Frank's fate and their two children's fate, is *also* an indictment of the world in which they lived—not just a judgment of their failures. And if we can indict a world, then we are not totally helpless.

In the end, every self-testing love-affair is a test not only of the lovers, but of the world that lovers inhabit. There are no 'pure' subjective acts of love or commitment which are not expressive of a social world and its possibilities, as well as the lovers' mettle and resources. At the heart of April's self-blame, between her and the equipment she sterilizes, there is an immanent critique of her society. But this is just another way of claiming that deep and profound social transformations are required, and hence also explicable, in view of the account of lovemaking I have been giving—love's emergence from the history of sexual practices governed by sexual reproduction and sexual domination. If social transformations such as new contraceptive rights and techniques, abortion laws, reproductive technologies and adoption laws continue to cause heated debate and dramatic social upheaval—indeed, a wholesale rethinking of what kinship means, what marriage means, what raising children implies and entails, what education responds to—then this is a further sign of just how much latitude we grant ourselves when we realize love as freedom.

Love-affairs are gaining reality and institutional acceptance in our time, irrespective of gender, in direct proportion to the *erosion* of the authority of sexual reproduction and sexual domination. In light of this erosion and its objective manifestations—changing adoption laws, reproductive technologies, new kinship formations—there is no longer any reason to regard love as gender-based. And without a need for gender-based love, is any gender-based practice going to continue to make much sense? Can gender help us make sense of anything, going forward?

I hope that my reflections have put us in a better position to explain—not that gender is 'troubled' or subject to indeterminacy as such—but *how* gender was first instituted and later became troubled by the achievement of love as freedom. The long, difficult past of gender-based divisions and the authority of sexual reproduction in the history of our love-lives remain the source of that trouble.

The frustrations that raged under the self-conceptions of the Victorian era, in Oscar Wilde or E. M. Forster, have given way to an unmistakably widening social agreement that love is real and actual in the world, irrespective of gender—not just that desires might be uncloseted, but that mutual recognition cannot be governed by gender-based divisions and hierarchies. When Therese and Carol manage to live out a self-testing relationship in Patricia Highsmith's *The Price of Salt* (1952)—no matter Carol's child and estranged husband—they do so not by confronting the obstacles of bourgeois marriage, maternity and sexual reproduction directly, but by installing a reality, a possible way of life, in view of which those obstacles appear less insuperable. And when Highsmith wrote her Afterword to the republication of the novel in the 1980s, she could affirm further that "blackmail has lost a lot of its teeth thanks to laws about mutual consent."[242]

In Annie Proulx's "Brokeback Mountain," Jack and Ennis inhabit a world like Laramie, Wyoming—our world, in which we know that some lovers must contend with the threat of what Ennis calls "the tire iron." When Jack dies, drowning in his own blood on the side of a dirt road, Ennis can neither refute nor accept the explanation given—that a tire had exploded while Jack was changing it.

Yet the lack of evidence does not leave Ennis, nor does it leave us, unsure of the past, nor of what might be done—institutionally, in the world. Changes in our laws, duties, habits, and our deepest norms can express not only what we know—that "it had been the tire iron" (282). Profound social transformations can also be how we, collectively, mourn and love another, unfatalistically.[243] Ennis can try to lay claim to Jack's dead body, for instance. And when that effort fails due to the tenacious grip of Jack's birth family, Ennis nevertheless recovers his lost shirt "hidden . . . inside Jack's own, the pair like two skins, one inside the other" (281). Improvised acts of mourning, new kinship formations and the erosion of gender remind us, individually and collectively, of the latitude that we have already granted one another, and hence the freedoms we might still grant.

But we should also recall that the sum of Jack's time with Ennis was marked not only by death, but by the immense difficulties they faced in struggling to understand one another. And by what seems—in their final encounter—like a shared acknowledgment at having *failed* to ever really 'get' one another. In part, this failure results from deceptions, lies, half truths, a breakdown of trust—"all them things I don't know," says Ennis bitterly, "could get you killed if I should come to know them." But there are also Ennis' own compromises, even his self-deceit: his failure to follow through on his stated desire to be with Jack, to follow him to Mexico or rearrange his other commitments. "Tell you what," says Jack, "we could a had a good life together. . . . You wouldn't do it, Ennis. . . . You're too much for me, Ennis, you son of a whore-son bitch. I wish I knew how to quit you" (277–78). No moral assessment or assigning of blame will suffice to resolve such attempts at mutual understanding. The love-affair just *is* the enacted attempt to understand; something the lovers put themselves through in order to even aspire to self-knowledge, to any satisfying knowledge of one another. Even where such knowledge remains heartbreakingly out of reach. "Nothing ended, nothing begun, nothing resolved" (278).

When Jack recalled "the time that distant summer on Brokeback when Ennis had come up behind him and pulled him close . . . as the single moment of artless, charmed happiness in their separate and difficult lives," he appraised the recollection not with regret, wistful nostalgia or a discreet love of the past, but with the realization that "nothing marred" the memory. Not even "the knowledge that Ennis would not embrace him face to face because he did not want to see nor feel that it was Jack he held." Not even if "they'd never got much farther than that" (279).

If the joys and failures of love remain in our past, unredeemed, then they may yet help us to make sense of freedoms now actual.

Notes

Part I: Prologue

1. *The Second Sex*, trans. Constance Borde and Sheila Malovanz-Chevallier (New York: Vintage, 2011); all citations are to this edition. I have been inspired by Beauvoir in more ways than I can acknowledge—as will hopefully be apparent in what follows. Nevertheless, my answers to these questions differ fundamentally from hers. Beauvoir posits a "will to dominate women," and a struggle between men and women modelled on the life-and-death struggle described by Hegel in *Phenomenology of Spirit*. She writes: "We have already posited that when two human categories find themselves face-to-face, each one wants to impose its sovereignty on the other. . . . It is thus understandable that man might have had the will to dominate woman" (ibid., 73).

2. See Irving Singer, *The Nature of Love*, vol. 1–3 (Cambridge, MA: MIT Press, 2009); also, Harry Frankfurter, *The Reasons of Love* (Princeton: Princeton University Press, 2004).

3. For a recent example, see Simon May, *Love: A History* (New Haven: Yale University Press, 2013). Also see Morton Hunt's *Natural History of Love* (New York: Knopf, 1959) or Dianne Ackerman's *A Natural History of Love* (New York: Random House, 1994), which claim that love is rooted in tendencies that can be found in animals, too, while nevertheless appearing differently when embedded in various historical contexts.

4. See, for example, Denis de Rougemont, *Love in the Western World* (Princeton: Princeton University Press, 1940); and John C. Moore, *Love in Twelfth-Century France* (Philadelphia: University of Pennsylvania Press, 1972); also see Marilyn Yalom, *How the French Invented Love* (New York: HarperCollins, 2012).

5. Eva Illouz, *Why Love Hurts* (London: Polity Press, 2012); and *Cold Intimacies* (London: Polity Press, 2007). From what she calls a "sobered modernist perspective," Illouz focuses on the importance of romantic love "in modernity" and "as modernity." She defends a sociological explanation of "the anxieties and disappointments inherent in so many experiences of love" by "find[ing] their causes in the social reorganization of sexuality, of romantic choice, of the modes of recognition inside the romantic bond

and of desire itself." I agree with many of the broadly Marxist and Weberian premises of Illouz's analysis—namely, that romantic love entails, even presupposes, some conception of individual autonomy (though we would need to spell out what is meant by that); that the "co-mingling of love and economic calculus at once makes love central to modern lives and is at the heart of the conflicting pressures to which love has been submitted"; and that an understanding of romantic love requires understanding "the cultural and institutional core of modernity" (*Why Love Hurts*, 5–17, 289–39). However, whereas Illouz claims that sociological *descriptions* of these cultural or institutional features of modernity provide a *causal* explanation of specifically 'modern' love-predicaments, I see such descriptions as dodging all the really interesting questions: *Why* have 'modern' notions of human autonomy been so closely tied to romantic love, such that the prizing of the former entails coming to grips with the latter? Why has romantic love become entangled with the kinds of economic calculus or "marriage markets" Illouz describes, and with what implications? Why do the 'modern' institutions and practices described by Illouz look the way they do—and might this have anything to do with older love practices, stretching back even to ancient times? I will provide my own answers to these questions at different points throughout.

6. There are also peculiar recent attempts to provide an "axiomatics of love," as in Alain Badiou's essay "What Is Love?" translated into English in *Umbr(a)* 39 (1996); and in his *In Praise of Love*, trans. Peter Bush (London: New Press, 2013). Badiou defines love as an "event" that "ruptures" social order. This will not be my approach here.

7. There are perplexing features of the world that can be explained just by determining what they are—from black holes and viral infections to traffic signals and pastries. We can say a lot about specific social practices as well, just by determining, for instance, what the scientific method is, or what *sprezzatura* in Renaissance Italian culture was. We can even ask, What is the good or the beautiful or the just?—while, like Socrates, starting a discussion about the kind of determinations we make when we examine how we live. In asking these questions, we also look for the right discourse, or disciplinary approach, for answering them; and along the way, we shape distinct fields of specialized study.

8. In Fichte's *Grundlage des Naturrechts* (1796), freedom and self-consciousness develop not in response to being blocked in the satisfaction of one's desires, but when one is "summoned" by another person who negates or rejects one's desires and interests. Rather than present such a situation as one that just requires compromise (as in Hobbes' "pact"), Fichte sees these challenging social relations as a condition of free agency. Hegel's own speculative notion of freedom is impossible to summarize. But such a summary is not necessary here. The points of orientation I am offering will, I hope, be enough to get my discussion rolling.

9. Compare Hegel's passing but frequent remarks on, for instance, the "free power" of the Universal in logic as "free love"; or his depiction of the achievement of self-knowledge as "the form of a feeling . . . in love, for instance," in G.W.F. Hegel, *Science of Logic*, trans. A. V. Miller (New York: Prometheus Books, 1969), 603; and *Elements of the Philosophy of Right*, ed. Allan Wood, trans. H. B. Nisbet (Cambridge: Cambridge

University Press, 1991), §7, Addition, p. 228. Hegel's *Logic* begins by noting that 'threats to sense' posed by temporal change produce the "simplicity" of "pure being"—or the split between true being (*Sein*) and appearance (*Schein*). Hegel goes on to propose love and friendship as forms of practical reason, wherein the ways of knowing (loving, being someone's friend) also realize what is known (love, friendship). For a discussion, see Michael Theunissen, *Sein und Schein: Die kritische Funktion der Hegelschen Logik* (Frankfurt: Suhrkamp, 1980), 1–95.

10. One example: if we ask whether human beings truly practiced ritual human sacrifice in certain times and places, the answer might come back, "Yes." But the knowledge provided by that answer is very different from the knowledge that might come from posing a different question: What *is* human sacrifice, really? The difference between these two questions is manifest not just in the 'knowledge' they offer, but in their assumption about what it is to know something. So, in figuring out 'what' we know—and in building on what others have helped us to know—we also need to think about *how* we know, or go on figuring things out and trying to get things right.

11. It is the persistence of this desire to understand in the face of temporal change, and not any immortal romance, that is expressed—I think—in Shakespeare's Sonnet 116:

> Let me not to the marriage of true minds
> Admit impediments. Love is not love
> Which alters when it alteration finds[.]
>
>   . . .
>
> Love's not Time's fool, though rosy lips and cheeks
> Within his bending sickle's compass come;
> Love alters not with his brief hours and weeks,
> But bears it out even to the edge of doom.

Shakespeare's Sonnets, ed. Stephen Booth (New Haven: Yale University Press, 1977).

12. I have in mind what the philosopher Robert Brandom, in "The Pragmatist Enlightenment (and Its Problematic Semantics)," *European Journal of Philosophy* 12, no. 1 (2004), has described as a "second Enlightenment," in which "it is possible to explain what remains, and is acknowledged as, contingent" (2).

13. I see Shakespeare's *Hamlet* as a particularly forceful piece of thinking on the implications of this transformation. I will return to this issue, with a broader panorama in mind, in Part II of this book. See also Paul A. Kottman, *Tragic Conditions in Shakespeare: Disinheriting the Globe* (Baltimore: Johns Hopkins University Press, 2009), chap. 2.

14. I find compelling—and am indebted to—Robert Pippin's formulation of the challenges we face in explaining this immense social transformation. See Robert Pippin, *The Persistence of Subjectivity* (Cambridge: Cambridge University Press, 2005), 7–19; *Hegel's Practical Philosophy* (Cambridge: Cambridge University Press, 2008), 276; and "Hegel on Political Philosophy and Political Actuality," *Inquiry: An Interdisciplinary Journal of Philosophy* 53, no. 3 (2010): 407.

15. A word about terminology. There is an interesting slippage between "sexual difference" and "gender" in many writings on these issues—which touches upon the way in which the so-called structuralist inheritance (in anthropology, especially) is taken

up in so-called post-structuralist writings on gender. (Therein lie other terminological troubles; I mention all this only for the sake of general orientation.) In Part III of this book, I will speak of *sexual difference* as an explanatory category which tries to make sense of reproduction in human life; I will use *gender* (man, woman, boy, girl, hermaphrodite, eunuch, transsexual) as a socially articulated position of activity and passivity that institutionalizes what I will call *sexual domination*. For more on these terms and their usage, see Gayle Rubin, "Sexual Traffic," interview by Judith Butler, *differences* 6.2+3 (1994): 67–68; also Joan W. Scott, "Gender: A Useful Category of Historical Analysis," *The American Historical Review* 91, no. 5 (1986): 1067.

16. Again, this is not to avoid acknowledging regressive social trends that deny these developments, although it would be important to treat any causal explanation for such regressions as part of the larger story under consideration here, and not as a separate history.

17. "Naturally," I mean, in light of the commitments held dear by those engaged in the polemics. This leaves open the question of how those commitments came to be held, and what authority they might exercise going forward.

18. To cite one widely circulated passage, in "What Is Critique?" Foucault investigated what he called "the connections that can be identified between mechanisms of coercion and elements of knowledge . . . such that a given element of knowledge takes on the effect of power" (59). This essay appeared in *The Politics of Truth*, ed. Sylvère Lotringer (Cambridge, MA: MIT Press, 1997).

19. This phrase belongs to Paul Ricoeur. For two accounts, to which my comments here are indebted, see Robert Pippin, "Natural and Normative," *Daedalus* (Summer 2009): 35–43; and Robert Brandom, "Reason, Genealogy and the Hermeneutics of Magnanimity" (unpublished paper, available for download). As Ricoeur put it in *Freud and Philosophy* (New Haven: Yale University Press, 1970), "Since Marx, Nietzsche and Freud . . . we have started to doubt consciousness" (32–33).

20. Robert Brandom frames the issue well in "Reason, Genealogy and the Hermeneutics of Magnanimity": "When the great genealogists dug down in the areas of discourse they addressed, they found causes underlying the reasons." On the one hand, genealogy could be a matter of addressing "systematic distortions" in various discourse, to borrow Jürgen Habermas' phrase—namely, those causal factors which determine the reason of particular subjects, rendering their thoughts and actions less than transparent: economic classes (Marx), expressions of the will to power (Nietzsche), or Oedipal relations in the family (Freud). On the other hand, there remains a more radical genealogy according to which causes not only distort reasons, but *masquerade as* reasons. As Brandom puts it, "Genealogy in its most radical form seeks to dispel the *illusion* of reason."

21. Hence, the rise of 'historicist' scholarship about what people once thought about this or that, at some particular point in time. I assume that the rise of such studies over the past two generations, across the humanities, is evident to anyone paying attention.

22. Judith Butler, *Undoing Gender* (New York: Routledge, 2004), 27.

23. Butler characterizes gender norms as "arbitrary" in her essay "Sex and Gender in

Simone de Beauvoir's *Second Sex*," *Yale French Studies*, no. 72 (1986): 35. See also Judith Butler, "Contingent Foundations: Feminism and the Question of Postmodernism," in *Feminists Theorize the Political*, ed. Judith Butler and Joan Wallace Scott (New York: Routledge, 1992), 3–21; and Judith Butler, Ernesto Laclau, and Slavoj Žižek, *Contingency, Hegemony, Universality* (New York: Routledge, 2000).

24. See Judith Butler, *Bodies That Matter* (New York: Routledge, 1993), 3. There is overlap here with the political theories of Antonio Gramsci, Ernesto Laclau and Chantal Mouffe. For an account of the Gramscian origins of the term *hegemony*, see Ernesto Laclau and Chantal Mouffe, *Hegemony and Social Strategy* (New York: Verso, 1985), chap. 1. Especially telling is Laclau's and Mouffe's insistence that hegemony takes hold as a theoretical notion precisely where a Hegelian notion of historical reason withdraws (see pp. 7–8).

25. I understand the central question of Beauvoir's *The Second Sex*, and of feminism itself, to be, "How, in the feminine condition, can a human being accomplish herself . . . not in terms of happiness but in terms of freedom" (17). And I agree that this is the right question. However, I am not convinced by Beauvoir's suggestion that Hegel's master-slave dialectic provides the right model for explaining the institution of a gender-based hierarchy for reasons I hope to make clear. For instance, I am not convinced by passages like the following: "when two human categories find themselves face-to-face, each one wants to impose its sovereignty on the other" (73). Instead, I will try to show how institutions of sexual domination and gender-based hierarchies are better explained (retrospectively) as integral to the sense-making efforts that emerge in the development of what I call our sexual self-education.

26. Butler's most recent formulations, in *Sense of the Subject* (Bronx, NY: Fordham University Press, 2015), suggest that, at the psychic-subjective level, too, we as individuals are both "formed" and "undone" by "what we come to sense and know," and that we "never quite get done with being undone" in this way (11, 16). This echoes her earlier account of subject formation in *The Psychic Life of Power* (Stanford: Stanford University Press, 1997).

27. For a thoughtful discussion, see Cinzia Arruzza, "Gender as Social Temporality," in *Historical Materialism* 23, no. 1 (2015): 28–52.

28. Michel Foucault, *Discipline and Punish* (New York: Random House, 1977), 24.

29. Kwame Anthony Appiah, *The Honor Code: How Moral Revolutions Happen* (New York: Norton, 2010).

30. For recent contributions, see Jay Bernstein's account of "moral modernity" and the abolition of torture in *Torture and Dignity: An Essay on Moral Injury* (Chicago: University of Chicago Press, 2015); George Kateb on human rights in *Human Dignity* (Cambridge, MA: Harvard University Press, 2010); and Lynn Hunt, *Inventing Human Rights* (New York: Norton, 2008).

31. This is a prevalent feature, for instance, in latter-generation Frankfurt school theorists. as discussed by Axel Honneth in *The Struggle for Recognition: The Moral Grammar of Social Conflicts* (Cambridge, MA: MIT Press, 1995); and *Disrespect: The Normative Foundations of Critical Theory* (Cambridge: Polity Press, 2007). For Honneth,

moral progress measures the desirability of social changes, in terms of their contribution to greater individualization, recognition and social inclusion.

32. Different need not mean better; recall, for instance, Marx's insistence on the particular awfulness of wage labor, as distinct from the systems of slavery it replaced.

33. This is not to say that more ambitious accounts of the historical meaning of slavery—such as Marx's—cannot be attempted or are prima facie invalid. There is much more to think about here.

Part II: Love of the Living and the Dead

1. Aristotle called this determinacy, or the quality whereby something is a "such and such." In his *Lectures on the Philosophy of Religion*, vol. 2 (Berkeley: University of California Press, 1996), Hegel sometimes called it "the finite," which helps us determine people as well as things—"a qualitative determination, a *quality* . . . such that (its) quality is a determinacy that is immediately identical with *its* being. . . . We say 'something red;' here red is the quality, and if this ceases to be, then it is no longer this . . . there are men and women of quite determinate character, and if this is lost, they cease to be. Thus the fundamental quality of Cato was to be a Roman republican; when this ceased, he ceased to be" (256).

2. Of course, this goes not only for people, but for anything subject to temporal change—anything that prompts a search for some identity or essence or reason that makes sense of the changes. At this level of generality, accounting for someone and accounting for something overlap.

3. The passage is worth quoting at length for its formulation of the distinction between, yet the inseparability of, sense-perception and reflective judgment:

> what judgment
> Would step from this to this? Sense, sure, you have,
> Else could you not have motion; but sure, that sense
> Is apoplex'd; for madness would not err,
> Nor sense to ecstasy was ne'er so thrall'd
> But it reserved some quantity of choice
> To serve in such a difference. What devil was't
> That thus hath cozen'd you at hoodman-blind?
> Eyes without feeling, feeling without sight,
> Ears without hands or eyes, smelling sans all,
> Or but a sickly part of one true sense
> Could not so mope. O shame! where is thy blush? (3.4. 70–81)

William Shakespeare, *Hamlet*, ed. Harold Jenkins, Arden Shakespeare (London: Metheun, 1982); all citations are to this edition.

4. For instance, Hamlet is, I think, unnerved and motivated by his dismay at being unable to say anything more about his own father than this: "He was a man, take him for all in all, / I shall not look upon his like again" (1.2.186–87).

5. Other 'threats to sense,' when it comes to understanding who we are, must have included (and still include) the experience of hunger or deprivation, of illness and dis-

ease, of want, appetite, scarcity. The list could go on. By starting with individual mortality, I hope to clear a path that goes very far back, and hence via which these other issues might eventually also be considered. To borrow Hegel's terms, I am suggesting that care for the dead is a primary form of objective spirit—primary because it is not just one ritual practice among many, but a practice without which institutional life cannot take shape as intergenerational.

6. Obviously, this did not prevent our ancestors from imagining so-called afterlives. Shakespeare was able to confront young Hamlet with the ghost of Old Hamlet. Images of life after death not only present visions of human happiness or misery; stories of life after death implicitly show death to be what we *take* it to be, rather than a natural process to which we are helpless witnesses.

7. See Aristotle, *On Youth and Old Age, On Life and Death, On Breathing*, pt. 10, in *Complete Works of Aristotle*, vol. 1, ed. Jonathan Barnes (Princeton: Princeton University Press, 1984). Hegel, in *Phenomenology of Spirit*, trans. A. V. Miller (Oxford: Oxford University Press, 1977), characterizes death as the "the quiet [*die Ruhe*] of simple Universality" (§450).

8. To illustrate once more with Shakespeare's help, this is why Gertrude's remarks about Old Hamlet at the outset of Shakespeare's play are so galling to Prince Hamlet—"all that lives must die,/passing through nature to eternity," she chides, "Why seems it so particular with thee?" Hamlet's response, of course, is to declare that his father's death does not 'seem' particular to him—"Seems, madam? Nay, it is. I know not 'seems.'" (1.2.72–76). To hold to the particularity of his father's passing—the death of this individual—is to look for an essence beneath the appearance of death as mere natural process. If Hamlet cannot say, or at least *try* to thoughtfully demonstrate, who his dead father 'really' was—beyond, as we have seen, merely listing his perceptible qualities ("*He was a man*, take him for all in all,/I shall not look upon his like again"; emphasis added)—then he cannot say who anyone 'really' is.

9. "[T]he movement of consciousness" must assert itself by "interrupting the work of Nature and rescuing the [dead individual] from destruction; or better . . . it takes on itself the *act* of destruction" (Hegel, *Phenomenology of Spirit*, §452).

10. On the other end of life, the *natural process* of birth is turned into a *human deed*—membership in a historical community—by naming a child, through baptismal ceremonies and the like, in view of which the child becomes 'one of us.'

11. In Sophocles' play *Antigone*, Antigone repeatedly emphasizes that she shares with her siblings the bond of blood, uterine origins in Jocasta. But she emphasizes this not just to assert that this 'fact' of blood just *is* their bond, but rather as justification for the duty to bury Polynices; see *Sophocles I*, ed. David Grene and Richard Lattimore, trans. David Grene (Chicago: University of Chicago Press, 1991). Human life (family life) cannot be intelligibly sustained *as* human unless it can furnish a nonnatural (cultural, familial) foothold within the passage from womb to death and decay.

12. Alexandre Kojève, *Introduction to the Reading of Hegel*, ed. Allan Bloom, trans. James H. Nichols Jr. (Ithaca: Cornell University Press, 1980), 61; emphasis in original.

13. When Antigone, for instance, declares that her wedding shall be to death, she is

just expressing the form that her love of others takes generally: love of the dead (family life) is not (yet) fundamentally distinct from sexual love or the marriage bond, at least in her view (Sophocles, *Antigone*, line 185). The notion that the death of an unmarried girl amounted to her 'marrying death' was a commonplace in ancient Greek and Roman epitaphs; it is repeated, as we shall see, down to Shakespeare's *Romeo and Juliet*. Antigone's claim, I take it, is not that she marries death *instead* of a living person (Haemon, say), but rather that she loves at all only inasmuch as she loves the living and the dead alike. I do not mean that Sophocles defends this view (Haemon's words and deeds, for one thing, reveal a critical perspective on Antigone's self-justification).

14. This is seen not only in the well-known 'heroic' view, according to which Achilles' death, for instance, shows how "only a man who does not survive his one supreme act remains the indisputable master of his identity and possible greatness, because he withdraws into death from the possible consequences and continuation of what he began," as Hannah Arendt says in *The Human Condition* (Chicago: University of Chicago Press, 1958), 193–94. It applies as well to Odysseus when he weeps at hearing his own deeds recounted at the court of the Phaeacians—or to Oedipus, when he hears the story of his origins. These episodes are famously discussed by Aristotle in the *Poetics*; in Chapter Sixteen, for instance, Aristotle offers Odysseus' weeping as an example of narrative recognition. For a thoughtful discussion, see Adriana Cavarero, *Relating Narratives: Storytelling and Selfhood*, trans. Paul A. Kottman (New York: Routledge, 2000).

15. Think, for instance, of the way that Attic tragedy displayed a split between the present and its legendary past.

16. Walter Benjamin, "The Storyteller," in *Selected Writings*, vol. 3 (Cambridge, MA: Harvard University Press, 2002), 151. All of this raises a familiar set of issues about artistic practices more generally—issues, of course, that artworks themselves often explicitly thematize—namely, the split between what we sometimes call the autobiographical and the biographical perspectives, or between the positions of protagonist and narrator, first-person and third-person, artist and subject. Needless to say, different artistic media and art forms 'take up' this indebtedness to individual mortality, to human separateness and connectedness, in different ways. While it would be worth reflecting on how different artworks and media—from Homeric narration to Roman funerary portraiture, from Shakespeare's sonnets ("No longer mourn for me when I am dead") to Rembrandt's self-portraits, from photographs to films—thematize their practical debt to the individual mortality of subject or artist, this is not the place to go into detail.

17. The list of such thoughtful innovations is, of course, long and various. Consider—as just a taste—the challenges that arise in maintaining gravesites or funerary memorials, in view of radically transforming landscapes and societies. After all, caring for the dead requires at least *some* vigilance, for some period of time, over the site of the dead's interment. But, then, what kind of vigilance? And under what authority can the living lay claim to the 'homes' of the dead? What if there are competing authorities—such as tribal memory, or legal property rights? And what if the ritual-material connection between vigilance over the gravesite and care for the dead is put into question—by competing

claims upon the ground itself, for example? In these cases, the 'work' of caring for the dead is itself transformed, necessarily innovative.

18. One tip of just one iceberg: Mark Smith, *Traversing Eternity: Texts for the Afterlife from Ptolemaic and Roman Egypt* (Oxford: Oxford University Press, 2009).

19. Sigmund Freud, "Mourning and Melancholia," in *The Standard Edition of the Complete Psychological Works of Sigmund Freud*, ed. and trans. James Strachey, vol. 14 (London, Hogarth Press, 1914–16), 243–58.

20. For a consideration of how Shakespeare's *Hamlet* presents the challenges that inhere in caring for the dead under conditions of radical social change, see my *Tragic Conditions in Shakespeare*, chap. 2.

21. Virgil, *Georgics* 4.453–527, in *Eclogues. Georgics. Aeneid: Books 1–6*, Loeb Classical Library (Cambridge, MA: Harvard University Press, 1999); Ovid, *Metamorphoses* 10.1–85, in *Ovid IV: Metamorphoses, Books IX–XV*, Loeb Classical Library (Cambridge, MA: Harvard University Press, 1916). Unless otherwise indicated, all citations are to these editions.

22. Some context: Aristaeus learns from Proteus that Orpheus' anger at Eurydice's death has led to the loss of his bees. Virgil is invoking a classical image of bees as paradigmatically social creatures, whose *fama* (tradition, way of life) was a lens through which human sociality was viewed, and whose cultivation signaled the possibility of an agriculture in harmony with nature, rather than the rapacious cultivation that generally characterizes how humans productively plow the earth. This view of bees was common in antiquity. Aristotle saw bees as *politikai*, and generically connected to human beings in this sense; see Aristotle, *Politics*, trans. Carnes Lord (Chicago: University of Chicago Press, 1984), 1253a; also, Aristotle, *On the Generation of Animals*, bk. 3; Aristotle, *History of Animals*, bk. 9; and Varro, *De re rustica*, bk. 3, chap. 16. See also, H. M. Fraser, *Beekeeping in Antiquity* (London, 1931); Hellfried Dahlmann, "Der Bienenstaat in Vergil's *Georgika*," in *Virgil: Critical Assessments of Classical Authors*, vol. 2, *Georgics*, ed. Philip R Hardie (New York: Routledge, 1999); M. Owen Lee, *Virgil as Orpheus: A Study of the* Georgics (Albany: State University of New York Press, 1996), chap. 8. It has also been suggested that bees were seen by Virgil as "guardians or symbols of chastity," and that Aristaeus is thus being punished for his attempted rape of Eurydice with this 'loss' of his chaste creatures; see the discussion in C. G. Perkell, "A Reading of Virgil's Fourth *Georgic*," *Phoenix* 32, no. 3 (1978): 211–21.Related to this, bees were thought to reproduce asexually (*Georgics* 4.200) and to require even their keeper to be chaste—a requirement violated by Aristaeus in his attempted rape of Eurydice. Unlike bees, human beings manifestly fail to reconcile their urges with the 'life-cycle' of nature—both with regard to the way in which human sexuality is not limited to the reproduction of the species and with respect to the way in which the deaths of individuals cause grief for human beings, while posing no such trouble for bees (*Georgics* 4.200–12). The rapacious violence of Virgil's Aristaeus stands in contrast not only to his own prior image as benefactor and cultivator, but also to classical representations of Orpheus' "harmony" with the natural world— his ability, for instance, to charm nature with his song. Virgil seems to see in Aristaeus something like the violent domination of nature inherent in the 'productive' labor of

human agriculture—an aspect also likely emphasized in Aristaeus' attempted rape of Eurydice. The first half of the Fourth *Georgic* is devoted to something like an anthropomorphic description of apiary life; whereas the second half of the book contrasts the woe and weal of individual human beings (Proteus, Aristaeus, Orpheus, Eurydice) to the fate of the bee life-world. The poem, in short, appears to be thematically organized according to what we have come to regard as the 'nature-culture' problem, or the self-estrangement of human life and activities from the *bios* of the botanical-animal life-cycle (the *fama* and the *amor* of the apiary life-world). This is arguably true of Ovid's *Metamorphoses* as well, which depicts transformations in the natural world as resulting from events in human history. On this issue, see the discussions in Marcel Detienne, "The Myth of Honeyed Orpheus," in *Myth, Religion and Society*, ed. and trans. R. L. Gordon (Cambridge: Cambridge University Press, 1981), 95–109; and Claude Lévi-Strauss's remarks on Virgil's poem in *From Honey to Ashes: Introduction to a Science of Mythology*, trans. John Weightman and Doreen Weightman (New York: Harper, 1973), 403 n17. On Eurydice as a figure for nature, see Charles Segal, "Orpheus and the Fourth *Georgic*: Vergil on Nature and Civilization," *American Journal of Philology* 87, no. 3 (1966): 307–25; André Oltramare, *Etude sur l'épisode d'Aristée dans les Géorgiques de Virgile* (Geneva, 1892), 158. On Aristaeus and productive domination, see Virgil, *Georgics* 4.326–28; and Segal, *Orpheus: The Myth of the Poet* (Baltimore: Johns Hopkins University Press, 1989), chap. 2.

23. "She fled headlong at the river to escape your / advances, the poor girl did not see death lurking at her feet / in the high grass—the huge water snake that guards the streambanks," as described in Janet Lembke's translation of Virgil's *Georgics* (New Haven: Yale University Press, 2006), 4.456–58.

24. Earlier versions of the myth, dating at least to the middle of the fifth century BCE, told of Orpheus' success in returning with Eurydice (see Segal, *Orpheus*, 8).

25. Orpheus, "famous in name," reads an archaic metope (570–560 BCE) on the Sicyonian treasury, Delphi, that represents the voyage of the Argonauts. Testimony to Orpheus' participation in the Argonauts' expedition leads some to assert that the figure of Orpheus is even more ancient than the Trojan heroes, older even than Homer. "For the Greeks [Orpheus] is dated one generation before the Trojan War, since he was associated with the expedition of the Argonauts; for us no evidence goes back beyond the middle of the sixth century," notes Walter Burkert, *Greek Religion: Archaic and Classical* (London: Wiley-Blackwell, 1991) 296. For a more recent discussion, see Umberto Curi, *Miti d'amore: Filosofia dell'eros* (Milan: Bompiani, 2009), 107. See also W. K. C. Guthrie, *Orpheus and Greek Religion* (London, 1935); Lee, *Virgil as Orpheus*, chap. 1; and Segal, *Orpheus*.

26. Segal (*Orpheus*, chap. 1) calls this the "magic of Orpheus."

27. If the surviving evidence is to be believed, this happened at a time between the Athenian tragedian Euripides' *Alcestis* (c. 438 BCE) and the composition of Virgil's *Georgics* (c. 29 BCE).

28. Segal discusses the private character of Orpheus' song here—its rejection of public ritual—in *Orpheus*, 22–24, 164–65. In his famous rewriting of the myth in "Orpheus, Eurydice, Hermes," Rainer Maria Rilke emphasizes this same aspect: "A woman

so loved that from one lyre there came / more lament than from all the lamenting women." See *The Selected Poetry of Rainer Maria Rilke* trans. Stephen Mitchell, English and German Edition (New York: Vintage, 1989).

29. *Georgics*, trans. Lembke, 4.459–66.

30. Ovid, *Metamorphoses*, trans. Mary M. Innes (London: Penguin, 1955), p. 226.

31. "Determinate negation" is Hegel's term, which I understand to mean not just what Robert Brandom has glossed as the "concept of material incompatibility"—or the medieval notion that *omnis determinatio est negatio* (to be determined as *this* is to be determined as *not that*)—but rather as meaning that new self-conceptions or theoretical orientations arise only as the (historically subsequent) denial or negation of a given theory, or self-conception. Hegel's examples typically come from the history of philosophy; but we could also think of what Thomas Kuhn described as "paradigm-shifts" in the sciences, where new scientific paradigms arise only as refutations of prior paradigms. See Paul Redding, *Analytic Philosophy and the Return of Hegelian Thought* (Cambridge: Cambridge University Press, 2007), chap. 3; mirrored in Markus Gabriel, *Transcendental Ontology: Essays in German Idealism* (London: Bloomsbury, 2011), n86.

32. In Ovid's version, we learn that Orpheus "mourned Eurydice to the full in the upper world." But, then, Ovid also depicts Orpheus' descent to the river Styx as springing from the failure of this mourning to satisfy him; more on this in a moment.

33. Love, then, is not the external 'cause' of Orpheus' failure to mourn Eurydice. So, I disagree with readings that see this line of Ovid's as an "avowal of (Orpheus') total submission to Amor" (Segal, *Orpheus*, 24).

34. I understand this to be Ovid's critical revision of Virgil's famous line *Amor vincit omnia, et nos cedamus Amori,* "Love conquers all things, so we too shall yield to love" (*Eclogues* 10.69).

35. "His music moved" (*at cantu commotae*; my translation) not only trees, animals and men but also the gods of the Underworld, "hearts impossible to soften with living prayers" (*Georgics*, trans. Lembke, 470).

36. Here is Virgil's account:

Yes, the homeplace of Death and the farthest crannies of Hell
were stunned by the song; the Furies, too, their hair entangled
with bile-green snakes, and Cerberus's three jaws fell agape,
while the wind-driven wheel of Ixion came to a dead stop.

(*Georgics*, trans. Lembke, 4.481–84)

Ovid's rendering goes even further, emphasizing the cessation of ritual practices associated with death and dying.

37. Modified from the Loeb translation.

38. The brief mention in Euripides' *Alcestis* is ambiguous. There is also the version of the Greek poet Conon (a contemporary of Virgil, who may therefore have used Virgil as his source and inspiration). See the discussion in Segal, *Orpheus*, 156. There are also several copies of a relief depicting Orpheus with his lyre, removing the veil from Eurydice's face while she looks into his eyes and rests her left hand on his shoulder. The most famous of these is housed in the Museo Archeologico Nazionale in Naples

(another copy is housed in the Louvre). I see the relief as depicting the moment of the turn—though, of course, others may see it differently. However, because it is a Roman copy of an (alleged) Greek original, it is difficult to know what kinds of historical conclusions to draw from its existence. See the discussions in Jacques Heurgon, "Orphée et Eurydice avant Virgilie," *Mélange d'Archéologie et d'Histoire* 49 (1932): 36; and in C. C. Bowra, "Orpheus and Eurydice," *Classical Quarterly*, 2, no. 3/4 (1952): 121.

39. Because it is not clear, in Virgil's telling, for how long Eurydice was to have followed Orpheus, the turn backward is somewhat difficult to decipher. One hint, however, is given by Virgil's use of the term *respicere* (look back), which carries the sense not only of looking backward but also of establishing contact—the word also carries the sense of fond regard or care. See Maurizio Bettini, *The Portrait of the Lover*, trans. Laura Gibbs (Berkeley: University of California Press, 1999), 149.

40. Ovid's and Virgil's portrayals of the "second loss" of Eurydice are—while the best-known—also somewhat unusual with respect to most other iterations of the tale. Recall, as mentioned, that the Greek sources sometimes portray Orpheus as having returned 'successfully' to the realm of the living, in a kind of comic resurrection—effectively taking Orpheus 'back to the happy wedding day.' This also seems to have been a prominent feature of lesser known medieval representations; see Peter Dronke, *Sources of Inspiration: Studies in Literary Transformation, 400–1500* (Rome, Edizioni di Storia e Letteratura, 1997), 263–83; and John Warden, ed., *Orpheus: The Metamorphoses of a Myth* (Toronto: University of Toronto Press, 1982). This *lieto fine* was then featured in the first operatic version of the Orpheus myth, Jacopo Peri's *Euridice* (1600), first produced for the wedding of Henry IV and Maria de Medici. The happy ending is, of course, also resuscitated, with a few differences, in the most popular of the many Orpheus operas—Gluck's *Orfeo ed Euridice* (1762)—and appears in the Balanchine-Stravinsky ballet *Orpheus* (1948). Incidentally, the reunion of Orpheus and Eurydice in the Underworld, narrated in Book 11 of Ovid's *Metamorphoses*, is less the happy ending of a return to earth than the manifest achievement of Orpheus' freedom with Eurydice, even after his own death: "now side by side they walk; now Orpheus follows her as she precedes, now goes before her, now may in safety look back upon his Eurydice" (*Metamorphoses* 11.63–66).

41. In Plato, the business of seeing in the cave is passive, imposed *upon* the prisoners—they are chained and cannot turn around—in contrast to the theoretical, noetic activity of the philosopher who looks upon the whole scene only after ascending. For more on this contrast with Homer's *Odyssey*, bk. 11, see Segal, *Orpheus*, 60.

42. That he does not "gaze," is I think, evidenced by the fact that Orpheus is "permitted" to turn and look only once, fatefully. This is a good point at which to distinguish my sense of Orpheus' turn from that provided by Maurice Blanchot in *The Gaze of Orpheus*, trans. Lydia Davis (Boston: Station Hill, 1981). Blanchot focuses on Orpheus' gaze (*le regard d'Orphée*)—which he understands as Orpheus' "desire" to see Eurydice shrouded in "night," in death. For Blanchot, Orpheus' gaze—his *regard*—shows him to be in the grip of a desire or "fascination," powerless to resist it. "Fascination is the gaze," writes Blanchot, "in which blindness is still vision, vision that is no longer the possibility

of seeing, but the impossibility of not seeing" (75). For more on the purportedly fetishistic character of Orpheus' desire, see the discussion of Blanchot in Simon Critchley, *Very Little . . . Almost Nothing* (New York: Routledge, 1997), 48–51. In contrast, I understand Orpheus' "look" not, as in Blanchot's book or Jean Cocteau's film *Orpheus*, as a fetishistic-compulsory desire in the face of which Orpheus himself is powerless, but as an action taken by him (a turn, a look backward) for which he holds himself responsible, and for which Eurydice holds him responsible. *Regard*, or "gaze," is thus not even the right characterization for the moment in question. Orpheus looks backward, yes—but in the sense that he actively turns or directs his eyes (*flexit amans oculos*, in Ovid's wording).

43. The answer lies in a deeply engrained—albeit, I think, mistaken—way of understanding of Orpheus' turn as the effect of some other causative force over which he is powerless: his anxiety about Eurydice, or his "desire," or his forgetfulness of the gods' command, or his fear. Indeed, Ovid's phrase *ne deficeret* is typically read as expressing the fear that Eurydice might "fail," grow weak and fall back. However, as some careful readers of have observed, *ne deficeret* "might refer to . . . Orpheus" as well as to Eurydice. Although her overall interpretation of the passage does not coincide with mine, see Victoria Rimell's reading of this Latin phrase, in *Ovid's Lovers: Desire, Difference and the Poetic Imagination* (Cambridge: Cambridge University Press, 2006), 110.

44. To mention only two of the well-known poems: Rilke's "Orpheus, Eurydice, Hermes," depicts Eurydice in botanical terms ("fruit," "flower," "root") following her death, but nevertheless allows her the question—uttered in response to Hermes' declaration, "he turned." "Who?" she asks. As if the question *why?* were not properly formulable unless one first asked *who?* The American poet H.D., in *Selected Poems* (New York: New Directions Books, 1988), 36–40, goes much further, imagining Eurydice holding Orpheus answerable, indefinitely: "why did you turn back, / that hell should be reinhabited / of myself thus / swept into nothingness?"

45. A related point, by way of clarification: in Aristotle's *Poetics*, the meaning of an action is revealed only in its unintended consequences (as in tragic plots). That is one kind of 'retroactive' reason-giving in human actions. But I am talking here about a different kind of retroactive revelation of an action's meaning or reason: namely, those acts which ask to be taken as reason-giving in situations where no authorizing or grounding reason is yet available.

46. These two works have, of course, long been invoked in the same breath by literary scholars, starting in 1598 with Francis Meres' observation of the propinquity of Shakespeare to Ovid—manifest, for instance, in the fact that Shakespeare's own use of Pyramus and Thisbe occurs in *A Midsummer Night's Dream*, a play that seems to have been written contemporaneously with *Romeo and Juliet*; see Jonathan Bate, *Shakespeare and Ovid* (Oxford: Oxford University Press, 1994), 2, 172–73 and passim. Ovid's *Metamorphoses* is the earliest known narrative source of the tale, though visual representations have survived from Ovid's era. See Peter E. Knox, "Pyramus and Thisbe in Cyprus," *Harvard Studies in Classical Philology* 92 (1989): 315–28.

47. This detail is perhaps relevant, in that the use of bricks in Roman domestic architecture also facilitated the rise of a commercial, civic real-estate market, because the

labor costs and prices for bricks could be more easily set and regulated than costs and prices for stones, wood or clay. The horizon for Ovid's story, I take it, is therefore a social world in which domestic architecture supplants public buildings and temples as a primary locus of worldly investment or value-measurement, and where a proto-capitalist world of individual ownership rights is also being elaborated.

48. "Their nearness made the first steps of their acquaintance" (*notitiam primosque gradus vicinia fecit*; *Metamorphoses* 4.55–59). Unless otherwise indicated, I cite from Ovid, *Metamorphoses, Volume 1, Books 1–8,* trans. Frank Justus Miller, rev. G. P. Goold, Loeb Classical Library (1916; repr. Cambridge, MA: Harvard University Press, 2004).

49. Continues Ovid: "[marriage] torches too would have joined [them] in law" (*taedae quoque iure coissent*; 4.60; my translation).

50. Claude Levi-Strauss, *The Elementary Structures of Kinship* (New York: Beacon, 1969), 3–28.

51. Ovid perhaps did not need to provide a substantial 'reason' for the parents' injunction, beyond their individual-sovereign will. Hegel, for example, in *The Philosophy of History*, trans J. Sibree (Kitchener, Ontario: Batoche Books, 1900; retrieved from https://www.marxists.org/reference/archive/hegel/works/hi/lectures3.htm) saw Rome as manifesting, in the Augustan age, "the cold abstraction of sovereignty and power, as the pure egotism of the will in opposition to others, involving no moral element of determination, but appearing in a concrete form only in the shape of individual interests." For more on Hegel's view of Rome as a social space which recognized the rational agency of individuals, see the section titled "Rome from the Second Punic War to the Emperors" in *The Philosophy of History*, and the discussion of the Roman "legal person" in *Phenomenology of Spirit*.

52. Compare Hegel: "in love as such no transgression is inherent"; see *Lectures on Fine Art*, vol. 1, trans. T. M. Knox (Oxford: Oxford University Press), 215.

53. "There was a slender chink in the wall which divided the two houses, which was part of its making" (*fissus erat tenui rima, quam duxerat olim, cum fieret, paries domui communis utrique*; 4.65–66; my translation).

54. William Shakespeare, *A Midsummer Night's Dream*, ed. Harold Brooks, Arden Shakespeare (London: Bloomsbury, 1979), 1.1.235–41.

55. One hears a lot, nowadays, about the increasing substitution of 'virtual' interactions for 'physical' conversations—smartphones and instant messaging rather than 'real' talking. Worries about the 'virtual' or the 'seeming' have a long philosophical pedigree—from Plato's theory of supersensible forms, to Descartes' "automata," to the concerns about the devaluation of sensuous experiences in the age of industrial-capitalist modes of production. However, I think that these worries fail to diagnose what is at issue in text messaging and chat rooms—particularly given that, in certain parts of the world, more love-affairs now begin online than in 'real life.' These new media, like the telephone or the written letter, also occasion (and can teach us something about) the connection between *erōs* and (self) knowledge to which Plato's *Symposium* was also attuned. Robert Brandom states the issue perfectly in *Reason in Philosophy: Animating Ideas* (Cambridge, MA: Harvard University Press, 2009), when

he writes about "sapience and sentience" and "distinctly *human* pleasures." "The more pleasure one takes . . . the more knowledge and understanding, the more carefully cultivated practices are involved. . . . And the point is most obtrusively and ostentatiously manifest for the case of sexual pleasure. Since . . . not just culturally, but just as much from the point of view of pure physiology . . . overwhelmingly the most important human sexual organ is the brain" (137). More on this connection between *erōs* and knowledge will be discussed in the section "Giving Birth in Wisdom," in Part III of this volume.

56. The expressive possibilities of the medium seem to have been on Shakespeare's mind when he took the additional step of presenting Ovid's wall as an living actor—"It is the wittiest partition that ever I heard discourse, my lord" (*A Midsummer Night's Dream*, 5.1.166–67).

57. This example derives from the characteristically thoughtful reflections offered by Glenn Gould in the first part of "The Question of the Instrument," an interview with Bruno Monsaingeon (CBC Toronto, November 19–26, 1979).

58. This was, arguably, the issue that most occupied Ovid's attention, starting with the *Amores* (16 BCE), a series of love poems that trace the practical challenges lovers face in their interactions, through the *Ars amatoria* (2 CE) and its sequel, *Remedia amores*.

59. For context, see Victoria Rimel, *Ovid's Lovers*; D. F. Kennedy, *The Arts of Love: Five Studies in the Discourse of Roman Love Elegy* (Cambridge: Cambridge University Press, 1993); and R.O.A.M. Lyne, *The Latin Love Poets from Catullus to Horace* (Oxford: Oxford University Press, 1980).

60. Modified from the Loeb translation.

61. Various forms of stoicism (in Seneca and Cicero, and before that in Marcus Aurelius and Epictetus) were influential fatalist philosophies of Ovid's time. Worldly fortunes were taught to be seen as external to the inner "calm" of the wise person, and this inner life (and its immunity to worldly fortune) had to be cultivated through various exercises, through education or philosophy (the wise man is free even if a slave and in chains). A significant portion of the writings of the Roman Stoics concern *how* one might undertake such cultivation—such a giving in to fatalism, as I am summarily calling it. See Marcus Aurelius' *Meditations*, for instance, and for more, see Pierre Hadot, *The Inner Citadel: The Mediations of Marcus Aurelius* (Cambridge, MA: Harvard University Press, 1998). Another recent and relevant discussion can be found in Richard Sorabji, *Self: Ancient and Modern Insights about Individuality, Life and Death* (Chicago: University of Chicago Press, 2006).

62. And the narrative structure of Ovid's *Metamorphoses* aims to depict just that tangle of events and circumstances.

63. . . . *demisit in ilia ferrum: illa–ium* means "flank or side extending from hips to groin, private parts," according to *The New College Latin and English Dictionary* (New York: Bantam, 2007). The blood spouting from the wound, as Ovid describes it, has seemed to commentators a medically accurate description of a puncture of the upper femoral artery, located on the inner thigh; see Peter Jones, *Reading Ovid: Stories from the Metamorphoses* (Cambridge: Cambridge University Press, 2007), 136.

Ovid's image of blood spouting from Pyramus' artery as if from a pipe was taken up by Shakespeare in *Titus Andronicus* (2.4.29–30), and by Chaucer, in his *Legend of Good Women* (2.851–52).

64. Compare Hegel: "self-knowing reason . . . divides *itself* into spirit and nature"; G.W.F. Hegel, *Encyclopedia of the Philosophical Sciences in Outline*, trans. Steven Taubeneck (New York: Continuum, 1990), §577). Ovid's procedure in the *Metamorphoses* (and Hegel's point in the passage just cited) is not to set out the difference between natural occurrences and human activities, but to see how that difference is one that we install (or tell ourselves) for various reasons.

65. To borrow Hegel's dramatic formulation: "This consciousness was not driven with anxiety about just this or that matter, nor did it have anxiety about just this or that moment; rather, it had anxiety about its entire essence. It felt the fear of death, the absolute lord. In that feeling, it had inwardly fallen into dissolution, trembled in its depths, and all that was fixed within it had been shaken loose" (*Phenomenology of Spirit*, §194).

66. As far as I can tell, Hegel subscribes to this, at least in the account of self-consciousness given in §185–94 of *Phenomenology of Spirit*. In the first instance, Hegel emphasizes that self-consciousness cannot be achieved without staking one's life or at least, that self-consciousness is not actual without such stakes. "The individual who has not risked his life . . . has not achieved the truth of being recognized as a self-sufficient self-consciousness" (§185). Only by staking one's life, says Hegel, is "freedom proven to be the essence." In the second instance, as the bondsman's predicament reveals, "fear of death, the absolute lord [*des absoluten Herrn*]" is the experience that explains his submission to the lord (see §194).

67. Jonathan Lear has recently expounded something like this undertaking as "irony," making a "case" for its fundamental importance to living a human life, in *The Case for Irony* (Cambridge, MA: Harvard University Press, 2011).

68. In saying this, I do not mean to discount the widening social authority of various amorous practices in Ovid's Rome, to which Ovid himself was keenly attuned. I mean only to make the defensible observation that love-based relations in Augustan Rome were not as expansive and entrenched as they are in many areas around the world today.

69. De Rougemont, *Love in the Western World*.

70. For example, Shakespeare's Antony fails to defeat Augustus Caesar, not just because he was outnumbered, or because the wind favored his opponents' sails, but because Cleopatra turned her ships in retreat:

O, whither hast thou led me, Egypt?

. . .

[T]hou knew'st too well
My heart was to thy rudder tied by the strings,
And thou shouldst tow me after.

William Shakespeare, *Antony and Cleopatra*, ed. M. R. Ridley, Arden Shakespeare (London: Metheun, 1964), 3.11.51–58.

71. Think, too, of Dido as depicted both in Virgil's *Aeneid* and Ovid's *Heroides*— depictions which contain many of the same elements I have followed in these pages,

and should, I think, be read in the same light. (Note that Virgil is the first to include the funeral pyre in the depiction of Dido's suicide.) Likewise, Roman depictions of Lucretia or Virginia can be taken to underscore how certain Roman women (unlike Homer's Helen, say, and in contrast to Stoic doctrine) are understood as trying to somehow take responsibility for their fate.

72. The following pages revise my earlier effort at understanding Shakespeare's play, in "Defying the Stars: Tragic Love as the Struggle for Freedom in *Romeo and Juliet*," *Shakespeare Quarterly* 63, no. 1 (2012): 1–38.

73. Romeo duels with Tybalt and Paris, and these battles have their place in the drama; but that place is neither central nor decisive. For a longer discussion, see my essay "Duel," in *21st Century Approaches to Early Modern Theatricality*, ed. Henry Turner (Oxford: Oxford University Press, 2014).

74. William Shakespeare, *Romeo and Juliet*, ed. Brian Gibbons, Arden Shakespeare (London: Metheun, 1999); all citations are to this edition.

75. Rosalind did not need to do anything with Romeo in order to be desirable to him, any more than a glass of water needs to do something with a thirsty person in order to be thirsted after.

76. "She'll not be hit / With Cupid's arrow; she hath Dian's wit, / And, in strong proof of chastity well arm'd / From love's weak childish bow she lives unharm'd" (1.1.206–9).

77. When Mercutio later quips that Romeo speaks "the numbers that Petrarch flowed in," he reminds us of the Petrarchan pedigree of both this rhetoric and its understanding of desire (2.2.40). "Numbers" refer to the metrical measures of a love poem. For more, see Heather Dubrow, *Echoes of Desire: English Petrarchism and Its Counter Discourses* (Ithaca: Cornell University Press, 1995), 263–67.

78. Conversely, if Romeo's desire were to limit itself to Rosalind, then that could signal the end of his libidinous investment in living—"Black and portentous must this humour prove / Unless good counsel may the cause remove" (1.1.139–40).

79. See the marvelous description of Juliet's development from this moment forward in Hegel, *Lectures on Fine Art*, vol. 1, 581–82.

80. A kiss, as usual, can stand for more. I mention this partly to explain why I do not think that Juliet's later insistence on marriage has anything to do with concerns on her part about legitimating sexual relations between them.

81. Benvolio and Mercutio, by contrast, plainly seek to remain unidentifiable at the masque. They remain revelers at heart—further and further estranged from Romeo, whose actions appear to them as increasingly confounding: "let [the ladies] measure us by what they will, / We'll measure them a measure and be gone" (1.4.9–10).

82. This should explain why the lovers' critique of the "name"—to the point of 'doffing' it entirely—must apply not only to "Capulet" and "Montague," but also to "Romeo" and "Juliet"—"Call me but 'love' and I'll be new baptized!" (2.2.50).

83. Alexandre Kojève, *Introduction to the Reading of Hegel*, 61 (emphasis in original).

84. That Romeo and Juliet are—by rank, age, and title and by Capulet's own admission (1.5.63–66)—eligible marriage partners for one another shows that the lovers are not, after all, divided by insuperable social obstacles. Compare Hegel: "the feud between

the families lies outside the lovers, their aim, and their fate" (*Lectures on Fine Art*, vol. 2, 1167).

85. This is why *West Side Story* is much less compelling than its Shakespearean source. In *West Side Story*, a fight to the death is essential to a broader ethnic tribal struggle or gang war, in which Tony and Maria are caught up and by which they are defeated. Their fate is merely wretched and regrettable—as if the lovers merely had the fortune of being in the wrong place at the wrong time among the wrong people.

86. Compare Hegel's description of Juliet as initially naïve but suddenly developing "the whole strength of this heart, of intrigue, circumspection, power to sacrifice everything and to submit to the harshest treatment; so that now the whole thing looks like the first blossoming of the whole rose at once in all its petals and folds, like an infinite outpouring of the inmost genuine basis of the soul . . . which now comes on the scene as an immediate product of an awakened single interest" (*Lectures on Fine Art*, vol. 1, 582).

87. I understand the 'doffing' of "Capulet" and "Montague" to be a negation of family life for the terms of their self-understanding (a determinate negation of that 'objective' form of life); the question of the proper name, "Romeo," is an attempt to rethink their individual belonging to that objective form of life.

88. This is what Kant, in the *Critique of Pure Reason*, called the "original synthetic unity of apperception." I mention this not to give the last word to Kant on these issues, but rather to suggest that this is a good way to situate ourselves with respect to Juliet's reflections here.

89. Juliet takes the man in darkness to be Romeo, with the understanding that she could also be mistaken, and therefore have to correct herself. She takes the man to be Romeo, not just by responding to sonorous clues, but also because smelling a rose or hearing Romeo talk is Juliet's way (a human way) of determining what is there; which means our sensuous 'determinations' or 'identifications' of one another are also knowledge-claims—expressions of what we know and how we know it—for which we can hold each other answerable. These comments might seem arcane, but the implications are practical and concrete. When Edmond Rostand revisited Shakespeare's balcony scene in *Cyrano de Bergerac*, for instance, he showed how much this kind of 'sensuous-knowledge commitment' matters for love-affairs and their practical possibilities (*how* Roxanne distinguishes Cyrano from Christian matters tremendously).

90. G.W.F. Hegel, "Love," in *Early Theological Writings*, trans. T. M. Knox (Philadelphia: University of Pennsylvania Press, 1971), 307.

91. See Hegel's subsequent comments on these same lines in the Berlin lectures on aesthetics, in which he notes the necessity of seeing the pathos of love in the context of "the most diverse relations"—to parents, friends, apothecaries, nurses (*Lectures on Fine Art*, vol. 1, 239).

92. Here is Romeo's anti-fatalist formulation:

>   come what sorrow can,
> It cannot countervail the exchange of joy
> That one short minute gives me in her sight:
> Do thou but close our hands with holy words,

Then love-devouring death do what he dare;

It is enough I may but call her mine. (2.6.3–8)

93. This does not contradict a view like Dympna Callaghan's , according to which "a certain formation of desiring subjectivity attendant upon Protestant and especially Puritan ideologies of marriage and the family required by, or at least very conductive to, the emergent economic formation of capitalism" is visible in Shakespeare's play. But my aim, in contrast to Callaghan's, is to inquire into how *Romeo and Juliet* might help us to better explain these kinds of large-scale normative transformations (rather than to ask how the play is explained *by* these historical transformations). See Dympna Callaghan, "The Ideology of Romantic Love: The Case of *Romeo and Juliet*," in *Romeo and Juliet: Contemporary Critical Essays*, ed. R. S. White (New York: Palgrave, 2001), 85.

94. This is not to say, by the way, that the parents would have forbidden the marriage had they been approached with the idea. As mentioned previously, on my reading, Capulet sees Romeo to be of marriageable rank, age and title (1.5.63–66).

95. Compare the exchange between Petruchio and Katharina in *The Taming of the Shrew*, where Katharina ends up declaring:

Then, God be bless'd, it is the blessed sun:

But sun it is not, when you say it is not;

And the moon changes even as your mind.

What you will have it named, even that it is;

And so it shall be so for Katharina.

William Shakespeare, *The Taming of the Shrew*, ed. Brian Morris, Arden Shakespeare (London: Metheun, 1981), 4.5.18–22.

96. As we see in the very next scene, Juliet is perfectly willing to accept the Friar's "remedy" in the hope that, when she wakes from the drug, Romeo shall "bear" her "hence to Mantua" (4.1.117). And yet she chooses not to flee at the moment, although she could have made her escape "disguis'd" (3.3.167) and without the use of exotic drugs. (As everyone knows, Shakespeare knew perfectly well how to stage an escape for a woman in disguise, and the Friar suggests as much.) So, the question is, why does she let Romeo leave?

97.

Friar Lawrence. In the meantime, against thou shalt awake,

Shall Romeo by my letters know our drift,

And hither shall he come: and he and I

Will watch thy waking, and that very night

Shall Romeo bear thee hence to Mantua.

And this shall free thee from this present shame.

. . .

Juliet. Give me, give me! O, tell not me of fear! (4.1.117–25)

98. Romeo's language throughout the final act makes this clear; for instance:

A grave? O no! a lantern, slaughter'd youth,

For here lies Juliet, and her beauty makes

This vault a feasting presence full of light.

Death, lie thou there, by a dead man interr'd.

[*Laying Paris in the tomb*]
How oft when men are at the point of death
Have they been merry! (5.3.84–89)

99. For example, paying the Apothecary, breaking into the Capulets' tomb, slaying Paris.

Part III: From the Propagation of Life to Lovemaking

1. Quotations from Genesis 1–2 are from *Genesis: Translation and Commentary*, trans. Robert Alter (New York: Norton, 1997). In relation to this discussion, see especially, Genesis 1:22–23, 28–29. The command to "be fruitful and multiply" is repeated to each order of life—plant, animal and human—as if to draw some distinction between these orders according to their *way* of multiplying fruitfully. When it comes to human beings, for example, Genesis seems to imply that fruitful multiplication in human beings is conditional upon the fruitful multiplication of other life-forms.

2. Even if we understand Genesis to present Eve as having been produced 'from' Adam, this sort of single-sex or divine-self reproduction is nevertheless not presented in Genesis as continuing indefinitely.

3. Aristotle, *Politics* 1252a, 27–30, slightly modified from Lord's translation.

4. I leave out of consideration, here, the account of Eve's origins (from Adam's rib) in the second chapter of Genesis, where anatomical and linguistic differences between them are given greater consideration. Over time, this view led to the popular notion that a natural link exists between sexual difference and procreation, as witnessed in the centuries following the rise of Christianity. See John Boswell, *Christianity, Social Tolerance and Homosexuality* (Chicago: University of Chicago Press, 1980), 12–17.

5. It is worth adding that, with the advent of cloning and new reproductive technologies, it is now clear that naturalistic-causal grasps of reproduction do not just neutrally describe biological facts. Our scientific understanding also brings about 'new facts,' and indeed makes cloning possible. To learn about the birds and the bees is not to learn timeless scientific knowledge about 'natural requirements' for life. Rather, the 'learning' or 'knowledge' is itself an intervention *at the level* of the putatively 'natural,' and thus in no way separable from normative moral-cultural issues.

6. After all, it was only at a certain point in history that human beings perceptively grasped the sperm plus egg process *as being* biological, as calling for a causal explanation. And the institutional authority of the modern sciences to offer such causal accounts is itself something that had to be achieved over time. The authority of the sciences is institutional; it does not descend from birds-and-bees "facts of life."

7. Hans Georg Gadamer, *Truth and Method* (London: Sheen and Ward, 1975) uses the German term *Horizontverschmelzung*—by which he meant to say that historically aware interpretation requires that we be neither overly limited by our own historical horizons nor overly concerned with getting at the objective 'truth' about the past. "A person who has no horizon is a man who does not see far enough and hence overvalues what is nearest to him. On the other hand, 'to have a horizon' means not being limited to what is nearby, but being able to see beyond it . . . working out of the hermeneutical

situation means the achievement of *the right horizon of inquiry for the questions evoked by the encounter* with tradition" (269; my emphasis).

8. In his notes to his translation of Genesis, in *The Five Books of Moses: A Translation with Commentary* (New York: Norton, 2008), Robert Alter notes that the English term "Him, as in the Hebrew, is grammatically, but not anatomically, masculine" (19).

9. In a relevant set of remarks on this same passage—which connects Genesis 1 to Aristotle's *Politics*—Hannah Arendt sought in *The Human Condition* to show that "plurality" is the *conditio per quam* of all political life. "The human condition of action is implicit in Genesis ('male and female he created *them*'), if we understand that this story of man's creation is distinguished in principle from the one according to which God originally created Man (*adam*), 'him' and not 'them,' so that the multitude of human beings comes before the rest of multiplication" (8). Arendt goes on to say, in a footnote, that "it is highly characteristic of the difference between the teaching of Jesus of Nazareth and of Paul that Jesus, discussing the relationship between man and wife, refers to Genesis 1:27, 'Have ye not read that he which made *them* at the beginning made them male and female' (Matt. 19:4), whereas Paul on a similar occasion insists that the woman was created 'of the man' and hence 'for the man' even though he somewhat attenuates the dependence: 'Neither is the man without the woman, neither the woman without the man'" (8n).

10. As already noted, above, this is perhaps a plausible conclusion to draw from the account of Eve's origins given in the second book of Genesis.

11. Clearly these are not the only possibilities. Plenty of further distinctions (size, shape, color) can be apprehended. Remember, too, the well-known passage from Plato's *Symposium* in which Aristophanes claims that the sexes were originally "not two, but three" in number. At any rate, my claim is not that the apprehension of *a particular* anatomical difference between genitalia was, as a matter of historical fact, what must have happened at some 'originary' or foundational moment—but rather that the apprehension of *some* anatomical difference must have raised the question of what explanatory power that apprehension can have. What explanatory problems does that apprehension provoke?

12. Obviously, other questions *could* also arise—such as What kinds of cultural values get attached to what kinds of observations of differentiation? But *that* question implies a level of social-historical awareness that is, I think, not necessarily implicit in every naked observation of anatomical difference. Think of the 'innocence' or hilarity with which young children make observations about human bodies without necessarily being attuned to social valences that might attach to such observations.

13. For example, Genesis, chaps. 7 and 8; and Aristotle, *On the Movement of Animals*.

14. "[T]he mortal nature seeks as far as possible to be forever and immortal. Mortal nature is capable of immortality only in this way, the way of generation, because it is always leaving behind another that is young to replace the old. For while each of the animals is said to live and be the same (for example, one is spoken of as the same from the time one is a child until one is an old man; and though he never has the same things in himself; nevertheless, he is called the same), he is forever becoming young in some respects as he suffers losses in other respects: his hair, flesh, bones, blood, and his whole

body"; Plato, *Symposium*, in *Plato's Symposium: A Translation by Seth Benardete with Commentaries by Allan Bloom and Seth Benardete* (Chicago: University of Chicago Press, 2011), 207d–e; all citations are to this edition.

15. See Genesis 1:19–25, 28–29; Aristotle, *Politics* 1252a.

16. See, again, Socrates' remarks in Plato, *Symposium* 207d–e, cited above.

17. Ideas about sexual reproduction were immensely importance to nineteenth-century debates about social organization, out of which modern anthropology emerges. Johann Jakob Bachofen (1815–87) was among the first to argue that knowledge of sexual paternity was a crucial step in the development of culture. Others, such as John Ferguson McLennan (1827–81), also discussed the importance of knowledge of paternity for marriage practices and female chastity. Lewis Henry Morgan argued for a connection between property inheritance and knowledge of paternity in ancient cultures—in work that influenced Engels' theses about the importance of knowledge of paternity for social organization in his "On the Origin of the Family, Private Property and the State" (1884). As Rosalind Coward notes, in *Patriarchal Precedents: Sexuality and Social Relations* (London: Routledge, 1983), "The role of paternity and the procreative family were obsessive themes in the discussion of familiar forms" in early anthropological studies (60). In the early twentieth century, anthropologists like Bronisław Malinowski investigated the so-called ignorance of paternity of the Trobrianders. In his book *The Sexual Life of Savages*, 3rd ed. (London: Routledge, 1932), Malinowski was at pains to emphasis that "knowledge" of paternity was not a matter of mere empirical knowledge, but was "overlaid by beliefs of an animistic nature, and influenced by the moral and legal principles of the community" (xxi.). Malinowski's work not only challenged the universality of the Oedipus complex, as then championed by Ernest Jones; it also occasioned what has come to be known as the "Virgin Birth" debate—in which the acquiring of "knowledge" of sexual reproduction came to be seen not as a scientific step from ignorance to knowledge, but rather as bound up with the immense question of *how* to account for sexual self-education and cultural development, across cultures, as more than a matter of empirical observation and instrumental rationality. The present work is one attempt to think through these same difficult questions—which remain open and unresolved for anthropologists—although my approach is neither ethnographical nor (strictly) anthropological. (My thanks to Michael Silverstein for pointing me to Malinowski.) See also the entry on "Conception" in *Encyclopedia of Social and Cultural Anthropology*, ed. Alan Barnard and Jonathan Spencer (London: Taylor and Francis, 1996); and Carol Delaney, "The Meaning of Paternity and the Virgin Birth Debate," *Man* 2, no. 3 (1986): 494–513.

18. "Image" of, or "likeness" of (as in "made in the image of"), are the terms used by Genesis and Aristotle to express species-level reproduction. Or so I will assume.

19. It does not seem a stretch to imagine that—just as our ancestors must have apprehended differences between living bodies—they also apprehended likenesses between offspring and forebearer. This is emphasized in both Aristotle's work and Genesis: "with man as with the other animals and with plants there is a natural instinct to desire to leave behind one another being of the same sort as oneself" (Aristotle, *Politics*, 1252a); "Let us make a human in our image, in our likeness" (Genesis 1:26–27).

20. Some have followed a certain 'structuralist' line—for example, the work of Claude Lévi -Strauss or Jacques Lacan—in seeing "sexual difference" (male and female, masculine and feminine, usually) as a constitutive element of social relations, or at least as a fundamental framework for thinking about social relations. (Although Lévi-Strauss recanted some of his positions; see Claude Lévi-Strauss, "Postface," *L'Homme*, April–September 2000, 154–55.) Critics of Lacan and Lévi-Strauss, such as Judith Butler, see sexual difference not as a symbolic (or literal) precondition for the intelligibility of human culture, but rather as resulting from "ongoing cultural interpretations of bodies . . . dynamically positioned within a field of cultural possibilities" (Butler, "Sex and Gender in Simone de Beauvoir's *Second Sex*," 35). I am offering a different approach.

21. John McDowell, *Mind and World* (Cambridge, MA: Harvard University Press, 1994), 39. I realize that McDowell's suggestion is a controversial and discussion-sparking one; and I cannot defend it or properly interpret it here. But I do want to try to 'test' his hypothesis, as it were, in the course of this discussion. For a lively debate about this very claim, occasioned by Hubert Dreyfus' response to McDowell, see the essays collected in Joseph K. Schear, ed., *Mind, Reason and Being-in-the-World: The McDowell-Dreyfus Debate* (New York: Routledge, 2013).

22. Compare Hegel's remark, in *Hegel's Logic: Being Part One of the Encyclopedia of the Philosophical Sciences*, trans. W. Wallace (Oxford: Oxford University Press, 1975): "The facility that we attain in any sort of knowledge, art, or technical expertise, consists in having the particular knowledge or kind of action present to our mind in any case that occurs, even, we may say, immediate in our very limbs, as an outgoing activity" (§66).

23. Robert Brandom describes this as a process of "material incompatibility and consequence" or "material inferential relations," in *Tales of the Mighty Dead* (Cambridge, MA: Harvard University Press, 2002), 49 and passim.

24. See the discussion in Beauvoir, *The Second Sex*, 25–26, not for an authoritative account of the history of science, but for a way of framing the importance of that history to the questions at hand.

25. Again, 'perceptual-grasping' is my way of trying to restate McDowell's suggestion that "conceptual capacities are already operative in the deliverances of sensibilities."

26. For an informed discussion of ancient divinities as articulations of sexual differences—independent of sexual acts—see Claude Calame's examination of iconographical material in *The Poetics of Eros in Ancient Greece*, trans. Janet Lloyd (Princeton: Princeton University Press, 1999), chap. 2.

27. Without delving into the thickets of comparative religion—and taking note of the fact that the name of the Hindu god Brahma, for instance, is linguistically presented as gender-neutral (although sexual differentiations among the other Hindu gods are pronounced)—my modest point is that the articulation of divinities across many cultures often takes the form of an articulation of sexual difference between male, female, neutral, androgynous and other. As already discussed, Adam and Eve, for example, are presented as sexually differentiated in the same moment at which they are said to be made in God's image. Likewise, the respective generative powers of 'male' and 'female' elements (Gaea, Uranus, Zeus) shape the origins recounted in Hesiod's *Theogony*.

28. Again, this takes us into the terrain mentioned in note 17, above. To repeat, my aim in these paragraphs is to provide hypotheses that might furnish terms for a new reckoning with these questions, which have been so fundamental to the formation of modern anthropology.

29. Beauvoir's account is relevant here:

The male deposits his sperm; the female receives it. Thus, although she plays a fundamentally active role in procreation, she endures coitus, which alienates her from herself by penetration and internal fertilization ... the fundamental difference between male and female mammals is that in the same quick instant, the sperm, by which the male's life transcends into another, becomes foreign to it and is separated from its body; thus the male, at the very moment it goes beyond its individuality, encloses itself once again in it. By contrast, the ovum began to separate itself from the female ... first violated, the female is then alienated; she carries the foetus in her womb for various stages of maturation depending on the species." (*The Second Sex*, 36)

Malinowski posited that a "greater emphasis on female chastity" might have provided "a greater opportunity for empirical correlation between the sexual act and pregnancy"— though he provides little evidence or argumentation for this (*Sexual Life of Savages*, xxiv): Beauvoir's speculations about the importance of the 'first-personal' strike me as more plausible.

30. And I hope it goes without saying that prejudiced claims about "savages" who are "ignorant" of sexual reproduction get us nowhere. See note 17 above.

31. Michel Foucault, "The West and the Truth of Sex," *SubStance* 6/7, no. 20 (1978), 5–8.

32. Ibid.

33. Aristotle made this point when he distinguished human vocalizations (*phone*) of pleasure or pain—as with other animals, the voice is a "sign" (*semeion*) of pleasure or pain—from the *logos* on which a shared way of life could take root (*Politics* 1252–53). A related thought can be found in Elaine Scarry's discussion of pain as de-worlding, in *The Body in Pain* (Oxford: Oxford University Press, 1987).

34. On the ambiguity of the Hebrew verb, which apparently signifies "intercourse" as a form of "legitimate possession," rather than erotic expression, see Robert Alter's note to Genesis 4:1 in *The Five Books of Moses*, 29.

35. "Sumerian Sacred Marriage Texts," in *Ancient Near Eastern Texts Relating to the Old Testament*, ed. James B. Pritchard, 3rd ed. (Princeton: Princeton University Press, 1969), 643.

36. See note 17, above. To grasp that reproduction occurs through birth or sexual reproduction must entail, already at the experiential level, grasping one's belonging to a life-form which can reproduce in that way—or so I am claiming. Further, since the way in which reproduction is grasped or 'made sense of' is essential to reflectively apprehending the distinctiveness of the life-form to which one belongs, it is also essential to the endurance and development of distinctive practices within that life-form. Grasping *how* one's form of life reproduces itself is, in other words, essential to any reflective understanding of belonging *to* a life-form at all, and it is also essential to the distinctive practical domains that a life-form installs over time at the level of bodily activity (what

certain limbs might do, say). For this reason, I disagree with strong 'constructivist' views among anthropologists, according to which, as Marshall Sahlins puts it in *What Kinship Is—and Is Not* (Chicago: University of Chicago Press, 2013), "kinship is not given by birth as such, since human birth is not a pre-discursive fact" (3). For a recent scientific account of practical ways in which apes and humans 'grasp' distinctive ways of reproducing—such that the 'practical reasoning' itself articulates salient 'behavioral' distinctions between life-forms—see Holly Dunsworth, "Do Animals Know Where Babies Come From?" *Scientific American*, January 2016, 66–69. As Dunsworth puts it, "If we could somehow teach our great ape cousins that sex produces babies, then we might expect their behavior . . . to change dramatically . . . knowing where babies come from . . . would have its own behavioral consequences. . . . If apes apprehended that sex leads to babies, they would act a lot more like people."

37. Genesis 3:3–4.

38. John Milton, *Paradise Lost* (Oxford: Oxford University Press, 2008), bk. 9, line 1115.

39. I think that it is not pleasure that is cultivated in *ars erotica* (as Foucault suggested) but something more like sexual 'reason-giving.' After all, pleasures can be shared—"passed from one individual to another," as Foucault put it—without thereby being cultivated as an art. One can share the pleasure of a ripe fruit without thereby cultivating a culinary art. Cultivation requires more than the mere "sharing" or "transmission" of pleasures or pains—it entails the collective acknowledgment of a *reason* for the undertaking of certain activities. See Didier Eribon, *Michel Foucault et ses contemporains* (Paris: Fayard, 1994), 271, cited in Arnold Davidson, *The Emergence of Sexuality* (Cambridge, MA: Harvard University Press, 2001), 213.

40. Incidentally, Beauvoir's conclusion was not dissimilar. She writes:

> the perpetuation of the species appears as the correlative of individual limitation, so the phenomenon of reproduction can be considered as ontologically grounded. But this is where one must stop; the perpetuation of the species does not entail sexual differentiation. That it is taken on by existents in such a way that it thereby enters into the concrete definition of existence, so be it. Nevertheless, a consciousness without a body or an immortal human being is rigorously inconceivable, whereas a society can be imagined that reproduces itself by parthenogenesis or is composed of hermaphrodites." (*The Second Sex*, 24)

41. The reproduction of human life depends, of course, on other conditions besides sex—such as adequate nutrition, genetic factors and suitable physical environments. I do not have the space to discuss these here, other than to say (contra a reductive naturalism) that we should not be quick to conclude that the healthfulness of the earthly environment or genetic codes, for instance, is not likewise determined by the scope of human practices and activities.

42. This is not to say that this is the only way we come to see ourselves an agents, but it is one way—even a fundamental way.

43. In speaking of "sexual acts and experiences," I mean the emergence of a distinctive social-historical practice. In using the term *sexual*, I do not mean to allude to what Foucault calls "an experience of sexuality" (something that, as Foucault shows, emerges

much later). I mean, simply, the discernment of erotic-sexual activities, apprehendable and regulatable as such. I will use the terms *sexual* and *erotic* more or less interchangeably in this section.

44. Sexual practices install and achieve regulatable, 'civilized' forms of life; only then can civilization regulate sex (contra Freud's account in *Civilization and Its Discontents*).

45. And these rules must have been formed well before anything like the incest taboo could set in.

46. The discursive articulation of nonprocreative erotic acts—and the vicissitudes of *erōs* generally—in procreative terms, even if just metaphorically, is a notable feature of ancient texts. Think, for instance, of how *erōs* is connected to the midwifery of ideas in Plato's *Symposium*. I will return to this in a moment.

47. It is striking that Simone de Beauvoir's other philosophical magnum opus, besides *The Second Sex*, was a reflection on aging called *The Coming of Age* (*La vieillesse*). Although Beauvoir had much to say about the particular importance of aging and growth in both books, and although she clearly intuited the importance and connection between these two topics, she seems not to have explicitly formulated the suggestion I am making here: that the social articulation of the "feminine condition," as well as the masculine or other conditions—and, indeed, of human sexual practices—must have been tied from the start to the apprehension of, and attempt to make sense of, growth and aging (first with respect to fertile women).

48. For relevant discussions of such "initiation" practices in Greece and other ancient cultures, see, as only a start, Claude Calame, *Choruses of Young Women in Ancient Greece: Their Morphology, Religious Role, and Social Functions*, trans. Derek Collins and Jane Orion (Lanham, MD: Rowman & Littlefield, 1997), chaps. 2 and 3; Bernard Sergent, *Homosexuality in Greek Myth* (New York: Beacon, 1986), 11–12, 40–45; K. J. Dover, "Greek Homosexuality and Initiation," in *The Greeks and their Legacy* (Oxford: Blackwell, 1988), 116–19, 124–26.

49. The excavation of these ancient 'wisdoms' has become a cottage industry among contemporary sex therapists and yoga instructors—although this has more to do with the relaxing of sexual mores in modernity than with the supposed timelessness of such wisdoms.

50. These different knowledges became normatively binding whether or not they turned out to be verifiably accurate according to modern scientific criteria.

51. As mentioned, Foucault was uncertain which (if any) normative domains—medicine, psychiatry, prisons, sexuality—best display how power operates. Indeed, we might wonder if there really is such a thing as *power* under which all kinds of social and cultural norms can be subsumed and understood. Or at least, we might suspect that each of these norms requires or instantiates its own dimension of power. But then, what (if anything) would count as a significant dimension of power? That is, *which* customs and activities might be understood not only to require and institute their own distinctive normative domains—probably all activities do *that*—but also to do so in ways that perhaps foreground and hence educate us as to the implications of such 'requiring and instituting' more generally?

52. "The world has always belonged to males, and none of the reasons given for this have ever seemed sufficient. By reviewing prehistoric and ethnographic data in the light of existentialist philosophy, we can understand how the hierarchy of the sexes came to be. We have already posited that when two human categories find themselves face-to-face, each one wants to impose its sovereignty on the other. . . . It is thus understandable that man might have had the will to dominate woman" (Beauvoir, *The Second Sex*, 73). "If being a woman is one cultural interpretation of being female, and if that interpretation is *in no way necessitated* by being female, then it appears that the female body is the arbitrary locus of the gender 'woman'" (Judith Butler, "Sex and Gender in Simone de Beauvoir's *Second Sex*," 35; my emphasis).

53. Once again, then, I am contesting the Foucaultian thought, endorsed by Butler, that "knowledge and power are not finally separable but work together to establish a set of subtle and explicit criteria for thinking the world" (Butler, *Undoing Gender*, 27). I want to say that knowledge would not have the power it does, to shape social life and install or enforce norms, were it not for its explanation of what we take as the deepest threats to sense. Indeed, power is not intelligible *as power* unless we are already engaging others and the world as sense-makers. Although knowledge invariably results in power, knowledge-formation (threats to sense) must determine power.

54. At the same time, it is important to remember that not all knowledge is equally powerful, or powerful in the same way. If socially powerful effects are measurably different, depending on the knowledge-regimes to which they are connected, then this is because power depends upon the extent to which these knowledges respond, not solely to localized threats to intelligibility—sense that needs to be made in view of some particular circumstance—but to threats to any sense we might make of anything whatsoever.

55. I agree with Butler that "when the unreal lays claim to reality, or enters into its domain, something other than a simple assimilation into prevailing norms takes place [and that] the norms themselves . . . become open to resignification" (*Undoing Gender*, 27). But, I want to say further, profound normative change requires not just this or that challenge to the way we 'know' our world, but profound challenges to the intelligibility of anything at all. So, we should consider power-formations as effects of threats to sense-making, not just as indistinguishable from an ongoing process of knowledge production.

56. Before Foucault, sociologists like Mary McIntosh and Kenneth Plummer had argued that sexual desire is socially constructed.

57. For one example of the variety of norms and institutions—and as evidence that patriarchy is far from universal—see Cai Hua, *A Society without Fathers or Husbands: The Na of China*, trans. Asti Hustvedt (New York: Zone Books, 2001).

58. This is not to say that other lessons were not learned along the way, or that certain knowledges were not consolidated and refined—only that these gains were not yet authoritative enough to fundamentally transform our way of life or our self-understanding across broad swaths of history.

59. I fully admit that I may well misdiagnose certain practices as local, rather than as broadly significant. I do not claim to be offering any last word, historically or anthro-

pologically, on historical cultures—far from it. I mean only to offer a correctable account that might, however, bring into view the *kind* of phenomenological-retrospective account that, I think, we should be trying to offer.

60. For a discussion of symposia in the late archaic period that emphasizes the connection between their 'erotic' character and their role as an arena of civic debate and education, see Calame, *The Poetics of Eros in Ancient Greece*, 84–98 and, on flute-girls, 111–14.

61. Plato, *Symposium* 173b. For discussions of the meaning of the term *erōs*, on which I have relied here, see Paul Ludwig, *Eros and Polis: Desire and Community in Greek Political Discourse* (Cambridge: Cambridge University Press, 200), 7–10; and Calame, *The Poetics of Eros in Ancient Greece*, chap. 1. For historical context and relevant dates, see Martha Nussbaum, *The Fragility of Goodness: Luck and Ethics in Greek Tragedy and Philosophy* (Cambridge: Cambridge University Press, 1986), 165–71.

62. Various speeches in Plato's dialogue *do*, of course, describe and defend local erotic practices—in particular, pederastic love. But these descriptions and 'apologies' are framed and contained by the overall context of this effort to discuss *erōs*, as if this *erōs* therefore comprehended these particular practices without itself being fully graspable in terms of their mere description or defense. At any rate, it seems clear that Plato's text is as much an effort to understand the symposia of his day (and their erotic character) as it is (for us) a central piece of textual evidence for the social significance of these rituals. For a historical discussion, see Calame, *The Poetics of Eros in Ancient Greece*, chaps. 5 and 5.

63. See Plato, *Symposium* 177b–c. Also see Alexander Nehemas, Introduction, in Plato, *Symposium* (Indianapolis: Hackett, 1988), xiv. Again, that the symposia were seen as erotically charged *and* educational-discursive arenas certainly seems to have contributed to Plato's presentation of the scene. Calame comments that "a symposium . . . was certainly a place for learning; learning by example, but also learning through poetry, from the praise of aristocratic values or the narration of exemplary tales"; see his discussion in *The Poetics of Eros in Ancient Greece*, 94–95 and passim.

64. Aristophanes says nothing about female-female relations at this point in the dialogue, though he does address them later. Many commentators have discussed the manifest political implications of pederasty, and the freedoms opened by erotic activity between men, in Aristophanes' speech and in Greek culture generally. However, none of these discussions take up the issue of erotic sense-making, as I try to do here. See the discussions in Paul Ludwig, *Eros and Polis*, esp. 27–35; S. Sara Monoson, *Plato's Democratic Entanglements: Athenian Politics and the Practice of Philosophy* (Princeton: Princeton University Press, 2000), 67–86; and Mary P. Nichols, *Socrates on Friendship and Community: Reflections on Plato's Symposium, Phaedrus, and Lysis* (Cambridge: Cambridge University Press, 2009), 25–90. On the isolation of women and reproductive sex from philosophy and politics, see the discussions in Stanley Rosen, *Plato's Republic: A Study* (New Haven: Yale University Press, 2008), 210–11; Stanley Rosen, *Plato's Symposium* (New Haven: Yale University Press, 1968), 148; and Leo Strauss, *On Plato's Symposium* (Chicago: University of Chicago Press, 2003), 130–36.

65. For context, see Ludwig, *Eros and Polis*, 27–32; Monoson, *Plato's Democratic Entanglements*, 67–76; Nichols, *Socrates on Friendship and Community*, 25–90. Also see Rosen, *Plato's Symposium*, 148; and Strauss, *On Plato's Symposium*, 130–36.

66. *Phaulos* is Plato's word. Alexander Nehemas translates it as "vulgar," Seth Benardete as "pandemian." "And here you have the one whom good-for-nothing human beings have as their love," says Pausanias in this passage, "Those who are of the same sort as this (pandemian) Eros are, first of all, no less in love with women than with boys; secondly, they are in love with their bodies rather than their souls, and thirdly, they are in love with the stupidest there can be, for they have an eye only to the act and are unconcerned with whether it is noble or not" (Plato, *Symposium* 181b).

67. Plato, of course, does not tell us what the flute-girl may have done or said with the women at Agathon's house. But he does not prevent us from supposing that they, too, had things to say to one another—matters that could not sensibly be discussed with men—as well as their own festivities to pursue. We get a glimpse of this when a flute-girl returns following Socrates' speech toward the end of the dialogue. While "songs celebrating the erotic charms of girls who had subsequently progressed to adulthood were not to be heard at symposia," claims Claude Calame, "[a]llusions to politics, and to the civic and social qualities of the *agathoi* (typical of symposia) were replaced, where women were singing, by evocations of beauty enhanced by ornamentation and apparel, appeals to the charm and elegances of feminine maturity, and invitations to enter into intimacy with Aphrodite." See Calame's discussion of the Sapphic counterpoints to the male-centered symposia, in *The Poetics of Eros in Ancient Greece*, 99 and passim.

68. The secondary literature is extensive, but so far as I can tell it focuses almost exclusively the question of how to "define" Platonic *erōs*, rather than on what *erōs* explains (as is my approach here). In addition to the discussion in Nussbaum's *The Fragility of Goodness* and the bibliography she engages, the interested reader could start with Giovanni Ferrari, "Platonic Love," in *The Cambridge Companion to Plato*, ed. Richard Kraut (Cambridge: Cambridge University Press, 1992), 248–276; Anthony W. Price, *Love and Friendship in Plato and Aristotle* (Oxford: Clarendon, 1988),chap. 2; Santas Gerasimos, *Plato and Freud: Two Theories of Love* (London: Wiley-Blackwell, 1988); and Kenneth Dorter, "The Significance of the Speeches in Plato's *Symposium*," *Philosophy and Rhetoric* 2, no. 4 (1969): 215–34.

69. Consider Freud's discussion of Eros and the comparison he draws between his own theories and Plato's *Symposium*: "anyone who looks down with contempt upon psychoanalysis . . . should remember how closely the enlarged sexuality of psychoanalysis coincides with the Eros of the divine Plato." See Sigmund Freud, *Three Essays on the Theory of Sexuality*, in *The Standard Edition of the Complete Psychological Works of Sigmund Freud*, vol. 7, trans. James Strachey (London: Hogarth Press, 1981), 134; cited in Jonathan Lear, *Freud*, 2nd ed. (New York: Routledge, 2015), 86. Lear's extremely helpful exposition of Freud on this point coincides with the approach to Plato I am advocating here; as when Lear writes, "Even the infant who sucks his thumb is . . . trying to make sense of the world and his position in it. There are primal gratifications in this urge . . . but there is embedded in this an elemental desire for understanding and for orientation."

Lear goes on to make the same claim about Plato: "This whole process of sexual attraction, dissatisfaction, realization, thinking and reorientation—all of this, from a Platonic perspective, is a manifestation of Eros" (86–87).

70. For Pausanias, the vulgar acts concern only sexual gratification or reproduction, whereas the noble acts concern care for the beloved's soul.

71. Agathon begins his own discourse by saying that the others have "explained what qualities [in *erōs*] enable *erōs* to give those benefits for which we praise him" (Plato, *Symposium* 195a).

72. There is an immense bibliography and debates among specialists on this topic; the interested reader could begin with the pages devoted by Martha Nussbaum to the *Symposium* and the critical bibliography she engages in *The Fragility of Goodness*, chap. 6; and with Alexander Nehamas, "Beauty of Body, Nobility of Soul: The Pursuit of Love in Plato's *Symposium*," in *Maieusis: Essays on Ancient Philosophy in Honour of Myles Burnyeat*, ed. Dominic Scott (Oxford: Oxford University Press, 2007), 97–135.

73. See, for instance, *Republic* 490b, or *Phaedrus* 251c.

74. Friedrich Nietzsche, *Beyond Good and Evil*, ed. Rolf-Peter Horstmann and Judith Norman (Cambridge: Cambridge University Press, 2002), 3. I take a cue here from Robert Pippin's discussion of Nietzsche, eros and Socrates. However, I note that Pippin's discussion does not make much of the fact that Nietzsche sees Socrates' clumsiness as concerning—not just the way philosophers act as lovers generally—but the way philosophers act as lovers of *women*. This detail from *Beyond Good and Evil* is crucial to understanding the issues, in my view, and I will say more about it in the following section. See Robert Pippin, *Nietzsche, Psychology, and First Philosophy* (Chicago: University of Chicago Press, 2010), 14–19; and *Idealism as Modernism* (Cambridge: Cambridge University Press, 1997), 357–64.

75. Pippin, *Idealism as Modernism*, 363.

76. Though it does not feature in the bachelor Nietzsche's considerations.

77. "[A]ll philosophers so far have loved their truths" (Nietzsche, *Beyond Good and Evil*, §43).

78. Nietzsche, *Beyond Good and Evil*, §44. This is, of course, a recurrent preoccupation of Nietzsche's, as in *Ecce Homo*: "Listen to me, for I am thus and thus. Do not, above all, confound me" (Preface, §1). See Friedrich Nietzsche, *Nietzsche: The Anti-Christ, Ecce Homo, Twilight of the Idols*, ed. Aaron Ridley and Judith Norman, trans. Judith Norman (Cambridge: Cambridge University Press, 2005).

79. Pippin puts it well when he comments: "Nietzsche is pointing to a striving that is not satisfied merely in the absence of pain and the establishment of security but one that always anticipates the satisfactions of a possibly better life, not the rendering more secure or comfortable of the one that one happens to be living" (*Nietzsche, Psychology, and First Philosophy*, 16).

80. Nietzsche, *Beyond Good and Evil*, §44.

81. "In all the countries of Europe, and in America as well, there is . . . a very narrow, restricted, chained-up type of spirit whose inclinations are pretty much the opposite . . . with respect to these approaching *new* philosophers. . . . They are all . . . solid folks whose

courage and honest decency cannot be denied—it's just that they are un-free and ridiculously superficial" (ibid.).

82. Ibid.

83. Hannah Arendt, *Love and Saint Augustine* (Chicago: University of Chicago Press, 1996), 18.

84. "[P]hilosophy . . . is its own time comprehended in thoughts" (Hegel, *Philosophy of Right*, §21).

85. In truth, Nietzsche knew this about Socrates, too. See, for instance, Nietzsche's comment on Socrates' admission (in *Charmides* 155d) of getting an erection after glancing down a boy's cloak (*Beyond Good and Evil*, aphorism 137).

86. The passage is worth quoting in full.

> [The philosopher] must lead [the beloved] on to the sciences, so that he [himself, the lover] may see the beauty of sciences, and in looking at the beautiful, which is now so vast, no longer be content like a lackey with the beauty of a boy, or some human being, or of one practice, nor be a sorry sort of slave and petty calculator; but with a permanent turn to the vast open sea of the beautiful, behold it and give birth—in ungrudging philosophy—to many beautiful and magnificent speeches and thoughts; until, there strengthened and increased, he may discern a certain single philosophical science. (Plato, *Symposium* 210d–e)

87. Sappho's professed love of women was seen, already in antiquity, as a kind of parallel to Socrates' preference for young men. As mentioned, Plato's references in the *Symposium* to the flute-girl and her playing for women makes a similar suggestion. The third-century philosopher Maximus of Tyre writes: "What else could one call the love of the Lesbian woman than the Socratic art of love? For they seem to me to have practiced love after their own fashion, she the love of women, he of boys. For they said they loved many, and were captivated by all things beautiful. What Alcibiades and Charmides and Phaedrus were to him, Gyrinna and Atthis and Anactoria were to her." David A. Campbell, ed. and trans., *Greek Lyric*, vol. 1, *Sappho and Alcaeus*, Loeb Classical Library 142 (Cambridge, MA: Harvard University Press, 1982), 21.

88. That said, Foucault's point was not that individuals, even in the ancient world, could not have had preferences or predilections, in the sense of finding certain bodies or experiences more pleasurable than others. The point is it would be mistaken to suppose that pleasures could be the basis of knowable "truths," that they could structure ways of knowing the world, or the formation of self-expressive individual subjects. In a helpful commentary on Foucault, Arnold Davidson puts the point well: "Although we (nowadays) have no difficult talking about and understanding the distinction between true and false desires, the idea of true and false pleasures is conceptually misplaced. . . . There is no coherent conceptual space for the science of sexuality to attach itself to pleasure . . . different pleasures do not imply orientation at all, require no theory of subjectivity or identity formation" (*The Emergence of Sexuality*, 212).

89. Michel Foucault, *The History of Sexuality*, vol. 2 (New York: Random House, 1985), 192.

90. This sort of argument is not found only in classical Greek sources, such as the

Symposium, but as late as Plutarch's *Dialogue on Love,* where it is contested and critiqued. See the speeches of Protogenes and Pisias (750d–c). Also see Foucault, *The History of Sexuality,* vol. 3. Of course, there were also those—like Epicurus and Lucretius—who thought appetite should be celebrated as such.

91. This is a point made repeatedly by Foucault in his discussion of *paiderastia;* namely, that "it gave rise to a whole cultural elaboration" and set of ritual practices. See, for instance, *The History of Sexuality,* vol. 2, 214 and passim.

92. Nussbaum, *The Fragility of Goodness.*

93. Here, again, I am contesting Judith Butler's sense that gender norms are contingent and arbitrary.

94. See Michel Foucault, *The History of Sexuality,* vol. 2, pt. 4, chap. 3.

95. The expression of such personal-historical trauma has become a driving theme in contemporary novels. One measure of the ongoing necessity of such expressions is the number of recent novels devoted to grasping the psychic and social fallout from the sexual abuse of children, in view of critiquing the institutions that give sexual domination shelter (the church, schools, nuclear families): from Jane Smiley's retelling of *King Lear* in *A Thousand Acres* (New York: Knopf, 1991) to Rafael Yglesias, *The Wisdom of Perversity* (Chapel Hill: Algonquin, 2015). Consider, as one illustration of the historical innovation of the novel in this respect, the difference between these representations and the registration of trauma in the work of Saint Augustine, where the earthly-bodily sufferings of victims of rape and abuse are made meaningful through a denial of their subjective significance, a redemption in the afterlife or the immortality of the soul.

96. *Self-*prostitution—whereby one sets the price for the sexual use of one's *own* body, or whereby one extracts payment from another in exchange for such use—differs from sexual domination in that it amounts to the forfeiture of one's sexual agency to an existing social power-structure; the self-subordination of one's sexual activity to the power structures that inhere in some other social or economic hierarchy (patriarchy or capitalism, say). Self-prostitution is a form of fatalism.

97. Again, the *locus classicus* is Claude Lévi-Strauss' *The Elementary Structures of Kinship.*

98. As Nancy Fraser points out, in "What's Critical about Critical Theory? The Case of Habermas and Gender," in *The Frankfurt School,* ed. J. M. Bernstein (New York: Routledge, 1994), "in most jurisdictions there is no such thing as marital rape . . . a wife is legally subject to her husband; she is not an individual who can give or withhold consent to his demands for sexual access," 216–17. See also Carole Pateman, *The Sexual Contract* (Stanford: Stanford University Press, 1988), chap. 6.

99. There are influential accounts of sexual domination, like the one offered by Catherine MacKinnon in "Feminism, Marxism, Method and the State: An Agenda for Theory," *Signs* 7 (1982), which present 'objectification' as the sexual domination of women. However, MacKinnon offers no explanation. She merely asserts: "Sexual objectification is the primary process of the subjection of women" (541).

100. It has been observed that the Knight prefigures the modern figure of the masochist in this regard—however this observation fails to explain the historical-practical

dimension of this prefiguration, and instead imagines both masochism and courtly love to be manifestations of a "libinal economy" that transcends particular historical practices. See the discussions in Gilles Deleuze, *Masochism: Coldness and Cruelty* (New York: Zone, 1989), and Slavoj Žižek, "Courtly Love; or, Woman as Thing," in *Metastases of Enjoyment* (New York: Verso, 1994). Both Deleuze and Žižek borrow terms for their discussion from Jacques Lacan's discussion of courtly love, to be found in *The Seminar of Jacques Lacan, Book VII, The Ethics of Psychoanalysis*, ed. Jacques Alain Miller (New York: Norton, 1992), chap. xi.

101. If my reflections above are not wrong, then sexual domination should be understood to institute the very gendered power-dynamic without which no 'battle of the sexes' could even make sense. But courtship, I am suggesting, is not the carrying out of such a battle, but a development through which the zero-sum game of gender hierarchies is subject to critique.

102. For example, as already noted, Simone de Beauvoir regarded the historical relations between men and women to have been determined by a fundamental power struggle, the stakes of which were akin to Hegel's life-and-death struggle. I contest that view throughout these pages.

103. Pierre Choderlos de Laclos' *Les liaisons dangereuses* (1782) presents the story of the Marquise de Merteuil and the Vicomte de Valmont as a tale of sexual domination that, finally, turns into a struggle between the protagonists. Given the ultimate fates of de Merteuil and Valmont, this tale should be understood as showing that thinking in terms of "struggle" was precisely the wrong way for them to think about what they were doing. At the same time, to anticipate a point to which I shall return, the novel is clearly interested in showing how lovemaking (in the love-affair between Madame de Tourvel and Valmont) ends up threatening the viability of Valmont's self-understanding as a sexual dominator.

104. Compare Hegel's remarks on the way in which this kind of love "is only the personal feeling of the individual subject," hence "contingent." But the importance acquired by such contingency in courtship, I am suggesting, also belongs a kind of historical necessity, whose unfolding I am tracing. The inner feelings of the lovers are externalized in their active courtship—and that process itself is not contingent, for reasons I am elaborating throughout (*Lectures on Fine Art*, vol. 1, 567).

105. I have in mind, especially, Beauvoir's novel *She Came to Stay* (1943), which presents courtship as a struggle to the death.

106. As already mentioned, the one who submits by, say, treating his lover as a princess—that is, who submits in a theatrical way, may well be in fact the active partner, the one who sets the terms by which the entire relationship plays out as a matter of practice.

107. This is why, significantly, Hegel did not—could not—articulate the lord and bondsman as gendered beings. And it is why Beauvoir's subsequent attempts to do so, in *The Second Sex* and in *She Came to Stay*, fail to be adequately explanatory. For the institution of a gender-based division of labor results not just from individuals' fear of death—nor from any originary struggle to the death—but from the provisional freedom and agency achieved, by some, through practices of sexual domination.

108. See Hegel's remarks on "love's contingency" in *Lectures on Fine Art*, vol. 1, 566–67. Hegel means 'romantic love,' *tout court*, here, but I take his remarks to be an apt commentary on the limitations of the secrecy of courtship (not on "love" generally).

109. The courtship might be invisible to others—indistinguishable from the appearance of sexual domination—as in Shakespeare's *Taming of the Shrew* (1590). Petruchio and Kate engage in which looks at times like sexual subjugation (as when Petruchio starves Kate), and at times like something else (as in the enigmatic kiss at end of the play). The enigma of Shakespeare's play is rooted in the suspicion that institutions of sexual domination—regimes of 'taming'—cannot but produce, from within, these kinds of ambiguities.

110. Andreas Capellanus, *The Art of Courtly Love*, trans. John Jay Parry (New York: Norton, 1969); my emphasis.

111. An alternative candidate could be early articulations of Tantra. For a discussion, see Wendy Doniger, *On Hinduism* (Oxford: Oxford University Press, 2014).

112. Plutarch, *Dialogue on Love*, in *Plutarch's Morals*, Project Gutenberg, retrieved from http://homepages.wmich.edu/~acareywe/engl3120plutarch.html.

113. Foucault sees Plutarch as privileging the reciprocity of two active lovers over the active-passive relation between *erastes* (an adult male) and *eromenos* (a younger male) which characterized pederasty (*The History of Sexuality*, vol. 3, 193–210, esp. 209).

114. Consider Plutarch's famous depiction of Cleopatra, in his *Lives of the Noble Romans*, as further evidence in this regard.

115. Such marriages, at least for some, were apparently not impossible to achieve in the proto-modern Roman world, as indeed in the broader Hellenistic world. For instance, the Roman Stoic Musonius Rufus—Epictetus' teacher and a contemporary of Plutarch—argued for the training of women in philosophy, for marital fidelity as a measure of sexual reciprocity, and for the importance of equality in male-female unions. As a perhaps more famous instance, think of the kind of education Cleopatra received, not to mention the kinds of relationships she was able to cultivate with Caesar and Mark Antony: see the recent discussion in Stacy Schiff, *Cleopatra: A Life* (New York: Little, Brown, 2010), 28–30 and passim.

116. This account is taken from Joseph Bédier, *The Romance of Tristan and Iseult* ["drawn from the best French sources"], trans. H. Belloc (London: George Allen), 1913, Project Gutenberg, retrieved from http://www.gutenberg.org/files/14244/14244-h/14244-h.htm.

117. Hegel, *Phenomenology of Spirit*, §175–176. For Hegel, being "a living self-consciousness" means seeing oneself both as living and as desiring (to keep living). Self-consciousness entails seeing "life" both as a process of which one is a part *and* as something with which one cannot completely merge. Or, as Terry Pinkard puts it, "The world 'shows up' for creatures with a capacity for self-consciousness in a way that it cannot for non-self-conscious creatures" (Pinkard, "Subjectivity and Substance: Hegelian Freedom and Nature in History," http://philosophy.unc.edu/files/2014/07/Pinkard_colloquium.pdf).

118. Hegel, *Phenomenology of Spirit*, §159. Indeed, Hegel focuses so intently on *desire*—

rather than, say, on the faculty of the will or thinking—partly in order to unmask the mind-body duality's inability to deal with this tension between self-consciousness and life.

119. This estrangement can take many shapes—ranging from the extremes that Hegel finds in the "unhappy consciousness" to Tristan's and Iseult's thirst for wine.

120. As Isak Dinesen put it, in her tale "The Dreamers," in *Seven Gothic Tales* (New York: Doubleday, 2011), 274.

121. "Only in this way," as Hegel puts it, "does the unity of itself in its otherness become explicit for it" (*Phenomenology of Spirit*, §177).

122. As Eric Thomas Chafe, in *The Tragic and the Ecstatic: The Musical Revolution of Wagner's* Tristan and Isolde (Oxford: Oxford University Press, 2005), points out, Wagner "makes explicit the fact that the love potion was, at least from the lovers' point of view . . . not the cause of their love" (55).

123. Chana Bloch and Ariel Bloch, *The Song of Songs: A New Translation* (Berkeley: University of California Press, 1994). In their Introduction, these authors comment that "metaphors of feasting" suggest sexual fulfillment in the Song of Songs, and that the word typically translated as "love" in the opening verse (shown in the epigraph for this section), is the Hebrew word *dodim*, which "refers specifically to sexual love."

124. Bloch and Bloch, Introduction, 12.

125. For this reason, I disagree with Denis de Rougemont's thesis in *Love in the Western World*, according to which the articulation of love in the West began with the troubadour poets' "heretical" response to the centrality of marriage in early Christendom.

126. De Rougemont calls the Tristan myth the "great European Myth of Adultery" (*Love and the Western World*, 18). Tony Tanner's definition of adultery in *Adultery in the Novel: Contract and Transgression* (Baltimore, MD: Johns Hopkins University Press, 1979) is vague: "any compulsion to make illicit remixings or reorderings within the existing framework is a version of 'adultery' " (219).

127. Think, for example, of the so-called bedtricks, felicitous or infelicitous substitutions of sexual partners that recur in Arthurian romance and medieval literature and on up through Elizabethan drama. This plot device is, of course, at least as old as Genesis 29, where Leah is substituted for Rachel on Jacob's wedding night, and Genesis 38, where Tamar tricks Judah into sleeping with her. Nevertheless, it is a particularly common feature of medieval elaborations of courtship—from Boccaccio's *Decameron* down through the drama of Shakespeare's England—reaching an apotheosis in Shakespeare's own *Measure for Measure* and *All's Well that Ends Well*. From Genesis to Shakespeare, bedtricks shift in their themes from concerns about paternity to concerns about the 'authenticity' of the lovemaking. See the expansive and informative discussion in Wendy Doniger, *The Bedtrick: Tales of Sex and Masquerade* (Chicago: University of Chicago Press, 2005).

128. Goethe is, of course, invoking this tradition with Werther's suicide, in the final sentences of *The Sorrows of Young Werther*. In that novel, too, it is Werther's failure to establish a socially 'real' life with Charlotte that makes his love of her seem otherworldly, mere fantasy. Goethe proves that Werther's suicide itself—the "bullet entering his forehead," the "vein opened in his right arm"—is the most 'real' act in the story, as the many copycat suicides that followed the publication of *The Sorrows of Young Werther* sadly

demonstrated. Intriguingly, two centuries later, many novels by the twentieth-century writer Jun'ichirō Tanizaki depict forms of sexual obsession directly drawn from a similar Japanese tradition of *Shinjū* (double suicide), but these novels also self-consciously surpass this tradition by showing how—in modern, 'Westernized' Japan (a recurrent preoccupation of Tanizaki's work)—intensely felt lovemaking, while passionate to the point of appearing obsessive or fetishistic, now turns out to be capable of installing objective, livable-practical ways of life for the lovers, however 'perverse.' Sexual-obsessional love becomes the basis for—indeed, the primary reason for—domestic, economic, political, and legal arrangements in Tanizaki's novels.

129. I do not mean public forms of what we now call harassment, but rather genuine public displays of sexual affection. Such displays have not always and everywhere been permissible; perhaps in some cases, they have not even been apprehensible enough to be regulated.

130. Peter Singer, *The Expanding Circle: Ethics, Evolution, and Moral Progress* (Princeton: Princeton University Press, 2011).

131. Pippin, "Hegel on Political Philosophy and Political Actuality," 407.

132. Beauvoir, *The Second Sex*, 17.

133. Chrétien de Troye, *Perceval: The Story of the Grail*, trans. Burton Raffel (New Haven: Yale University Press, 1999), 22, lines 681–83.

134. William Shakespeare, *Othello*, in *The Norton Shakespeare: Tragedies*, ed. Stephen Greenblatt, Walter Cohen, Jean E. Howard, and Katharine Eisaman Maus, 2nd ed. (New York: Norton, 2008); all citations are to this edition.

135. Stanley Cavell, "Skepticism and the Problem of Others," in *The Claim of Reason* (Oxford: Oxford University Press, 1999), 7 and passim.

136. Hume rejected what he called "excessive scepticisme," on the simple grounds that it makes life unlivable, practically. Everyday life, therefore, is the proper riposte to Cartesian skepticism. See David Hume, *Enquiries Concerning Human Understanding and Concerning the Principles of Morals* (Oxford: Oxford University Press, 1975), 158–59.

137. See Cavell, *The Claim of Reason*, 341 and passim.

138. Ibid, 422.

139. Ibid., 384–93.

140. Cavell also presents this as the inseparability of what he calls "active" and "passive" skepticism—active skepticism being the way I deal with trying to know another; passive skepticism being the way I try to make myself known to another. See the helpful discussions in Richard Moran, "Cavell on Outsiders and Others," *Revue internationale de philosophie*, 256, no. 2 (2011), 239–54; and in Robert Pippin, "Active and Passive Skepticism in Nicholas Ray's *In a Lonely Place*," nonsite.org no. 5 (March 18, 2012).

141. "He cannot forgive Desdemona for existing, for being separate from him, outside, beyond command, commanding, her captain's captain" (Stanley Cavell, "Othello and the Stake of the Other," in Kottman, *Philosophers on Shakespeare*, 164). The avoidance of acknowledgment is key to Cavell's reading of Shakespearean tragedy, as also seen in his essay on *King Lear*: "The Avoidance of Love," in *Disowning Knowledge in Seven Plays of Shakespeare* (Cambridge: Cambridge University Press, 2003).

142. Cavell, "Othello and the Stake of the Other," 165.

143. Ibid., 164. This is what Cavell means when he asserts that "the idea of Desdemona as an adulterous whore is more convenient to [Othello] than the idea of her as chaste," or when he claims that Desdemona's faithfulness is worse that her faithlessness. Believing in Desdemona's adultery is convenient in that it gives Othello cover, a chance to doubt what he knows—that Desdemona desires him (ibid., 161–62).

144. After all, if Othello is nothing more than the gullible victim of a nefarious villain, then the entire story starts to look like just a sad misfortune (ibid., 162).

145. Ibid., 164; and see n135, above.

146. Cavell suggests, further, that Othello and Desdemona might not have made love, asking: "Well, were the sheets stained or not? Was she a virgin or not?" (ibid., 163).

147. Ibid., 161–62; and see n135, above. Harry Berger Jr. follows Cavell's reading, casting this moment in terms of sinning, in "Three's Company: The Specter of Contaminated Intimacy in *Othello*," *The Shakespearean International Yearbook* (2004).

148. Cavell, "Othello and the Stake of the Other," 164.

149. Cavell, "Hamlet's Burden of Proof, " in *Disowning Knowledge*, 188–89.

150. "Nothing could be more certain to Othello than that Desdemona . . . is flesh and blood; is separate from him; other. This is precisely the possibility that tortures him. The content of this torture *is* the premonition of the existence of another, hence of his own . . . as dependent, as partial" (Cavell, *Disowning Knowledge*, 138).

151. And not only that but there is also Othello's self-conception as a Moor, his place in Venice, as well as his sense of how others see him, all connected to his sense of others (Iago, Cassio, Brabantio). The dialectical gymnastics required for a fuller assessment of Othello's self-conception would require more space than is available here.

152. None of this is meant to underplay or obscure the significance of Othello's being a Moor. But I understand these 'multiple' self-conceptions—Othello as general, Moor, lover, man, older, all of which mean bearing in mind a difference between how he sees himself and how others see him—to reflect the complexity of the 'modern' world that is Shakespeare's Venice.

153. For expressions of this concern about public honor, see *Othello* 4.1.190–200 and 3.3.391–93, and also in this regard, compare *Othello* with the focus on 'honor' and sexual fidelity in Spanish drama of this period; and see as well the remarks to this effect in Hegel, *Lectures on Fine Art*, vol. 1, 560.

154. Othello notes what is bearable and what is not:

> to make me
> The fixéd figure for the time of scorn
> To point his slow and moving finger at—
> Yet could I bear that too, well, very well.
> But there where I have garnered up my heart,
> Where either I must live or bear no life,
> The fountain from the which my current runs
> Or else dries up—to be discarded thence. (4.2.55–62)

155. Iago draws attention to these different kinds of "bonds" through his repeated use of the words "bound" and "bond"). See the discussion in David Schalkwyk, *Shakespeare, Love and Service* (Cambridge: Cambridge University Press, 2008), 275.

156. Following through on this logic would, of course, require Othello to enforce strict control over Desdemona's movements, her sexual agency, and ultimately, her life.

157. No one in the play—with the possible exception of Emilia—is really interested in objectively establishing Desdemona's guilt or innocence, her honor or her shame. And it is not entirely clear that Emilia's interest in this is altruistic. To a large extent, her own public standing is bound up with that of Desdemona.

158. In other words, Othello "*knows* [Iago's insinuations] to be false"—so, for Cavell, the trance is something like Othello's "massive denial" of what he knows: we hear

> the words of a man in a trance, in a dream state, fighting not to awaken; willing for anything but light. By "denial" I do not initially mean something requiring psychoanalytical, or any other theory. I mean merely to ask that we not, conventionally but insufferably, assume that we know this woman better than this man knows her—making Othello some kind of erotic, gorgeous, superstitious lunkhead; which is about what Iago thinks. However much Othello deserves each of these titles, however far he believes Iago's tidings, he cannot just believe them; somewhere he also *knows* them to be false. (Cavell, "Othello and the Stake of the Other," 157, 161)

159. Othello refers to Desdemona as a "devil" at several points (see, e.g., 3.3.481). The term is also applied to others in the play; indeed, it is frequently repeated. But Othello uses the term only in reference to Desdemona. Even after Iago's deception has come to light, Othello calls him only "demi-devil" (5.2.307).

160. To Lodovico and Desdemona, and to the others present, Othello's actions and motives are unclear. Othello makes no explicit accusation, nor does he attempt to justify his actions. Hence, Lodovico's bewilderment: "My lord, this would not be believed in Venice, / Though I should swear I saw't. 'Tis very much. / Make her amends, she weeps" (4.1.236–38). And after Othello departs, Lodovico inquires, "Are his wits safe? Is he not light of brain? . . . What, strike his wife?" (4.1.266–69). And again, "Is it his use [to strike Desdemona], / Or did the letters work upon his blood / And new-create his fault?" (4.1.271–72).

161. Where physical violence is not effective or possible or desirable, one might nag or harangue. And in saying this, I am, clearly, not defending such actions; I am trying to explain Othello's actions in view of the historical possibilities open to him.

162. Provided, however, that the quarrel is not a genuine duel or battle to the death, wherein destructive intent or a will to mastery is recognized on both sides. This is a crucial point to bear in mind, not only for the divergence I am proposing from Hegel's *Phenomenology of Spirit* and its emphasis on the life-and-death struggle, but also for our understanding of the denouement of *Othello*, where Desdemona perceives Othello's murderousness but does not fight back or attempt to flee.

163. As Michael Neill points out, the line "she can turn and turn" refers to sex. According to Neill, editor of the Oxford Shakespeare edition of *Othello* (Oxford: Oxford University Press, 2006), "the 17th century pronunciation of *obedient* would allow an

actor to disclose the mocking word *bed* concealed in its second syllable." See his remarks in the Introduction to that edition, 172–73.

164. If—as Cavell has it—Othello is "denying" Desdemona's innocence by calling her "whore" or "strumpet," then we have to wonder: why should Othello bother to involve Desdemona in this denial, by baldly provoking her repeatedly? If Othello is denying what he knows about Desdemona, then why seek to engage her at all, let alone in this direct and intimate manner? Why not just go straight to erasing her?

165. When Othello mocks Desdemona for weeping—"O well painted passion"—we should, I think, hear echoes of Hamlet's provocation of Ophelia: "I have heard of your paintings, too, well enough" (*Hamlet*, 3.1.142). Like Desdemona, Ophelia is confused by Hamlet's outburst: "O what a noble mind is here o'erthrown" (3.1.149). By accusing Ophelia of falsity—"God hath given you one face, and you make yourselves another" (3.1.142–43)—is not Hamlet challenging Ophelia to demonstrate that she is an *authentic*, independent, creature, not merely the obedient extension of Hamlet's own (or of Polonius' or some other man's) desire? Hamlet seems to have frightened Ophelia with his earlier use of force against her—which I am tempted to understand as another attempt to 'get a rise' out of her, to demonstrate *her* self-certainty:

> He took me by the wrist and held me hard,
> Then goes he to the length of all his arm,
> And with his other hand thus o'er his brow
> He falls to such perusal of my face
> As a would draw it. Long stayed he so.
> At last, a little shaking of mine arm,
> And thrice his head thus waving up and down,
> He raised a sigh so piteous and profound
> That it did seem to shatter all his bulk
> And end his being." (2.1.88–97)

It used to be believed that *Othello* was written just after *Hamlet*, as "confirmed by similarities of style, diction and versification" (Bradley, *Shakespearean Tragedy* [New York: Penguin, 1990], 175).

166. I hear this as well in Hamlet's berating of Ophelia: "You jig and amble and you lisp, you nickname God's creatures and make your wantonness your ignorance." (3.1.146–48).

167. Whereas Cavell ("Othello and the Stake of the Other," 162) sees the invocation of "monumental alabaster"—and, indeed, the murder—as the "turning of Desdemona to stone," it seems to me that matters unfold in just the opposite direction. Othello wants to rouse her with his kisses—he wants reassurance that she is not only pleasing to the senses, or a breathing monument, but that she also acts independently. Cavell also begins his reflections on *Othello* by invoking the end of *The Winter's Tale* and the fact that Leontes had accepted Hermione's having become a statue as "the right fate for her disappearance from life" (ibid., 154).

168. And if Othello knows *this*, then he must also realize that there is nothing that he can do on his own to 'prove' that his desire is not impulse or sensuous appetite. This

is why simply robbing Desdemona of breath unilaterally, while she sleeps, will not suffice. To prove anything, he must rouse her.

169. As mentioned, it can be tempting to see sex as one of those activities—like sleeping—to which we sometimes succumb, during which urges and impulses supplant full consciousness. But if sex entails a suspension of self-awareness, then in what sense is the lover the one having sex? Even if he "succumbs" to his desires, doesn't he need to be able to say to himself, at a minimum, that *he* succumbed? If he cannot even affirm *that*, then of what can he be certain? Likewise, while he may fall asleep without fully intending to do so, he still has to be able to recognize that *he* slept or that he had such-and-such a dream. Otherwise, to twist a trope from Descartes, he cannot take himself to be awake, to be living his life. If Othello is acting out his fantasies about Desdemona here, then this is not in order to make his dreams come true, but rather as a bid to gain assurance that he is indeed awake, living his life. To live out a fantasy is to seek assurance that one was not simply fantasizing.

170. I hear this to mean, 'I hope *you* will not kill me.' If this is to be read as 'I hope you will not *kill* me,' then I cannot understand why Desdemona does not call for help. If it is to be read as 'I hope you will not kill *me*,' then we have to conclude that Desdemona does not understand the danger she is in—which, of course, she clearly does (see 5.2.39–41).

171. "A maiden never bold, / Of spirit so still and quiet that her motion / Blushed at herself" (1.3.94–96).

172. Cavell seems to echo Brabantio's view of Desdemona's obedience when he writes, of the final tableau, that Desdemona "obediently shares [Othello's] sense that this is their final night" ("Othello and the Stake of the Other," 162).

173. In 1980, the French philosopher Louis Althusser strangled his wife of 30 years, apparently while massaging her neck. (He was then declared mentally ill and institutionalized.) He later wrote about the events—wondering if his wife had wanted to die, if she had "passively accept[ed] death at [his] hands"; if it had been a case of "suicide via intermediary." See Louis Althusser, *The Future Lasts Forever*, trans. Richard Veasey (New York: New Press, 1993), 281. For a reading of Shakespeare's *Othello* that entertains a similar supposition, see Elizabeth Gruber, "Erotic Politics Reconsidered: *Desdemona's* Challenge to *Othello*," in *Borrowers and Lenders: The Journal of Shakespeare and Appropriation* 3, no. 2 (2008), retrieved from http://www.borrowers.uga.edu/781790/show. A less circumspect proposal of the same thesis is advanced in Robert Dickes, "Desdemona: An Innocent Victim?" *American Imago* 27 (1970): 279–97.

174. In a rare instance of A. C. Bradley seeming to me to be wildly off the mark, he says: "Desdemona is helplessly passive. She can do nothing whatever. She cannot retaliate even in speech; no, not even in silent feeling . . . [her] suffering is like that of the most loving of dumb creatures tortured without cause by the being[s] he adores" (*Shakespearean Tragedy*, 145). Both in the secondary literature and in the play's performance history, Desdemona is regularly presented as a passive victim. See Michael Neill's discussion in his Introduction to *Othello*, 103 and passim.

175. "I cannot say 'whore.' / It does abhor me now I speak the word; / To do the

act that might the addition earn / Not the world's mass of vanity could make me" (4.2.160–63).

176. This shows in her halting exchange with Emilia (4.2.95–113), which follows immediately upon Othello's accusation.

177. Catherine Clément misdiagnoses opera as the "eternal undoing" of women precisely because she is "determined to pay attention to the language, the forgotten part of opera." "I am going to talk about women and their operatic stories," she writes in *Opera, or the Undoing of Women*, trans. Betsy Wing (Minneapolis: University of Minnesota Press, 1988), "I am going to commit the sacrilege of listening to the words, reading the libretti, following the twisted, tangled plots" (5, 12). Had she heard Shakespeare's words as musically as Verdi did, she would not have so neatly separated the plot from the woman's vocalized experience of it. For a critique of Clément, see Adriana Cavarero, *For More Than One Voice*, trans. Paul A. Kottman (Stanford: Stanford University Press, 2005), 117–30.

178. In *The Dyer's Hand* (New York: Random House, 1962), W. H. Auden puts the thought this way: "The singer may be playing the role of a deserted bride who is about to kill herself, but we feel quite certain as we listen that not only we, but also she, is having a wonderful time . . . whatever errors the characters make and whatever they suffer, they are doing exactly what they wish" ("Notes on Music and Opera," 465–74). In his commentary on this remark in *On Opera* (New Haven: Yale University Press, 2008), Bernard Williams suggests that Auden's diagnosis is only correct insofar as it concerns the "musical artistry and achievement" of "the aesthetics of opera" (102–3). I disagree; I think (and I think Auden thinks) that opera manages to present, and make sense of, the way in which sexual agency is achieved by women through their *self*-undoing—perhaps the only form of agency available to women under stark patriarchal conditions.

179. Richardson distilled the events of his novel from many real-life accounts. And readers of *Pamela*, in turn, seem to have imitated the actions of the novel. See the discussion in Giles Worsley, "The Seduction of Elizabeth Lester," *Women's History Review* 13 (2004): 289–30; and Faramerz Dabhoiwala, *The Origins of Sex* (London: Penguin, 2012), 170–71. In his subsequent novel *Clarissa*, Richardson seems to have aimed for another verisimilitude in his depiction of the actions of the libertine Robert Lovelace as harsher and less redeemable—as if challenging readers to 'choose' between the modernity promised by Mr. B or that augured by the likes of Lovelace.

180. "By 1750, most forms of sex outside marriage had drifted beyond the reach of the law" (Dabhoiwala, *The Origins of Sex*, 77). Just as women appeared on the English stage for the first time in Restoration drama, so, too, England witnessed in these years the first emergence of women as a lasting part of literary world. As Jane Austen later put it, works written by women "afforded more extensive and unaffected pleasure than those of any other literary corporation in the world" (cited in Roger Lonsdale, ed. *The New Oxford Book of Eighteenth-Century Verse* [Oxford: Oxford University Press, 1984], 683). Scholarship on this period has focused on the articulation of issues that later became central to feminism, politically and philosophically: the sexual subordination of women, economic and political subjugation, maternity, shifting marriage practices and con-

ceptions of marriage, and challenges to religious tradition. For two recent surveys, see
Susan Staves, *A Literary History of Women's Writing in Britain, 1660–1800* (Cambridge:
Cambridge University Press, 2006); and Sarah Apetrei, *Women, Feminism and Religion
in Early Enlightenment England* (Cambridge: Cambridge University Press, 2014).

181. Nowadays, we would call this a *rape culture*.

182. For instance, in his *Letters Written to and for Particular Friends: On the Most
Important Occasions* (1741; available at http://quod.lib.umich.edu/e/ecco), Richardson
recounts the story of a young woman who tearfully tells the story of her entrapment,
rape and enforced prostitution (79–84). Richardson is at pains to emphasize the truth-
fulness of the account, as the sheer number of such published accounts also attests.

183. For discussions, see Dabhoiwala, *The Origins of Sex*, 173–74; and Rita Goldberg,
Sex and Enlightenment: Women in Richardson and Diderot (Cambridge: Cambridge
University Press, 1984).

184. I will focus in this section on the erosion of sexual domination, and will turn
in later sections to the erosion of the normative authority of sexual reproduction. That
said, the vicissitudes of the normative authority of sexual reproduction remain important for everything I say in these next few pages: think, as only one instance, of the role
played by Moll Flanders' offspring in Defoe's novel.

185. In *The Sexual Contract*, Carole Pateman argues that political rights were secured
for men by the patriarchal exclusion of women, creating conditions for the domestic
and sexual exploitation of women in prostitution and the marriage contract. Weaving
together Marxist and structuralist-anthropological reflections, Gayle Rubin has argued
that the gender "woman" emerges in economic exchange (in the sexual 'giving' or pro-
curing of women by men). However, Rubin also emphasizes that "no analysis of the
reproduction of labor under capitalism can explain foot-binding, chastity belts, or any
of the incredible array of Byzantine, fetishized indignities, let alone the more ordinary
ones, which have been inflicted upon women in various times and places"; see Rubin
"Traffic in Women: Notes on the 'Political Economy' of Sex,'" in *Toward an Anthropology of Women*, ed. Rayna Reiter (New York: Monthly Review Press, 1975).

186. Although it is true that people in positions of social power can do all kinds
of things, there is no news there, and no explanatory purchase, either, since we have
neither accounted for how such power was attained nor why it ought to have been exercised in certain ways rather than others.

187. In which case one wonders why *she* facilitated the assault. All citations of this
work are to Samuel Richardson, *Pamela: or Virtue Rewarded* (Oxford: Oxford University
Press, 2008).

188. To look for causal explanations for sexual domination is to misunderstand its
transcendental genesis. As I have argued throughout, while awful, institutionalized sexual domination is a way in which human beings have made sense of their lives and their
world, a way that can be critiqued and overcome only when its sense-making *fails*. It is
for this reason that I see the many debates in the sciences and social sciences which ask
whether rape is 'natural' (part of evolutionary biology or innate aggressions or instincts)
or 'social' (*just* a matter of power and social recognition, or lack thereof) as unhelpful and

misleading. It is important to think about sexual domination within the frame of what we sometimes call 'moral education,' so long as we understand that our moral self-education is as much a product of the practices it studies as it is a means for studying them.

189. This thesis is already nascent in Karl Marx's *Capital*—see *The Marx-Engels Reader*, vol. 1, ed. Robert C. Tucker (New York: Norton, 1978), 302–438—and forms the basis of Friedrich Engels' *Origins of the Family, Private Property and the State*; and it is one reason many so-called first-wave feminists in the nineteenth century emphasized demands for living wages, safe working conditions, and democratic governance of the marketplace. Economic equality was seen as a path to gender equality—or at least as a path to protection from sexual and domestic abuse. Marxist-feminist critiques have also produced analyses of affective labor, sexual oppression and market forces. See, as only a start, Gayle Rubin, "The Traffic in Women": Heather Brown, *Marx on Gender and the Family: A Critical Study* (New York: Haymarket Books, 2013), 52–98; Heidi Hartmann, "The Unhappy Marriage of Patriarchy and Capitalism: Toward a More Progressive Union," *Capital & Class* 3, no. 2 (1979): 1–33; Nancy Fraser, "Heterosexism, Misrecognition and Capitalism: A Response to Judith Butler," in *Fortunes of Feminism* (London: Verso, 2013), 175–86; Rosemary Hennessy, *Profit and Pleasure* (London: Routledge, 2000), 37–73; and Michael Hardt, "Affective Labor," *boundary* 26, no. 2 (1999): 89–100. See also Cinzia Arruzza, *Dangerous Liaisons: The Marriages and Divorces of Marxism and Feminism*, trans. Marie Lagatta and Dave Kelly (Wales, UK: Merlin Books, 2013).

190. See the discussion and citation in Rubin, "The Traffic in Women," 163.

191. He goes on: "Nor care I to look upon a woman now . . . for there can be nobody like her. Sure . . . the devil's in this lady!" (342). All citations of this work are to Samuel Richardson, *Clarissa* (New York: Penguin, 1986). There are many such passages in the novels of this type, as anyone who has made it through these lengthy texts will remember.

192. This kind of single-minded pursuit recurs as a theme in later novels as well; think, for example, of *Les misérables*.

193. In her influential commentary, *Desire and Domestic Fiction* (Oxford: Oxford University Press, 1987), Nancy Armstrong defines "virtue" as the result of "Mr. B's attempt to penetrate the servant girl's material body" which "magically transforms that body into one of language and emotion, into a metaphysical object that can be acquired only through consent" (6). But there is, I think, nothing "magical" or "metaphysical" about the detection of women's virtue in this context.

194. Fielding wrote two novels in direct rebuttal to *Pamela*—one of which he titled *Shamela*. The intensity of Fielding's objections is instructive, since it shows the lengths to which he and his readers felt compelled to go, literally, to issue this rebuttal. Fielding also felt the novel, as a form, was of limited help when it came to the depiction of normative-moral dilemmas. See the excellent discussion of this issue in Thomas Pavel, *The Lives of the Novel* (Princeton: Princeton University Press, 2013), 135–41.

195. The question of what Mr. B "ought to do" is one that he himself poses, in precisely those terms, at various points (e.g., 252).

196. *This* is the importance of women's lived experience to the history of the novel.

If the modern novel was largely developed out of increased female literacy, in women's writings and the first-personal expression of women's sexual subjugation (and I agree with those who argue, against Ian Watt, that this is manifestly so), then this is not just because "written representations of [women] allowed [them] to become an economic and psychological reality" (Armstrong, *Desire and Domestic Fiction*, 8). It also is because the development of the *form* of the modern novel—its written production and read consumption—responds to the first-personal experiences of individuals (this *content*) in a way which impresses upon all of us normative-moral dilemmas that could not, at the time, have been impressed otherwise. Thomas Pavel (in *The Lives of the Novel*, 134) makes a version of same point I am making about Richardson's role in this development.

197. The logic of the reading I am pursuing here is, I believe, borne out by the way the novel proceeds on the page. Look, for instance, at the passage in which Pamela discusses her acceptance of Mr. B's proposal: "he insisted upon a more explicit answer to his question, of what I thought he *ought* to do . . . but were I the first lady in the land, instead of the poor abject Pamela Andrews, I would, I *could* tell you" (252; emphasis in original).

198. From a political and legal point of view, love-based marriage was a recent development in Hegel's time—although its significance had already been explored in the Scottish Enlightenment, in the work of Adam Ferguson (1723–1816) and John Millar (1735–1801). In England, the 1753 Marriage Act, for instance, tried to continue to make it impossible for the young and in love to marry without the consent of their elders—as if to stem the tide. See the discussion in David Lemmings, "Marriage and the Law in the Eighteenth Century," *The Historical Journal* 39, no. 2 (1996): 339–60. For an excellent account of the important of the Scottish Enlightenment to Hegel, see Lawrence Dickey, *Religion, Economics, and the Politics of Spirit: 1770–1807* (Cambridge: Cambridge University Press, 1989).

199. "[L]ove, as a feeling [*Empfindung*], is open in all respects to contingency, and this is a shape which the ethical may not assume. Marriage should therefore be defined more precisely as rightfully ethical [*rechtlich sittliche*]" (Hegel, *Philosophy of Right*, §161).

200. Ibid., §162.

201. Ibid, §158, Addition, p. 199.

202. Ibid.

203. Hegel, *Enzyklopädie der philosophischen Wissenschaften im Grundrisse*, in *Werke*, vol. 8, §24a, ed. E. Moldenhauer and K. Michelet (Frankfurt: 1970), quoted in Robert Pippin, "What Is the Question for Which Hegel's Theory of Recognition Is the Answer?" *European Journal of Philosophy* 8 (2000): 156.

204. This needs to be mentioned in light of a peculiar resurgence of sophistic works that vainly attempt to answer the question of what love 'is'—for example, recent writings by Simon Critchley and Alain Badiou. Critchley's recent interviews and writings tackle the What is love? question; and an earlier work, too—*Ethics, Politics, Subjectivity: Essays on Derrida, Levinas and Contemporary French Thought* (New York: Verso, 1999)—(mistakenly) suggests that Hegel was engaged in a definitory exercise in the *Philosophy of Right*: "Hegel defines love as 'the consciousness of my unity with another'" (5).

205. This, of course, implies the opposite of what is sometimes claimed about the modern era—namely, that its fundamental institutions (democratic government or the liberal state) prove incapable of satisfying the "infinite demands" of subjectivity. Versions of this thesis animate Jacques Rancière's work, and also Simon Critchley's *Infinitely Demanding: Ethics of Commitment, Politics of Resistance* (New York: Verso, 2007), to give two contemporary examples; but they also nourish pseudo-Freudian critiques of bourgeois marriage, such as Lawrence Lerner's view, in *Love and Marriage* (New York: St. Martin's, 1979), that no social arrangement can shelter the intense eroticism of lovers. By this point the reader will, I hope, see that profound, ongoing institutional transformations—like the emergence of love-based marriage—are nothing other than objective articulations of subjective demands, attempts at to make sense of what would otherwise remain practically unintelligible.

206. It is possible, of course, to read Hegel as concluding that love and freedom *do* come to rest in the family, or in the institutions of bourgeois society. Robert Pippin suggests this at various points in his work: for example, in *After the Beautiful* (Chicago: University of Chicago Press, 2013), 37. But I would like to think (as Pippin, too, often does) that the direction I am proposing is closer to Hegel's actual line of thought, if not always to the letter of his text.

207. The famous opening of Tolstoy's *Anna Karenina* can perhaps be of help here: "Happy families are all alike; every unhappy family is unhappy in its own way." I do not see this statement as categorizing the difference between those particular families that are happy and those that are unhappy by dividing them into two camps: the homogeneous (all alike) versus the heterogeneous (unhappy in its own way). Rather, I understand this novel to take, as its point of departure, the view that families are a practical domain in which the demands of mutuality or satisfaction are worked out—sometimes successfully (and since the demands are world-historical as well as personal, the happy results will resemble one another), but often with varying and unhappy results. If this were not so, Tolstoy would not have needed to write the novel.

208. Critiques of bourgeois marriage are legion; compelling vindications of its significance are very few. In addition to Hegel's discussion—and earlier works such as Shakespeare's comedies and romances, Milton's tract "Doctrine and Discipline of Divorce," Jane Austen's novels, Tolstoy's novella *Family Happiness* and so on—perhaps the only interesting philosophical attempts are Stanley Cavell's *Pursuits of Happiness: The Hollywood Comedy of Remarriage* (Cambridge, MA: Harvard University Press, 1981) and Richard Eldridge's essay on Austen in *On Moral Personhood: Philosophy, Literature, Criticism, and Self-Understanding* (Chicago: University of Chicago Press, 1989), 141–80.

209. Hegel obviously lived at a time when the male head of the household controlled the resources; long before shared bank accounts, equal pay, and so forth. So, I am extrapolating in this paragraph to form a thesis on the basis of what I see in Hegel's remarks.

210. Kottman, *Tragic Conditions in Shakespeare*, 107–14.

211. Hegel, *Philosophy of Right*, §173–80.

212. Here, again, an important harbinger is Shakespearean drama. In *Pericles* and,

above all, in *The Winter's Tale*, Shakespeare depicts the fate of children—of their very being, but also of their treatment, their education and upbringing—as deciding or demonstrating the fate of the love-relation of which they were born. Shakespeare was the first, so far as I am aware, to treat the love of children—whether one disowns them, or acknowledges them, or lets them live in one's home—as potentially offering a test of whether the parents of the child love each other, freely embrace one another. Even *Hamlet* might be understood to present Hamlet as dismayed by his mother's remarriage (or, even, by suspicions that Claudius is his biological father) not only because of concerns about legitimacy and worldly inheritance, but because it would mean that Gertrude did not love Old Hamlet, the dead king.

213. Hegel, *Philosophy of Right*, §174, Addition, p. 211 (my emphasis).

214. "Children are free *in themselves*, and their life is merely the immediate existence [*Dasein*] of this freedom; they therefore do not belong as things [*Sachen*] to others or to their parents" (ibid., §175).

215.   Ralph Waldo Emerson gives us a moving exposition of this, in light of his own son's death, in his essay "Experience." Conversely, testimony to the resilience of cultural practices in which children are not loved, or acknowledged as independent beings, simply by virtue of being born, can be found in Nancy Scheper-Hughes *Death without Weeping: The Violence of Everyday Life in Brazil* (Berkeley: University of California Press, 1992). I mention these examples to give an indication of how important the decline in infant mortality rates has been for the rise of the love-based children I am discussing.

216. "On the whole, children love their parents less than their parents love them" (Hegel, *Philosophy of Right*, §175, Addition, p. 213). I do not think that Hegel presents this statement as a universal axiom, but only as the way things work if and when children are raised in love-relations (in practical relations that take on the challenges of mutual recognition).

217.   Hence Hegel's lengthy critique of Roman law in the *Philosophy of Right*: "the position of Roman children as slaves is one of the institutions which most tarnishes the Roman legal code" (§175).

218. See Hegel's discussion of maternal love, in *Lectures on Fine Art*, vol. 1; for instance, 541–43.

219. Hegel, *Philosophy of Right*, §174.

220. "Human beings do not arrive by instinct at what they are destined to become; on the contrary, they must attain this by their own efforts" (ibid., §174).

221. For instance: "Marriage differs from concubinage inasmuch as the latter is chiefly concerned with the satisfaction of the natural drive, whereas this drive is made subordinate within marriage" (ibid., §163, Addition, p. 203). Hegel is here responding to what he calls Kant's "crude" view of marriage as a "civil contract" which "entitles the parties concerned to use one another"; he is also responding to Schlegel's *Lucinde*, which argued that marriage should incorporate natural drives and passions (see §161, Addition). Hegel's point is that marriage is not *just* subject to natural impulses and, hence, cannot be disrupted by the natural drives or the natural functionings of the body. (His

curious support for this claim is the fact that, "within marriage . . . one may speak un-blushingly of natural functions"; §163.)

222. Hegel's most extensive discussion of sexual reproduction occurs in the *Philosophy of Nature*.

223. More relaxed sexual mores may be one symptom or manifestation of the erosion of the normative authority of sexual reproduction, but they are not the cause.

224. Having just written this sentence, I find in the newspaper an advertisement for Kate Bolick's *Spinster: Making a Life of One's Own* (New York: Crown, 2015).

225. Strikingly, Hegel thought that "modern dramas and artistic presentations in which love between the sexes is the basic interest" were limited by the "total contingency"—"for the whole interest is represented as resting solely upon *these* particular individuals. This may well be of infinite importance for *them*, but it is of no importance *in itself*" (Hegel, *Philosophy of Right*, §162). I think my observation here might go some way toward explaining Hegel's fascination, and confusion, in the face of Shakespearean drama.

226. Would it be inappropriate to mention that Hegel himself fathered a child out of wedlock? Though he eventually acknowledged his son, to some degree, it seems to have been a fraught issue for him. I mention this not as being of mere biographical or prurient interest, but precisely because the *kinds* of challenges faced by Hegel himself and his family, as particular individuals, *are* world-historical challenges of interest to others. See the account in Terry Pinkard, *Hegel: A Biography* (Cambridge: Cambridge University Press, 2001). For another angle on the "place for the bastard . . . in the Hegelian family", see Jacques Derrida, *Glas*, trans. Richard Read and John Leavey (Lincoln: University of Nebraska Press, 1986), 12a/6a and passim.

227. For an attempt in this direction, see Sarah Vandegrift Eldridge, *Novel Affinities: Composing the Family in the German Novel, 1795–1830* (Rochester: Boydell & Brewer, 2016).

228. I am not convinced by Tony Tanner's more ahistorical thought about the novel in this era—namely, the thought that contracts invariably breed transgression (see his *Adultery in the Novel*).

229. I will focus on these two novels because of their broad influence. That said, as Thomas Pavel has taught me, Balzac's novels are an even richer source for reflection on the issues I shall raise. And then there is Goethe's *Faust*, Part I (1808), with its rejection of childbearing, and Anne Brontë's *The Tenant of Wildfell Hall* (1848) and Victor Hugo's *Les misérables* (1862).

230. Gustave Flaubert, *Madame Bovary*, trans. Lydia Davis (New York: Viking, 2010); all citations are to this edition.

231. This is the view of a number of Flaubert's most well-known critics, such as Dominick LaCapra, *"Madame Bovary" on Trial* (Ithaca, NY: Cornell University Press, 1982), Louise Kaplan, *Female Perversions: The Temptations of Emma Bovary* (New York: Bantam, 1991), Judith Armstrong, *The Novel of Adultery* (London: Macmillan, 1976), Michael Black, *The Literature of Fidelity* (New York: Harper and Row, 1975) and Tony Tanner, *Adultery in the Novel*.

232. "Léon walked about in the room; it seemed strange to him to see this lovely lady in her nankeen dress in the midst of all this wretchedness. Madame Bovary blushed; he turned away, thinking that perhaps his eyes had expressed some impertinence. Then she laid the child back down; it has just spit up on her collar" (81). Mère Rollet, of course, later facilitates the affair.

233. Leo Tolstoy, *Anna Karenina*, trans. Richard Pevear and Larissa Volokhonsky (New York: Penguin, 2000). All this—I should mention—leads Anna to glance at Vronsky's picture, and to feel an "unexpected surge of love" for him.

234. The importance of financial independence is, of course, not to be underestimated. This is an issue to which American novelists of this period, like Henry James and Edith Wharton, appear especially attuned when compared with their European counterparts. (Whereas Wharton herself had few financial worries, the American novelist Kate Chopin—who bore six children before she turned twenty-eight, and before being left in debt following the death of her husband—turned to writing stories, mostly at night as her children slept, as a source of income.) However, to say that love requires certain financial preconditions in order to be 'real' and 'lived' is not to say that love expresses nothing other than financial necessities (the view of some of James' and Wharton's protagonists). As already suggested, we should remember to think about financial needs as responding to the dynamics of love and reciprocity and not just the other way around. For a concurring discussion of Henry James on this issue, see Robert Pippin, *Henry James and Modern Moral Life* (Cambridge: Cambridge University Press, 2001), 174–75.

235. Richard Yates, *Revolutionary Road* (1961; repr. New York: Vintage, 1989), 426; all citations are to this edition.

236. "I don't know who I am" (358), she says, later reflecting that "then you were face to face, in total darkness, with the knowledge that you didn't know who you were" (417). All this as Frank continues to yell things like, "you know God damn well you love me" (381).

237. Cavell, *Pursuits of Happiness*, 2.

238. Cavell compares these situations to Shakespearean romance: "It is as though you know you are married when you come to see that you cannot divorce, that is, when you find that your lives simply will not disentangle" (ibid., 127).

239. In *American Beauty*, the married couple never seem to mourn the loss of whatever joy they might once have had together—making their relationship seem less like a mistake than, so to speak, something that happened *to* them. But if they—like the closeted military officer, his troubled son, the teenage daughters, or the wife's clandestine lover—are mere victims of circumstance, then we are just watching a puppet show whose strings are being pulled by an ultimately unintelligible force.

240. I am thinking of passages like the one that begins, "What a subtle, treacherous thing it was to let yourself go that way! Because once you'd started it was terribly difficult to stop" (416).

241. As when Theodor Adorno writes, in *Minima Moralia*, that "marriage as a community of interests unfailingly means the degradation of the interested parties, and it is the perfidy of the world's arrangements that no-one, even if aware, can escape such

degradation" (A10). While I recognize—and have gone to lengths to argue—that forms of sexual domination are ruinous for lovemaking, and are indeed what love 'negates,' I do not think that there is any "perfidy of the world's arrangements" which makes escape from degradation impossible.

242. Patricia Highsmith (writing as Claire Morgan), *The Price of Salt* (1952; repr. Tallahassee: Naiad Press, 1984), 278. I wrote these pages before becoming aware of the film version of this novel. But the very existence of the film (and its distribution through a major Hollywood studio) make Highsmith's hopefulness in her 1984 Preface to this novel seem prescient.

243. Annie Proulx, "Brokeback Mountain," in *At Close Range* (New York: Simon & Schuster, 1999); all citations are to this edition.

Index

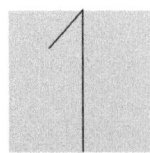

SQUARE ONE
First Order Questions in the Humanities

Series Editor: **PAUL A. KOTTMAN**

Square One steps back to reclaim the authority of humanistic inquiry for a broad, educated readership by tackling questions of common concern, regardless of discipline. 'What do we value and why?' 'What should be believed?' 'What ought to be done?' 'How can we account for human ways of living, or shed light on their failures and breakdowns?' 'Why should we care about particular artworks or practices'?

Pushing beyond the trends that have come to characterize much academic writing in the humanities—increasingly narrow specialization, on the one hand, and interdisciplinary 'crossings' on the other—Square One cuts across and through fields, to show the overarching relevance and distinctiveness of the humanities as the study of human meaning and value. Series books are therefore meant to be accessible and compelling. Rather than address only a particular academic group of experts, books in the Square One focus on what texts, artworks, performances, cultural practices and products mean, as well as how they mean, and how that meaning is to be evaluated.

Adriana Cavarero, *Inclinations: A Critique of Rectitude*